The Year the Music Died

1964-1972: A commentary
on the best era of pop music, and an
irreverent look at the musicians and social
movements of the time.

www.AnimalsToZombies.com

Stew, thanks for your interest

Dwight Rounds

Dwight Rounds

Bridgeway
Books

The Year the Music Died
Published by Bridgeway Books
P.O. Box 80107
Austin, Texas 78758

For more information about our books, please write to us, call 512.478.2028, or visit our website at www.bridgewaybooks.net.

Printed and bound in China.

Library of Congress Control Number: 2006933198

ISBN-13: 978-1-933538-69-3
ISBN-10: 1-933538-69-4

Dedication

To my wife, Laurie, son, Brock, and daughter, Virginia.
For all these years, you have put up with listening to my very limited range of music, especially in the car.

To my mother Gingie.
While very strict in other areas, you gave me complete freedom in buying whatever music I wanted. You knew that I had enough sense to be my own person, and to not be influenced by whatever lyrics I was listening to.

Contents

Foreword by Bob Cole

Bob Cole began his career as a rock 'n' roll DJ in Miami in 1971, when he was only fourteen years old. He is currently the co-host of the number one radio show in Austin, Texas, "Sam and Bob in the Morning" on KVET-FM. A member of the advisory board of the Texas Heritage Songwriters Association, Bob has been the recipient of the Trailblazer Broadcaster award and a former Billboard Magazine Program Director of the Year. He was inducted into the Country Radio Hall of Fame in 2003.

Many people of my generation believe that good rock music hasn't been produced since, well...that depends on the way you remember it. However, Dwight Rounds makes a good case for a milepost that marks the end…and I would probably agree. It was in the early '70s when the signal began to fade for all of us—all of us who were lucky enough to experience firsthand the most enduring, prolific, and defining music era in history. Back then, all of us were too caught up in the barrage of music and its message to society to truly understand and appreciate it. *The Year the Music Died* reclaims the essence of the era, and its author, Dwight Rounds, brings to light a newfound appreciation for the music that defined a generation.

This music was not just about the rebellion and confusion of the times or a social statement of rebellion and youth—it was an enduring soundtrack for a generation that believed the message of peace and understanding in the music they loved was their release during a time of war and political turbulence. *The Year the Music Died* provides the catalyst for the reemergence and cultural embrace of this music for a new generation.

In the '60s and early '70s, there was no MTV, no E! Network, no *Inside Edition*—only a very, very young *Rolling Stone Magazine*. We hardly knew with any reliability the inside skinny, or the "true Hollywood story" behind the music and the performers themselves. Dwight finally fills that void and provides that long-awaited insight into the personalities and their music.

Dwight peels back the layers of time to reveal the music in a way readers can understand. I have seen many attempts by writers to recapture the essence of this era, and most fall well short of my expectations. Dwight, on the other hand, took me backstage for 307 pages and left me with a long-needed, honest, intellectual understanding of something I've loved all my life.

Dwight Rounds is not a run-of-the-mill music buff, but rather the Jacques Cousteau or Neil Armstrong of the everyday music fan of that era. He has explored, chronicled, and assembled the evolution of this great music with detail and passion, bringing it all to life again, and the experience far transcends reminiscence. It's a musical resurrection, one I predict you too will experience when you immerse yourself into *The Year the Music Died*.

Preface

This book deals with the era when "Bono" meant the gregarious Sonny Bono, not the humorless U2 singer. I was nine years old when the Beatles first appeared on the Ed Sullivan show. I can vaguely remember watching that night and being frustrated with having to watch the whole show in order to see them perform at the end. (That was a clever move by Sullivan to get people to watch the non-Beatles part of the show). The main topic of conversation in fourth grade the next day was the Beatles and who your favorite Beatle was. I did not have one, but I do remember a friend saying that his was George because he could take the others in a fight.

I had no interest in music before that February 1964 night. I had one 45 RPM record, "Monster Mash," but do not remember liking it much. I had never heard of the top group in the United States at the time, the Beach Boys. Our mother bought *Meet the Beatles* for the family, but somehow I ended up taking possession of it, and still have it. I received the *Beatles' Second Album* for my tenth birthday, and bought every successive album (the mono, $2.99 version, rather than the $3.99 for stereo; I am not even sure I knew what stereo was). The only singles I bought were "Paperback Writer/Rain" and "Eleanor Rigby/Yellow Submarine." I enjoyed about every song that I heard on the radio (KFRC in San Francisco), but did not buy a non-Beatles album until *The Monkees* and *More of the Monkees* in 1967, and *Bookends* in 1968. As time went along, I grew to like the other groups more and more. This music spoiled me. It didn't occur to me at the time that there would never again be groups as talented as the Beatles or that, overall, music would change for the worse. When the Beatles stopped recording together, I hoped their separate efforts would be as good. I was hugely disappointed, with the exceptions of *McCartney, Imagine,* and *All Things Must Pass.* Another great music year was 1970, with only a slight decline from 1969. Starting with 1971, though, the seeds of destruction were being planted. Number-one songs "Knock Three Times," "One Bad Apple," "Want Ads," "Go Away Little Girl" (the worst one), "Gypsies, Tramps and Thieves," "Family Affair," and "Brand New Key" were warning songs of what was to come.

I purchased Neil Young's *Harvest* in early 1972, not knowing that would be the end of my interest in popular music. I could not wait to buy Young's next studio album, *On the Beach.* I liked the first song, "Walk On," but the rest of the album was no good. Driving back to college in the summer of 1974, I listened to the radio because I did not have a cassette player. There was not one song I cared for. The last straw was buying Paul Simon's *Still Crazy after All These Years* album, thinking it was garbage, then finding out it won an Album of the Year award. The only albums that I thought were worth buying after 1972 were Bob Dylan's *Blood on the Tracks,* the Eagles' *Hotel California,* and The Rolling Stones' *Some Girls.*

I am still living in a musical time warp. All I listen to is pre-1973 music. I could not tell you one number-one song after 1985, or name a song by U2 or Nirvana.

Most music books I have read are written by musicians and are written in an abstract language. For example, "Classical music, once an art of expression, became a pseudo-scientific, quasi-architectural craft of technique whose principles of design, opaque to the ear, were appreciable only by examining the 'blueprint' of the score. Similarly, the rapid succession of conceptual *coups* in the world of painting and sculpture, so novel at the time, turned out to be merely the end of modernism, and as such, the dying fall of Western art." This is from the book *Revolution in the Head* by Ian McDonald. I enjoyed the book, at least the parts I could understand.

This book is not written like that. I am not a musician, nor is the book written in the abstract. However, a majority of music-listening enthusiasts are not musicians either, and I hope this book will especially appeal to them.

Another very different thing about this book is that many music book authors, being musicians themselves, tend to idolize those they write about. They have the same values, political opinions, and mindsets, which can give a very unrealistic view of the subject matter. I obviously have my own biases, which I know are present in the book, and at least I will admit that up front. I am not trying to present opinion as fact. I believe very simply that people should make their own choices about their own lives, including their own pocketbooks, rather than having those choices taken away through coercion. This is real freedom, in my opinion, not the civil-liberties-only freedom espoused by most in the music industry.

Obviously, there is no such thing as a "good" song or a "bad" song; it is all subjective. Much of the commentary in the book is just my opinion, which is no more important or less important than anyone else's opinion. Please remember this if you are going to try and prove me "wrong."

There is no way that this book has all the answers. For example, the only musicians I know of from that era who have not been divorced are Paul McCartney, Charlie Watts and Richie Furay. I am sure there are others, but it was not possible for me to research that. I encourage you to e-mail me at DCRounds@aol.com for any corrections, additions, or opinions that you strongly agree with or disagree with.

Dwight Rounds

Acknowledgments

I would like to acknowledge a friend of mine, Frank Boswell, who has easily been my biggest original supporter with this book project. He had many encouraging comments, including, "I think you have something here." He shares my love of the music of this era, and was very prompt to respond and comment on any small segments of the book I sent to him. He gave me a perspective from two points of view, from what I call the "elite" listener and the "proletariat" listener (see page xviii). As a pastor, Frank was despondent when he could not figure out any of the "religious rock" lyrics in the book's trivia section. He made noises about going back to seminary, but I reminded him that rock lyrics were probably not the main focus in seminary!

I would also like to thank Marianne Van Zandt who, after reading the first version of this book, has been a non-stop source of encouragement. She is one of the few people I know who likes this music as much as I do.

To give you an example of what might be of interest in this book, here are some questions about pop-rock music from 1964-1972. The answers are in the book's text, with the page numbers on the right. There is more trivia on page xxv.

1. Name the Beatles' songs with the following lyrics:	
"Float upstream"	
"Float downstream"	
"Turn you on"	
"Turn me on"	
2. Name two album covers that were three-dimensional.	
3. Who was the lead singer for Santana? (p. 164)	
4. Name the song and group for the following lyrics:	
a. "I seen a lot of things I ain't never seen before (pg. 132)	
What is it about bad grammar and lyrics, anyway? See p. 215 for more examples	
b. Boom-lacka-lacka-lacka (p. 166)	
c. Get your motor running (p. 130)	

Introduction

The Best Era of Pop Music

Why 1964-1972?

Even without the Beatles, this era easily had the best music. However, when you include the Beatles, there is no contest. Having the Beatles as part of the era is like having Wilt Chamberlain as part of the Boston Celtics in the early 1960s. The Beatles split up in late 1969, but their last album appeared in 1970. Their four best solo albums appeared before 1972. This book "breaks the rules" that music must be classified by decades starting with zero.

Specifically, the dates are February 1, 1964 (when "I Want to Hold Your Hand" replaced "There! I've Said It Again" (Bobby Vinton) at number one through April 15, 1972 (when "The First Time Ever I Saw Your Face" replaced "A Horse with No Name"). In early 1972, there were two other great songs at number one, "American Pie" and "Heart of Gold." The number-one songs after "The First Time," "Oh, Girl," "I'll Take You There," and "The Candy Man," showed no improvement. The music was dead.

There are other reasons why the music of this era is the best. The songs had melodies; bands relied on good music, rather than stage antics, pyrotechnics, and theatrics (with the exception of go-go girls!); and most of the popular groups wrote their own music. For what it's worth, forty-one percent of the top five hundred songs, according to *Rolling Stone* magazine, were from the years 1964-1971, while these eight years were only sixteen percent of the fifty-year total. Pete Townshend described 1970s music as "the fall of the Roman Empire." In the book *100 Great Albums of the Sixties* by John Tobler, eighty-nine percent of the albums are in the six years from 1964-1969.

Some dreadful songs at the top of the chart in 1963 were "Go Away Little Girl" (Steve Lawrence), "Sukiyaki" (Kyu Sakamoto), "Blue Velvet" (Bobby Vinton), "Sugar Shack" (Jimmy Gilmer and the Fireballs), and "Dominique" (The Singing Nun). The Beatles' timing could not have been better.

The year 1972 is "The Year the Music Died." Don McLean's line of "the *day* the music died" (released in November 1971) could have easily referred to April 15, 1972, as mentioned above. Also in 1972, were "Oh Girl," "The Candy Man," "Brandy," "Alone Again (Naturally)," and "Me and Mrs. Jones." And worst of all was the advance of glitter rock, with David Bowie as Ziggy Stardust.

Listeners: The Elite and Proletariat

There are two entirely different types of music-listening enthusiasts, and various combinations of the two. The first will be titled the "elite" or the "intelligentsia." These are usually musicians themselves, self-appointed experts, intellectuals, or others somehow involved with the music business. To be hip, their favorite groups will always include ones that were not commercially successful, and their favorite songs of the commercial groups will often not be singles, but more obscure songs. To them, the thought of a song selling well actually degrades the song because the general buying public does not know good music. They listen very closely to the lyrics to pick up hidden meanings and political messages (even ones that the writer does not intend). A huge day for them was when the *Sgt. Pepper* album came out. Not only were the lyrics printed on the cover, but they believed that the songs were intertwined, making it a "concept album." They like the words "genre," "artist," "rhythm section" (the latest cliché for bass and drums), and "front man." They enjoy talking about how certain songs "changed their consciousness," prefer FM radio, and will choose "Stairway To Heaven" as their favorite Led Zeppelin song.

The elite will list their favorite groups as Cream, Jimi Hendrix, and Bob Dylan, and to really be hip, the MC5, Fugs, and the Velvet Underground. They will also claim to have liked Buffalo Springfield and the Yardbirds when they were active groups, rather than after the fact. They like the Beatles (one of the few groups popular with just about everyone), but for usually different reasons than the rest of the population. John Lennon, as the intellectual one, is their favorite, of course, and they consider his solo music at least as good as his Beatles music because he was being honest. Their favorite Beatles song is "A Day in the Life," giving honorable mention to "Tomorrow Never Knows," "In My Life," and the second side of *Abbey Road* (which is considered one song to them). They will rarely list a single as a favorite song.

There is a certain lingo that one must master to be considered an elite. The first rule is, never use the term "Bob Dylan," but rather only "Dylan." Do the same with the "Stones," the "Spoonful," and the "Dead." The usual rule is to drop the first word, but be careful! The hip term for Creedence Clearwater Revival is not "The Revival," but rather "Creedence." This can also be helpful in the sports world by using the "'Horns," "'Canes," "'Huskers," "'Niners," "'Sixers," and so on. If you use the full name, your comments will probably be ignored in either arena. For locations, say the "Village" (for Greenwich Village), and the "Haight" (for Haight-Ashbury).

The elite enjoy calling musicians "artists," along with musicians using that word for each other. However, the dictionary definition of "art" is "the conscious use of skill and creative imagination in the production of aesthetic objects." The key word here is "objects," which implies something tangible. From this, musicians are not artists. Vincent Van Gogh and Pablo Picasso were artists. If musicians are artists, they are one of dozens of subsets, and the term "musician" is a much more definitive word.

> Keith Richards said, "I don't think rock-and-roll songwriters should worry about art. I don't think it comes into it. A lot of it is just craft anyway, especially doing it for a long time. As far as I am concerned, art is just short for Arthur."

The second type of music-listening enthusiast is the "proletariat." Members of this group are more casual music fans and enjoy listening to music for entertainment. They are not much interested in the lyrics, except for their entertainment value. The melody and rhythm are mostly what make the song for them. Groups popular with them, but not the elite, are the Monkees, Herman's Hermits, and Three Dog Night. The elite would consider these groups simpleminded.

There are a *lot* more proletariat than elite (elite, by definition, means "few"). That is why the Grass Roots, Partridge Family, and Carpenters sold significantly more music than the Yardbirds, Velvet Underground, and Fugs.

For proletariats, people who create music are called musicians. They like the Beatles, not because they changed people's consciousness, but because the music made them feel good. They prefer "Penny Lane" over "Strawberry Fields Forever," and they liked "Hello, Goodbye."

Both groups have songs they secretly like, but will not admit to anyone else. When someone is listening to this type of song in the car, and someone else opens the door, she will turn off the CD player. If the doorbell rings at home, she will replace the current CD with Cream or Jimi Hendrix. I certainly have these songs on my iPod, but they will remain a secret (to get to those songs, one needs a password). There are millions of people who purchased records of the 1910 Fruitgum Company, Ohio Express, Bread, the Carpenters, and others whose music has not aged so well, and most of them are still alive. The elite have their own groups, ones like the Monkees, Sonny and Cher, and Lovin' Spoonful.

Group Commentary and Sales Statistics

For simplicity, the word "group" will be used for both individuals and groups, as individuals almost always had accompanying musicians, with the exceptions of early Bob Dylan, Joni Mitchell, and Neil Young (live). Even Donovan had accompanying musicians, as seen while playing live on *Shindig*.

It is interesting, though, that both Dylan and Donovan used themselves for backup and harmony vocals.

The idea of a song being good or bad is purely subjective. The *commercial* success of a song, album or group, however, can be objectively measured by record sales and chart comparisons with other songs.

"Gold" is a Record Industry Association of America (RIAA) designation of five hundred thousand sales. "Platinum" is an RIAA designation of one million sales; the number after "platinum" indicates how many millions; i.e., "platinum 3" is three million in sales.

Single/album "ranking peak" is the *Billboard* top position reached. This number is based on both sales and radio play (for singles). All albums shown are gold or higher, and singles are peaking at ten or better. "Weeks" is the number of weeks at that top position, if the song has ranked number one or two.

Single/album rank by calendar year is according to *Billboard.* For singles, it is in the year released, and for the top forty songs of the year. For albums, it is the top one hundred of the year, and the album can make the list for two or more years. The ranking for albums is based on the chart positions and number of weeks on the charts, rather than sales. This book ranks albums only through 1971.

Single all-time ranking is according to *Billboard*, through the year 2000.

Group all-time single rank is by *Billboard* as of June 30, 2001, and is for sales of singles.

Album all-time unit sales rank is from RIAA. This is based entirely on sales, rather than the rating system that *Billboard* uses. The RIAA and *Billboard* rankings are quite different. For example, Frank Sinatra is sixty-sixth on RIAA and third on *Billboard.* Most of Sinatra's career was during an era where the total album sales were much lower than in later years. Thus, he did much better on a ranking based on album chart positions than total sales. An opposite example, during a much higher period of albums sales, is Led Zeppelin. They are ranked third by *RIAA*, but only forty-fifth by *Billboard.* They tended to have a lot of sales over many years, rather than in spurts.

"RS" is the song's rank in the *Rolling Stone* magazine of top five hundred songs (November 2004).

"Total sales" (platinum and gold) is the strongest evaluator of album success. "Peak" is the least meaningful ranking for albums; it is a relative position, meaning that it will show well with weak competition, and poorly with strong competition. If an album came out at the same time as *The Beatles (White Album)*, forget about number one; whereas, a different release date might make that ranking possible. An album can peak at a high position, but not be on the charts for long, or might have good sales over a long period, but not achieve a high peak. The weakness in the calendar-year ranking is that an album might be split evenly amongst two or more years, and not rank high in any year.

Singles have almost no sales after their "hot" period, so single peak rankings mean a lot more than albums, which can have significant sales for years.

Often, the terms "pop" and "rock-(and-roll)" are interchangeable. However, this is not correct. There is no "rock" chart, only "pop," which includes all albums. This book's rankings are the pop rankings, and it includes some non-rock-and-roll music. Christmas albums are not included.

When comparisons and lists are made, they are only from the 1964-1972 era.

Sample Chart

Year	Top Ten Single(s)	Peak	Weeks	RCY	All Time Ranking	Gold Album(s)	Sales	Peak	Weeks	RCY
1966	California Dreaming* (A)	4				If You Can Believe Your Eyes and Ears (A)	Gold	1	1	1966 (6) 1967 (25)
1966	Monday Monday*	1	3	5	315	The Mamas & The Papas	Gold	4		
1966	I Saw Her Again*	5								
1966	Words of Love	5								
1967	Dedicated to the One I Love (B)	2	3	21		Deliver	Gold	2	7	
1967	Creeque Alley* (C)	5								

All-time single rank #252

* Written by John Phillips

(A) RS 89; featured a flute

(B) Written by Ralph Bass and Lowman Pauling. Bass later invented the Bass guitar (not really)

(C) "good vibrations"

Survey

"Name recognition," and anything else that pertains to the "survey," is the result of a questionnaire that I gave to twenty-nine friends who said they had an interest in the music of this era. Participants were age forty-eight or older.

Name Recognition

How well do you recognize musicians' names from this era? Sure, you've probably heard of Brian Wilson of the Beach Boys, but how about Al Jardine? Survey participants were tested to see how many names they could list from a selection of groups. For those groups the survey covered, you'll find the results as the first bulleted item above the group's song chart. It will look like this example from the Beach Boys, showing how well each member's name is recognized:

- Name recognition: Brian Wilson, ninety percent; Mike Love, forty-five percent; Carl Wilson, forty-one percent; Al Jardine, thirty-four percent; Dennis Wilson, twenty-one percent.

How Well Do You Know The Music?

The page numbers where the answers are located are shown in parentheses. The answers for those without page numbers are all on pp. 305-307.

1. Name the Beatles songs where the song title is not part of the lyrics. (pp. 25-42)
2. Name a group where the lead singer of the first single, which reached number ten, was not even in the group when the second single was released. (p. 125)
3. The Beatles by numbers: Name the songs that had these numbers in the lyrics: "1-2-3-4," "1-2-3-4-5-6-7-8-9," "1-2-3-4 and 5-6-7-8-9-10," "1-2-3-4-5-6-7," "1+1+1=3" (pp. 25-42)
4. What is the significance of the numbers 2006 and 910, relating to the Beatles? (pp. 25-42)
5. Which groups had four lead singers (at least three songs each)?
6. Which album cover had a toilet on it? (p. 99)
7. Which Beatles songs had split-lead-solo vocals? (pp. 25-42)
8. Which group had a lead singer that played the bongo drums? (p. 133)
9. Which band had two drummers? Two keyboard players? (pp. 151, 139)
10. Name groups whose first top-forty hits were written by Bob Dylan.
11. Pick the two that were not a band: Four Tops, Box Tops, Four Boxes; Five Americans, Jay and the Americans, Jay and the Five Americans.
12. Which song was released almost simultaneously by two different groups? One reached number fifteen, and the other number forty.

13. Name group members who were not the primary lead learned how to snap their fingers, or play the tambourine. To learn the tambourine takes years of specialized training, which includes deciding on whether to bump against the wrist or hip.) This does not include Motown groups, where instrument playing was rare.
14. Which Bob Dylan songs could also be called "Wet Weather Ahead" and "Spinning Your Wheels"?
15. Who was the biggest success in the U.K. who never did catch on, this side of the Atlantic Ocean? He/they had sixty-eight top-twenty songs from 1961-1999 in the U.K., but zero in the U.S.
16. Which 1966 single was the name of another group?
17. Who was the first to wear wire-rimmed granny glasses? [Probably not who you think.] (p. 122)
18. Which two Bob Dylan songs had almost exactly the same beginning?
19. Name two number-one songs (from 1964 and 1965) whose lyrics were written before 1930.
20. Name five songs that have the word "together" in the title.
21. What songs have a party going on in the background?
22. Name two people (besides Elton John) whose primary instrument was the piano.
23. Which band lost its primary songwriter, who was also one of its lead singers, but continued with two strong albums?
24. Name a song that was the title of the group's preceding album. (p. 67)
25. Which album had the lyric "Lenny Bruce" on two different songs? (p. 103)
26. Which song character died June 3, 1967? (p. 193)
27. Name groups whose first top-forty hit was written by Bob Dylan.
28. Which song title (two entirely different songs) was a number-one hit in both 1959 and 1970? (p. 194)
29. Who was the first musician to part his hair down the middle (well before John Lennon in 1968)?

Which songs contain these lyrics?

1. “Electrically, they keep a baseball score” (p. 129)
2. “Declare the pennies on your eyes” (p. 31)
3. “I never understood a single word he said” [No, not a Bob Dylan interviewer] (p. 132)
4. “I can almost taste it” (p. 127)
5. “Magic carpet ride” [Other than Steppenwolf] (p. 127)
6. “Good vibrations [Other than the Beach Boys] (p. 100)
7. “Get while the gettin’s good” (p. 89)
8. “When you return, it’s the same old place” (p. 192)
9. “I’ve been droolin’” (p. 121)
10. “Who’s your daddy” [Pedro Martinez’s favorite song] (p. 170)
11. “Nothin’ I do don’t seem to work” (p. 56)
12. “Hey, hey, hey” [two number-one songs] (pp. 56, 102)
13. “Grateful Dead”
14. “Some people born silver spoon in hand, lord, don’t they help themselves. But when the tax man comes to the door, lord, house look like a rummage sale, yeah.”
15. “He can’t even run his own life, I’ll be damned if he’ll run mine.”
16. “The bathroom is clear”
17. “I saw someone on the street who was really shook”
18. “Be sure to hide the roaches”
19. “He died, but it did not show”
20. “I look pretty tall, but my heels are high”
21. “I’m going to take my problems to the YOUnited Nations” [no, not John Kerry]
22. “If it’s square, we ain’t there”
23. “Light my fire” [other than the Doors or Jose Feliciano]
24. “Eight miles high” [two songs, other than the Byrds]
25. “She was practiced at the art of deception”
26. “Stuck around St. Petersburg, when I saw it was a time for a change”
27. “Blood in the streets, town of Chicago”
28. “Mom met Dad in the back of a rock and roll car”
29. “Keep your eyes on the road, hands on the wheel”

30. "Negroes in the forest" [for extra credit: what do they say?]
31. "Love your neighbor, until his wife gets home"
32. "I don't care if she waddles like a duck" (p. 214)
33. "Move over, Rover, and let Jimmy take over"
34. "They've got the guns, but we've got the numbers"
35. "When I was young, I carried a gun"
36. "From me to you" [other than the Beatles]
37. "Two and two is three"
38. "Beatniks" (Cool, Daddy-O)

Religious lyrics

39. "I'll pray there ain't no hell"
40. "And I pretend to pray"
41. "Get on my knees and pray"
42. "Jesus Christ" [not J.C. Superstar, 1973]
43. "The church service makes me nervous"
44. "Don't forget to say grace"
45. "Devil's on the loose"
46. "Glory hallelujah"
47. "Allah" [no, not Cat Stevens; I consider this the most difficult lyric question]
48. "I've got a friend in Jesus"
49. "If the Bible tells you so"
50. "The resurrection"
51. "Lord have mercy"
52. "Before you can see Jesus"
53. "Great God in heaven"
54. "Doesn't anybody know how to pray?"
55. "I'd kill him with my Bible"
56. "I think it's a sin"
57. "Jesus loves you"
58. "Child of God"
59. "I am the god"

For picture answers, please see p. 307

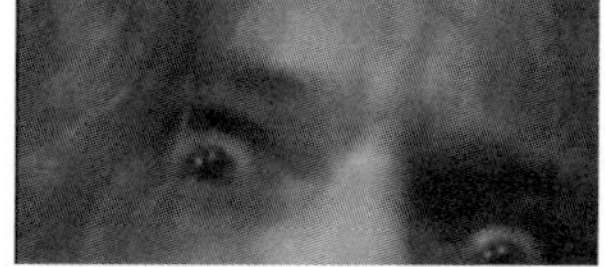

Whose eyes?

Whose glasses?

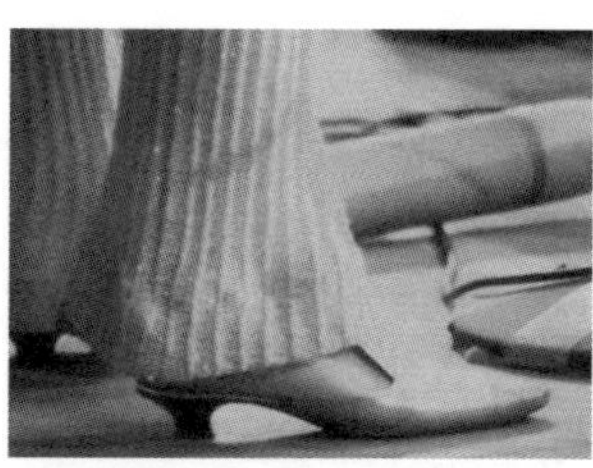

Whose shoes?

Whose shoes?

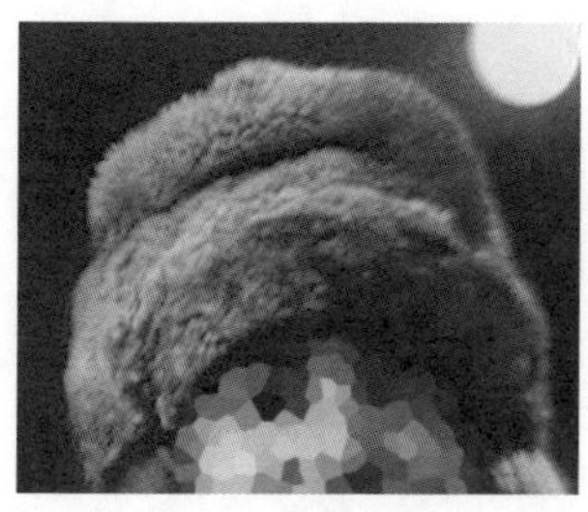

Whose hat?

Whose hat?

The First Tier

The Beatles

Chapter One

The Beatles

The Beatles are so tremendously popular because they appeal both to the elite and the proletariat. Writer Peter Stamfel said, "Since the Beatles came along, all the professional failures who said it was impossible to be good and sell at the same time have been answered finally."

It is hard to "imagine," if you were not alive at the time, or old enough to remember, what a phenomenon the Beatles were. They had the top five songs in the Top 40 *all at once.*_They had four singles out on different labels. Overnight, they changed men's hairstyles. Their hair was as big of a topic as their music. They were on trading cards and lunch boxes. They were the main characters in two movies and a cartoon show. They sang songs in two different languages. They were the first group to play in a stadium (which seated fifty-six thousand, and they filled it with no advertising). They were the first group with a music video ("Rain/Paperback Writer" and "We Can Work It Out/Day Tripper" preceded "Penny Lane/Strawberry Fields Forever," but the latter was the first one widely seen [on the Ed Sullivan Show]) and the only group that could afford not to tour.

As if they did not have everything else going for them, it is interesting that all three guitarists were the same height (5'11"). This certainly helped for stage presence, and in the many songs that two of them would sing into the same microphone. When bands like the Animals got on stage where a guitarist was 9 inches taller than the singer it looked awkward. The same problems were had with the short singer of the Lovin' Spoonful playing with taller guitar players.

Great Songwriting

It is hard to believe that the two greatest musicians of the rock era were both in the same band. Nothing else had happened like that since Babe Ruth and Lou Gehrig were on the Yankees together. Keith Richards, who was the third most talented musician of the era, was not in the top tier with John Lennon and Paul McCartney.

Musical Talent, Second Tier:

3. Keith Richards
4. John Fogerty
5. Paul Simon
6. Bob Dylan
7. Neil Young
8. Pete Townshend
9. Roger McGuinn
10. Brian Wilson

The above list is weighted heavily toward songwriting, which is the most valuable musical talent. There are hundreds of very talented singers and instrument players for every great songwriter. Roger McGuinn is the only one of the above who was not an outstanding songwriter. However, he was the founder of folk rock and psychedelic rock, and his twelve-string guitar had the best sound of any instrument.

Songwriting is the backbone of any musical group. There are perhaps many singers and instrumentalists that could have been used to make a certain song a hit, but the same cannot be said for songwriters. The Monkees and Three Dog Night are good examples of this; they were successful because they found good songwriters.

They could have been interchanged with scores of other musicians, and the songs would have been just as successful.

Lennon and McCartney wrote more superior songs as the Beatles than they did as soloists, even though most songs were written entirely by either one or the other. This was due to the competition between them, writing what the market wanted to hear, and George Martin's producing.

Most other songwriting pairs, such as Goffin-King, Gilbert-Sullivan, Rice-Webber, Love-Wilson, and Taupin-John, consisted of one person writing the lyrics, and the other the music.

During the Beatles' tenure, it was sometimes assumed that Lennon wrote the lyrics and McCartney the music (the lyricist is usually mentioned first). Lennon and McCartney were unusual, in that on the songs where they collaborated, they wrote both lyrics and music together. Songs that they truly combined on were "From Me to You," "Thank You Girl," "I'll Get You," "She Loves You," "I Want to Hold Your Hand," and "Baby's in Black." The rest were primarily written by one or the other. Lennon and McCartney had agreed to share songwriting credits, regardless of the writer, back in the early 1960s. When Lennon's "Give Peace a Chance" had a Lennon-McCartney songwriting credit, people started to realize that they were not co-writers on at least some of the songs.

Musicianship

Were the Beatles good musicians? Good enough. Does it really matter to just about anyone if they are each in the ninety-ninth percentile of all instrument players, rather than the 99.5 percentile? George Harrison was ranked as the twenty-first best guitarist on the *Rolling Stone* list. Would the songs really be any better if he were in the top five? How many people heard "Back in the USSR" or "Ballad of John and Yoko," and immediately noticed that Ringo Starr was not playing (this is assuming Starr was a better drummer than McCartney)? Did anyone notice right away that Lennon, Harrison, and Starr were not playing on "Lady Madonna"? The Beatles were great, primarily because they were great songwriters and singers, not because they were the best at their instruments.

Lennon

John Lennon was the greatest rock musician overall, especially through the period of *Revolver*. He was the primary songwriter for all the Beatles' number-one songs until "We Can Work it Out," in late 1965, with the exception of "Can't Buy Me Love." ("She Loves You" and "I Want to Hold your Hand" were considered co-written by Lennon and McCartney.) After "We Can Work it Out," McCartney passed him up, with only "All You Need is Love" and "Come Together" reaching number one for Lennon.

Something happened after *Revolver*. Maybe it was meeting Yoko Ono. Maybe it was his massive use of lysergic acid diethylamide (LSD), which caused lethargy. His music moved down a notch, even though he was still the number-two overall musical talent until the end of the Beatles. Sorry, but "Being for the Benefit of Mr. Kite" and "Yer Blues" were not in the same class as "Ticket to Ride" and "Day Tripper." He was tired of not being himself and became more interested in writing songs that he wanted to write, rather than what would necessarily be popular.

McCartney

McCartney was the second-best rock musician and was number one from 1967 to 1970. He also assumed the leadership role in the group after manager Brian Epstein died and after Lennon lost interest. McCartney was the master of public relations and had the most common sense in the group.

Harrison and Starr

George Harrison, as the number-three player, was also incredible, especially from *Revolver* forward (after a midterm slump from *Sgt. Pepper* through *Yellow Submarine*). He is close to making the prior list of talented musicians.

Ringo Starr had the best personality and sense of humor and sang some good songs himself. His answer to the following question is classic:

> Interviewer: "How do you determine who sings each song?"
>
> Starr: "Whoever knows the words."
>
> The answer is not as silly as it sounds, for whoever sang lead on the songs generally was the principal songwriter.

There are no other groups in which all the members sang lead at one time or another, or all wrote songs. There were no other groups in which all the members handled interviews well, or did not do encores. (Encores are a waste of time. Why go through the nonsense of going off stage and then coming back, and then possibly doing it again? A standing ovation means nothing either, as it is done all the time). They did the first music video with "Penny Lane" and "Strawberry Fields Forever." Actually, there were videos for "Paperback Writer," "Rain," "Day Tripper," and "We Can Work It Out," but these were not widely seen They also had the sense to quit touring, which was unheard of at the time. Most groups complain about touring, but the Beatles actually did something about it (and could afford to quit). That was the best decision that any group ever made.

Ed Sullivan Show

On the Beatles' first two appearances on *The Ed Sullivan Show* (February 1964), the song lineup was "All My Loving" (twice), "Till there Was You," "She Loves You" (twice), "I Saw Her Standing There" (twice), "I Want to Hold Your Hand" (twice), "This Boy," and "From Me to You." I am sure it was no accident that McCartney sang the lead on five of these songs, and Lennon only once, to more appeal to the young female audience. Has there ever been another entertainment show where the host only introduces the acts (and moves his arms around a lot)? The Beatles were only paid $2,400 for their Sullivan appearances. However, for what it did for their career, they would have come out far, far ahead, even if they had paid to be on the show. Of course, there were critics of their music after their first performance on *The Ed Sullivan Show*.

> Noel Coward, actor, had this to say. "I've met them. Delightful lads. Absolutely no talent."

> Ray Block, orchestra leader on the *Sullivan* show said, "The only thing different is the hair, as far as I can see. I give them a year."

> Nat Hentoff, music critic, declared, "Musically, this reviewer cannot understand the fervor of Beatles' admirers, or the scorn of their detractors. Except for their visual uniqueness, the Beatles are a run-of-the mill rock-and-roll attraction."

Not being content with being wrong once, Hentoff soon after gave this comment:

> "The Searchers seem to be the most professional British rock group to have appeared in America. To this viewer, the initial impression was more favorable musically than had been the case with the Beatles or the Dave Clark Five. They sustained an exuberant mood, punctuated by several unison jumps in the air. They showed a more subtle command of dynamics than the two groups that preceded them."

Moptops

When the Beatles first appeared, their hair was just as big a topic of discussion as their music. It all started when bassist Stu Sutcliff's girlfriend, Astrid Kirchherr, started combing his hair over his forehead, and letting it grow a little to give him more of an "artist" look. Later, the others, except for Pete Best, adopted the same look when Brian Epstein encouraged them to drop their "grease" look.

Roadies

The Beatles had only two road managers, where later bands had dozens. Mal Evans was more high profile for some reason, and helped occasionally with some of the songs (without songwriting credit). He was also the ice swimmer in the movie *Help*. Neil Aspinall, their first road manager, got stuck managing a lot of the ill-fated Apple projects. He was the primary non-Beatles speaker (the one wearing all of the goofy hats) on the *Anthology* video series.

Manager

The most important thing Brian Epstein did was recognize the talent and charisma of the Beatles. Without him, they might have remained only a local band. He did an incredible job promoting the band and getting them on the *Palladium* and *Ed Sullivan shows*. Unlike many bands, the Beatles received significant money from mid-1963 on. There was never the common band question of "where did all the money go?" Before Apple Records, there was never a hint of financial problems. Epstein probably did a poor job of negotiating their first publishing contract and the same has been said for the EMI record contract. But after being turned down by other labels, they were not in a strong bargaining position in 1962. Brian also mismanaged the novelty royalties, which cost them tens of millions of dollars on their first U.S. tour.

British Invasion

The Beatles, first in so many things, were the first English group to have success in the United States, and the second group, behind the Dave Clark Five, to tour here. This started the "British

Invasion," which described all the English groups to have success in the United States from 1964-1966. (It should have been called the "English Invasion," because none of the groups were from Wales, Scotland [except Donovan], or Northern Ireland.) Of course, many felt threatened by this, and the U.S. government attempted a protectionist measure against free trade. Maybe the Beach Boys had their own lobbyist☺. The Department of Labor declared, in January 1965, that no UK rock groups would be granted H-1 visas, which were necessary for a U.S. tour. This did wipe out a Zombies tour, but common sense prevailed soon after and this restriction was eliminated.

The arrival of the Beatles was thought to be the death knell for most American groups. This was certainly true for folk music, even though Peter, Paul, and Mary remained popular. Here are the popular 1963 groups that fell by the wayside: the Rooftop Singers, Steve Lawrence, Chubby Checker, Bobby Vee, Bobby Darin, Johnny Mathis, Kingston Trio, and Dion. The survivors, however, seemed to pick up steam, as overall record sales increased with the advent of the Beatles, who created an overall increase in music. Included in this group were the Beach Boys, Jan and Dean, and Bob Dylan, who all had more success after 1963.

Post-1972 albums are usually not listed in this book, but it is interesting to note that even with huge sales of non-compilation albums, *The Beatles 1962-66* was platinum (15), and *The Beatles 1967-70* was platinum (16). Both albums were released in 1973. *Anthology 1*, *2*, and *3* each reached platinum (8), (4), and (3), respectively in 1995-1996. On top of that, their album 1 reached platinum (8) in 2000.

Beatle Album Rankings

For the following, I rated each Beatles song from five to one, the top quintile of songs being a five, the second a four, and so on. (See song ratings beginning on p. 25.)

Using those ratings, each album is ranked below on the average rating per song. (Sorry, no extra points for a "concept" album or a good album cover). Obviously, the rating of the songs is highly subjective, but once this is established, the album rankings are objective.

UK Versions

(The average is not exactly 3.0 because there are some songs on more than one album.)

Rank/Album:	Average song rating:
1. *Revolver*	4.00
2. *Past Masters Two*	3.87
3. *Magical Mystery Tour*	3.64
4. *Help!*	3.43
5. *Past Masters One*	3.31
6. *Beatles for Sale*	3.21
7. *Yellow Submarine*	3.17
8. *Hard Day's Night*	3.15
9. *Rubber Soul*	2.86
10. *Let it Be*	2.83
11. *Please Please Me*	2.71
12. *Sgt. Pepper*	2.69
13. *Abbey Road*	2.53
14. *The Beatles*	2.37
15. *With the Beatles*	2.36

U.S. Versions

Rank/Album:	Average song rating:
1. *The Beatles Again*	4.00
1. *Revolver*	4.00
1. *Yesterday and Today*	4.00

The original cover of *Yesterday and Today* pictured the group dressed in white butcher's outfits, with slabs of meat, glass eyeballs, and nude, decapitated dolls. Capitol Records sent this cover out to radio stations and some large stores (one copy each), and once the word got out, the 750,000 already-produced covers were pasted over with the trunk picture. Contrary to popular belief, the original covers were never sold in stores. The new cover could be meticulously peeled off, which resulted in the existing butcher covers in existence today. (For some reason, steaming it off with an iron was the method that I had heard would work, and of course I destroyed the whole cover trying it.) In the lower-right-hand corner of the paste-over cover, one could see the bleed-through of Starr's V-neck shirt. The Beatles' protest of the "butchering" of the UK albums *Rubber Soul* and *Revolver* was rumored as the reason for the cover. However, the Beatles had never planned for the original picture to be used on the album. They were tired of the same old photo shoots and wanted to rebel a little.

4. *Magical Mystery Tour*	3.64
5. *Hard Day's Night*	3.62
6. *Help!*	3.43
7. *Second Album*	3.36
8. *Yellow Submarine*	3.17
9. *Rubber Soul*	3.08
10. *Beatles 65*	3.00
11. *Something New*	3.00
12. *Let it Be*	2.91
13. *Beatles VI*	2.82
14. *Sgt. Pepper*	2.69
15. *Early Beatles*	2.64
16. *Abbey Road*	2.53
17. *The Beatles*	2.37
18. *Meet the Beatles*	2.33

- Songs that were on UK albums (including *Past Masters*), but not on U.S. Capitol/Apple albums: "Misery," "There's a Place," "I'm Down," and "From Me to You."

Singles

The week ending April 4, 1964, had Beatles songs at the top five positions on the singles chart. "Can't Buy Me Love" was at the top and had not previously been released in the UK; "I Want to Hold Your Hand" was on its way down; two of the songs were hits in the UK in 1963 and were being re-released in the United States ("She Loves You" and "Please Please Me"); the fifth song, "Twist and Shout," was also a 1963 song, but was being released for the first time.

Nothing has ever come close to matching this, nor have the backlog of songs that they had. The Beatles were able to release a single while the previous singles were still in the top ten. What was even more amazing is that they could also release three other singles (old songs) at nearly the same time. The only other group with two singles in the top ten was the Dave Clark Five with "Bits and Pieces" and "Glad All Over." Even the Beatles would not again have two in the top ten, other than the above songs, unless they were flip sides of each other.

The first non-Beatles song that reached number one was "Hello, Dolly!" on May 16, 1964, after fourteen straight weeks of a Beatles song holding the spot. The first time the Beatles were not in the top ten at all, after "I Want To Hold Your Hand" was released, was June 27, 1964.

Singles vs. Albums

The Beatles were the first, and one of the few, groups that could easily sell albums without their latest single on it.

In the UK, "I Want to Hold Your Hand," "From Me to You," "I Feel Fine," and in both the United States and the UK, "Paperback Writer," "We Can Work it Out," "Hey Jude," "Ballad of John and Yoko," "Penny Lane," and "All You Need Is Love," were not on the contemporary albums.

There was a delay of eleven months for "Get Back/Don't Let Me Down" until it appeared on the *Let it Be* album. There was a six-month gap between "We Can Work It Out/Day Tripper" and the *Yesterday and Today* album. The only other group that often left singles off of U.S. albums was the Rolling Stones, with "Jumpin' Jack Flash," "Honky Tonk Women," and "19th Nervous Breakdown."

One line of thinking is that not having the single on the album would increase single sales (the only way to own the song is to buy the single). Another line of thinking (which was used by Led Zeppelin) was that not putting out singles from an album would increase album sales. For example, if "Norwegian Wood" were released as a single, it would decrease the *Rubber Soul* sales. You could own the song without buying the album.

The Beatles released three albums that had no singles on them: *Rubber Soul* (United States), *Sgt. Pepper*, and *The Beatles*. Following the logic of not having singles on albums increasing album sales (you had to buy the albums to get the best songs from that album), *The Beatles* was the number one-selling Beatles album, platinum (19); *Sgt. Pepper* was number two, platinum (11); and *Rubber Soul* was number four, platinum (6).

The single "B-side" was also part of this. A better flip-side would marginally increase the sales of that single, and slightly decrease album sales. "Penny Lane" sold more with the "Strawberry Fields Forever" flip-side than it would have with "Being for The Benefit of Mr. Kite."

It would make sense that singles were released before albums (they all were except "Something/Come Together," which was released six days after the *Abbey Road* album, and "Hard Day's Night," which was released seventeen days after the album). If people know it is going to be on the album, they are less inclined to buy the single. They could assume that they were going to like the non-single album cuts. Since the Beatles' albums contained so many good non-singles, it is surprising the singles sold as well as they did. Obviously, price is a factor. Some could not afford to buy albums. Singles were about $1 and albums were $2.99 (mono) and $3.99 (stereo).

Electrical Music Industry (EMI) owned Parlophone (UK) and Capitol (U.S.), the labels on which the Beatles' records were released (Apple was later the distributor).

A group usually needs a hit single to get off the ground. Even the Beatles did, issuing the singles "Love Me Do" and "Please Please Me," along with including both songs on their first UK album; it was the same with "I Want to Hold Your Hand" and *Meet the Beatles* in the United States. Exceptions to the hit single rule are Jimi Hendrix Experience, who got started in the United States with the Monterey Pop Festival; Bob Dylan, who had album success before his first single release; and Led Zeppelin, who did not have a single on their first album. However, Dylan went to a much higher level with the single release "Like a Rolling Stone." However, all lesser groups would not have the luxury of not including the single on the album. I doubt Zager and Evans considered not putting "In the Year 2525" on their album.

Since most albums had the hit singles on them, and a lot of "skip-over" songs, more people were inclined to buy the lesser groups' singles, rather than their albums.

Record Companies

Vee Jay records was the most successful black-owned record company before Motown. "Love Me Do" was not released as a single in the United States until 1964, but Vee Jay released "Please Please Me" in March 1963. Capitol Records had the first option to release a Beatles single in the United States, but they passed, and Vee Jay picked up the option. The song did get some airplay from Chicago station WLS and was placed on their top-forty charts for two weeks. The band's name was misspelled "Beattles" on both the record label and the top-forty charts.

"From Me to You" was released, again by Vee Jay, in May 1963. Nationwide, the airplay was only enough to push it to number 116 in Billboard, with this peak coming on August 10, 1963.

Vee Jay passed on "She Loves You," and it was picked up by Swan Records and released in September 1963. It also went nowhere.

In December 1963, Capitol Records launched the largest promotional campaign in music history for the single "I Want to Hold Your Hand/I Saw Her Standing There." Of course, this was a huge hit, which left Swan and Vee Jay in interesting positions.

Swan re-released the "She Loves You" single, which was number nine for all of 1964. Vee Jay re-released the "Please Please Me" single, which was number thirty-five for 1964. They also re-released the *Introducing the Beatles* album, which was the number thirteen album for the year. Tollie Records released "Twist and Shout," which was number twenty-four for 1964. Amazingly, MGM re-released "My Bonnie," in which the Beatles were only backup musicians for Tony Sheridan, and it peaked at number twenty-six. Atco released "Ain't She Sweet" (also with Tony Sheridan), which reached number nineteen and featured Lennon as lead singer.

Why did these singles do so much better the second time around? Firstly, they were not originally marketed very well. However, there are a lot of songs that do well that are not marketed, but rarely by unknown groups. Songs by UK bands had never done well in the United States. Probably more important was familiarity. Once people decided that they liked the Beatles' sound from the *Meet the Beatles* album and the "I Want to Hold Your Hand" single (which were hugely promoted), they were much more likely to purchase other Beatles music, including songs that were previously recorded. The same happened with the Doors and their first single release, "Break on Through," which became much more popular after "Light My Fire"; Don McLean's first album, *Tapestry*, after "American Pie" was released; and Simon and Garfunkel's "Wednesday Morning, 3 AM," which went nowhere in its initial release.

Song Rights

Music-publishing companies obtain ownership of songs in exchange for providing publicity and copyright protection, obtaining record contracts, paying for demonstration recording, and providing funds for the group before sales money comes in. In early 1963, the Beatles gave up the rights to their songs to Northern Songs. Thus, when any of their songs were used on albums or song sheets, it was that company that collected one-half of the money, with the songwriter(s) getting the other half. To start with, Dick James and his partner owned fifty percent of Northern Songs, while Brian Epstein and the Beatles owned the other fifty percent. When the company started trading publicly, James and partner Charles Silver owned 37.5 percent combined; Lennon, fifteen percent; McCartney, fifteen percent; Epstein, five percent; Starr, 0.8 percent; and Harrison 0.8 percent. James and Silver sold out to ATV in 1969, as did Lennon and McCartney. Michael Jackson bought out ATV in 1985 and he sold half of his interest to Sony in 1995. Thus, today, for almost every Lennon-McCartney song sold, Jackson/Sony receives fifty percent and the Lennon estate and McCartney, twenty-five percent, each. Before Northern Songs was formed, McCartney bought the rights to "Love Me Do," "Please, Please Me," "P.S. I Love You," and "Tell Me Why." George's songs were initially owned by Northern Songs, but he formed Harrisongs when the initial Northern Songs contract expired in 1968. The owner of the publishing rights actually owns the song and decides on whether the song can be used for a commercial. When a musician complains about his song being played on a commercial, he has only himself to blame.

Apple Corps Ltd.

The Beatles, like most musicians, had little business aptitude and they had naïve ideas about how to run Apple Records. Starr liked the idea that people would not have to beg to get music recorded. Lennon said they would spin it like a top and see where it went; people who just want to make a film about anything do not have to get on their knees in somebody's office. They said that no one would be turned down.

> McCartney explained, "We are in the happy position of not needing any more money. So, for the first time, the bosses are not in it for profit. We have already bought all our dreams. We want to share that possibility with others."

After being in the real world a few months, McCartney said, "If we carry on like this, we will all be broke in six months." Neil Aspinall said that they got inundated with tapes, poetry, etc.

The two Apple Boutiques closed within three months; there were filmmakers who did not make films; there were poets who did not write poems.

> Starr said, "There was a tent for a guy to do a "Punch and Judy" show on a beach. They'd take the money and say, 'Well, maybe next week.'"

> Harrison said, "We had every freak in the world coming in there."

> Lennon said, "We owned a house which no one can remember buying. … The staff came and went as they pleased and were lavish with money and hospitality." There was an executive jet.

> "Apple rented me a gorgeous flat," said Doris Troy, whose single was a commercial failure.

> "Furnishings are an unbelievable expense," said Alistair Taylor, who was not above lavish spending himself. "One guy has an all-white office which cost the Earth. Another has real antique furniture in his office and expensive old paintings all over the walls. I thought to myself, why shouldn't I have what I want? So I went out to Ryman's and bought a set of their office furniture which really took my eye. I didn't bother to ask the price. Anyway, Apple now provides Lesley and me with a marvelous flat in Montague Place."

The liquor bill was $7,600 per month (in 2004 dollars), and the phone bill was $51,000 per quarter.

There was a subsidiary label set up, Zapple, for poetry and experimental music. Allen Ginsburg, Richard Brautigan and Ken Kesey were to record.

> Harrison said, "It seized up before it really got going, as with so many things with Apple. Both the Zapple albums that did come out were a load of rubbish." (Lennon and Yoko Ono's *Unfinished Music Number Two*, and Harrison's *Electronic Sounds*).

Apple Records, a record label, was also formed. EMI/Capitol still maintained ownership rights to the Beatles records, but issued the records under the Apple label, starting with the album *Yellow Submarine* in 1968. The Capitol logo still remained, in small print, on the Apple records. EMI/Capitol was chosen to distribute Apple records until 1975. Obviously, this part of the Apple company was immensely successful. It offset the frivolities mentioned above.

Apple did sign Mary Hopkin, Badfinger, and James Taylor, but no one was hired who sent an application through the mail, as they had promised. They also signed eighteen other, mostly unknown, bands.

Retirement

The Beatles are also one of the few groups that officially announced their retirement. (Buffalo Springfield had an album called *Last Time Around*, and Cream had one called *Farewell Tour.*) At the time, the end of the group seemed to be the release of McCartney's first solo album (it really *was* solo) in April 1970 (one week prior to the release of "Let It Be"), and his announcement that he was quitting. However, Lennon told the rest of the group he was leaving on September 13, 1969. He was persuaded by Allen Klein not to announce it for business reasons. The only studio work after that was the January 3, 1970, recording "I Me Mine," without Lennon.

Miscellaneous

- Two of the worst predictions ever made were made in relation to the Beatles: 1. Lennon's Aunt Mimi said that he would never make a living playing a guitar. 2. When Decca Records turned down the Beatles, Decca executive Dick Rowe said that groups of guitars were on their way out.

- Regarding French audiences in 1964, McCartney said, "The funny thing about France is that it was boys screaming." Harrison said, "Hanging around the stage door were slightly gay-looking boys."

- Best songs: 1. "Ticket to Ride" 2. "Norwegian Wood" 3. "Help!" 4. "Day Tripper" 5. "Paperback Writer" 6. "We Can Work It Out" 7. "I Feel Fine" 8. "Rain" 9. "She Said She Said" 10. "Twist and Shout"

- Best Harrison songs: 1. "Taxman" 2. "Here Comes the Sun" 3. "Something" (Frank Sinatra's favorite Lennon-McCartney song)

- Underrated: 1. "I Don't Want to Spoil the Party" 2. "Two of Us" 3. "Drive My Car"

- Worst Songs: 1. "Revolution 9" 2. "You Know My Name"

- Worst real songs: 1. "Within You Without You" 2. "Yes It Is" 3. "I Want You" 4. "Mr. Moonlight" 5. "Good Night" 6. "Long, Long, Long"

- Best singles (factoring in both A and B sides):
  1. A — "We Can Work It Out,"
     B — "Day Tripper," the best overall single released by any group
  2. A — "Paperback Writer,"
     B — "Rain"
  3. A — "Hey Jude,"
     B — "Revolution"

- Worst number-one song: "Can't Buy Me Love"

- The album *One (27 Number One Hits)* is stretching the truth, at least according to *Billboard* charts. "Love Me Do" did reach number one in the United States, but only number seventeen in the UK, when first released. "From Me To You" reached only number forty-one in the United States, but did reach number one in the UK. "Day Tripper" reached number five as a B-side to "We Can Work It Out." "Eleanor Rigby" reached number eleven as the B-side to "Yellow Submarine." "The Ballad of John and Yoko" reached number eight. "Something" reached number three as the flip-side (they were both considered A-sides) to "Come Together." Not included on the album was "Nowhere Man," which reached one, two and three on the three charts. On a side note, "Penny Lane" was the first song not to reach number one in the UK It did reach number one in the United States for a week.

- Two B-sides that did not make albums were "The Inner Light" and "I'm Down."

- At their last concert at Candlestick Park in San Francisco on August 29, 1966, there were five warm-up acts (I do not envy these people), ten thousand empty seats, and nothing from the *Revolver* album (to be released in a week).

There's every reason to believe that the Beatles' 1967 schedule will mix together most of the '65 and '66 ingredients in similar proportions. There's *no* question of the Beatles putting a stop to their tours.

"The traveling bit isn't always enjoyable," admits Ringo, "but touring is still one of the most important things we do. It's very bad for an artist to sit back and think he's got it made. If it weren't for fans, his whole security would fall about him and it would all be over. Fans want to *see* groups — not just listen to their records or watch TV shows. Also, it's exciting for the group to do concerts and hear the reactions of an audience. After a break, there's nothing quite so wonderful as the sound of a live audience shouting, screaming and having a ball. It makes you feel great. That's what show business is all about. We wouldn't miss concerts tours for anything, so you can forget the rumors!"

16 Magazine, August 1966

Neil Aspinall says they all agreed to Pete's firing, but that it was George who gave the final push because George was Ringo's biggest admirer. Pete's mother has a simpler theory: "Pete's beat had made them. They were jealous and they wanted him out." It is not

There may be some truth to the tale that the **Beatles** will change their official name to **Sgt. Pepper's Lonely Hearts Club Band** for tax purposes. ~~As "Beatles" they are in~~

Tiger Beat, October 1967

Beatle Paul McCartney is Mike's brother — but he is dead-set on making it to the top all on his own.

Spec, January 1967

Year	Top Ten Single(s)	Peak	Weeks	RCY	ATR	Gold Album(s)	Sales	Peak	Weeks	RCY
1964	I Want to Hold Your Hand (A)	1	7	1	51	Meet the Beatles	Plat 5	1	11	1964 (8) 1965 (31)
1964	She Loves You (B)	1	2	9	392	Second Album	Plat 2	1	5	24
1964	Please Please Me (C)	3		35		Hard Day's Night	Plat 4	1	14	1964 (37) 1965 (36)
1964	Twist and Shout (D)	2	4	24	982	Something New	Plat 2	2	9	1964 (51) 1965 (51)
1964	Can't Buy Me Love (E)	1	5	2	131					
1964	Do You Want to Know A Secret (F)	2	1	32						
1964	Love Me Do	1	1	22	889					

1964	P.S. I Love You (B-side)	10								
1964	Hard Day's Night (G)	1	2	15	489					
1964	I Feel Fine	1	3	8	345					
1965	Eight Days a Week (H)	1	2	16	599	Beatles '65	Plat 3	1	9	2
1965	Ticket To Ride	1	1	22	897	Beatles VI	Plat	1	6	10
1965	Help! (I)	1	3	6	353	Story	Gold	7		46
1965	Yesterday (J)	1	4	2	218	Early Beatles	Plat	43		93
1966	We Can Work It Out	1	3	6	343	Help!	Plat 3	1	9	27
1966	Nowhere Man (K)	3				Rubber Soul	Plat 4	4	6	4
1966	Paperback Writer	1	2	18	598	Revolver	Plat 5	1	6	17
1966	Yellow Submarine (L)	2	39							1966 (8) 1967 (56)
1967	Penny Lane (M)	1	1	18	924	Sgt. Pepper	Plat 11	1	15	1967 (10) 1968 (6)
1967	Strawberry Fields Forever (B-side) (N)	8								
1967	All You Need Is Love (O)	1	1	16	823					
1967	Hello Goodbye	1	3	10	316					
1968	Lady Madonna (P)	4				Magical Mystery Tour	Plat 6	1	8	4
1968	Hey Jude (Q)	1	9	1	23					

1969	Get Back	1	5	3	128	The Beatles	Plat 11	1	9	8
1969	Come Together (R)	1	1	14	667					
1969	Something (Harrison) (S)	3	3	38		Yellow Submarine	Plat	2	2	57
1969	Ballad of John and Yoko	8								
1970						Abbey Road	Plat 12	1	11	4
1970	Let It Be (T)	1	2	10	393	Again	Plat 3	2	4	49
1970	The Long and Winding Road	1	2	17	590	Let It Be	Plat 3	1	4	31

All-time single rank #2

Songwriters were Lennon-McCartney

(A) "You Don't Own Me" (Lesley Gore) had the misfortune of peaking at the same time at number two for three weeks; RS 16

(B) RS 64

(C) RS 184

(D) Behind "Can't Buy Me Love" for four weeks

(E) RS 289

(F) Behind "Hello, Dolly!"

(G) RS 153

(H) RS 384

(I) RS 29

(J) RS 13

(K) Behind "19th Nervous Breakdown," "Ballad of Green Berets"

(L) Behind "You Can't Hurry Love"

(M) RS 449

(N) RS 76

(O) RS 362

(P) Behind "Young Girl," "Honey," "Cry Like a Baby"

(Q) RS 8

(R) RS 202 3

(S) Behind "Come Together," "Wedding Bell Blues," double A-side

with "Come Together" the first ever double A-side; RS 273

(T) RS 20

Total album sales 166.5 million (first)

- There were also seven non-single RS rankings, making the total twenty-two in all.

Rating the Songs

For the following, each Beatles song was rated from five to one, the top quintile of songs being a five, second a four, and so on. The UK versions of the albums are used.

Album:	Song Rating Average:
Please Please Me	2.71
Rating: Songs:	Comments:
3 "I Saw Her Standing There"	1-2-3-4
3 "Misery"	Not on any U.S. album
3 "Anna"	Written by Arthur Alexander, who also wrote *You Better Move On* for the Rolling Stones
2 "Chains"	Written by Goffin-King; previously released by The Cookies in 1962
2 "Boys"	Dixon-Farrell; previously released by The Shirelles, the first American all-girl group

1 "Ask Me Why"	One of four songs played at their first recording session at EMI studios; thankfully, George Martin nixed it as their first single
5 "Please Please Me"	In the last verse, after "Last night I said these words to my girl," Lennon and McCartney mistakenly sing different lyrics. Somehow, on the later releases, this was eliminated
4 "Love Me Do"	Lennon was supposed to sing lead, but a harmonica was decided on, which gave the lead to McCartney; no electric guitar; only two chords
2 "P.S. I Love You"	McCartney's voice covers more than an octave, while Lennon stays on one harmony note in the bridge
1 "Baby It's You"	"Cheat, cheat"
3 "Do You Want to Know a Secret"	Written by Lennon, sung by Harrison. "I thought it would be a good vehicle for him because it only had three notes and he was not the best singer in the world."
1 "A Taste of Honey"	Written by Scott-Marlowe; previously released by Lenny Welch
3 "There's a Place"	Written by Lennon, but he sings low harmony vocal, except for the first and third lines of the bridge; not on any U.S. album
5 "Twist and Shout"	Charted a second time in 1986; no rhythm guitar on instrumental break

Album:	**Song Rating Average:**
With the Beatles	2.36
Rating: Songs:	Comments:
4 "It Won't Be Long"	"Yeah" is said fifty-six times
1 "All I've Got to Do"	Lennon's attempt to do Smokey Robinson; no lead guitar
4 "All My Loving"	Prominent rhythm guitar with triplets; first song that had significant radio airplay that was not a single; reached number forty-five in Canada
1 "Don't Bother Me"	First song written by Harrison
1 "Little Child"	50/50 Lennon-McCartney composition
1 "Till There Was You"	From the play *Music Man*
4 "Please Mr. Postman"	Number one for the Marvelettes in 1962; starts with "Wait;" a song title from *Rubber Soul.* No lead guitar.

5 "Roll Over Beethoven"	Written by Chuck Berry, whose songs the Beatles recorded more than those of any other songwriter; reached only number sixty-eight in Canada
1 *Hold Me Tight*	Inaudible bass; McCartney coming as close to singing out of tune as any song; backup harmonies precede the lead vocal
3 "You've Really Got a Hold on Me"	Only Harrison on background vocals; longest song to date at 2:58
2 "I Wanna Be Your Man"	The Rolling Stones' first charting single in UK
2 "Devil in Her Heart"	Written by Richard Drapkin; released as a single by the Donays in 1962; tom-tom drum introduction
1 "Not a Second Time"	William Mann, music critic: "Harmonic interest is typical of their quicker songs too, and one gets the impression that they think simultaneously of harmony and melody, so firmly are the major tonic seventh and ninths built into their tunes, and the flat-submediant keyswitches, so natural is the Aeolian cadence at the end of *Not a Second Time*." No lead guitar, bass; George Martin on piano
3 "Money"	Exact opposite lyric message from "Can't Buy Me Love"

Album:	**Song Rating Average:**
A Hard Day's Night	3.15
Rating: Songs:	Comments:
5 "A Hard Day's Night"	Not performed in film; split lead vocals; McCartney sang the bridge because Lennon could not reach the high notes
5 "I Should Have Known Better"	John's first falsetto
4 "If I Fell"	Written by Lennon, but McCartney sings melody with Lennon on low harmony (when both voices are together)
2 "I'm Happy Just to Dance with You"	Written by Lennon, sung by Harrison; ten "ohs" as backup vocals
2 "And I Love Her"	First song with two acoustic guitars
4 "Tell Me Why"	Written to provide an upbeat song for the movie; bizarre falsetto background vocals on bridge
3 "Can't Buy Me Love"	Exact opposite lyric message from "Money"; opens with chorus; first single to feature only one singer

2 "Any Time at All"	Dual lead vocal. McCartney sings the second "any time at all"
4 "I'll Cry Instead"	Only song on the U.S. *Hard Day's Night* album that was not in the movie
2 "Things We Said Today"	Acoustic guitar more dominant than electric lead throughout the song
2 "When I Get Home"	"Cows" and "trivialities"
3 "You Can't Do That"	Two lead guitars; Harrison dominates on backup vocals
3 "I'll Be Back"	McCartney on high harmony in the verses

Album:	Song Rating Average:
Beatles for Sale	**3.21**
Rating: Songs:	Comments:
3 "No Reply"	No lead guitar; music publisher Dick James told Lennon that this was the first song that told a complete story; Lennon's first song without an electric guitar
4 "I'm a Loser"	First Bob Dylan influence, with more introspective lyrics; i.e., "Beneath this mask, I am wearing a frown."
3 "Baby's in Black"	50/50 Lennon-McCartney composition and vocals; last duet until the *Let It Be* album; written in 12/8 meter
5 "Rock and Roll Music"	No lead guitar
4 "I'll Follow the Sun"	Written in 1960
1 "Mr. Moonlight"	Harrison on African drum; rare Hammond organ solo; ascending three-note bass solos
3 "Kansas City/Hey,Hey,Hey,Hey"	"1-2-3-4-5-6-7-8-9"
5 "Eight Days a Week"	First song with a fade-in; written primarily by McCartney, but song by Lennon (double-tracked until the bridge); not issued as a single in UK; no lead guitar
3 "Words of Love"	Written by Buddy "Huh-Huh" Holly, but was not a hit for him; when Holly died, he was attempting to revive his career. No major musician would be playing in an Iowa ballroom in February at the top of his career. His first single, "That'll Be the Day" reached number two, but his following releases were 3,10,17,37,27,32; Starr slaps a suitcase with a loose fastening (which makes a clapping sound)

1 "Honey Don't"	Sung by Lennon until Starr joined the group in 1962
2 "Every Little Thing"	Starr plays kettle drums after the lyric "she does;" sung by Lennon, but written primarily by McCartney
5 "I Don't Want to Spoil the Party"	Lennon double-tracked on first part of verses; solo on "There's nothing for me here" and then double-tracked again; bridge: McCartney sings melody, and John harmony; best harmonizing of all Beatles songs
4 "What You're Doing"	Best drum introduction; Lennon harmony on first verse words "look," "I'm," "you've," "and," "please," "you've;" McCartney double-tracked on "me"
2 "Everybody's Trying to Be My Baby"	An improved version live at Shea Stadium with an electric rhythm guitar, rather than acoustic

Album:	Song Rating Average:
Help!	**3.43**
Rating: Songs:	Comments:
5 "Help!"	B-side "I'm Down" was not on the album; no bridge; repeat of first verse with only John as acoustic guitar; starts with chorus
3 "The Night Before"	Background vocals only on "Ah, the night before;" Lennon on electric piano, which sounds very much like a guitar, only guitar is on instrumental break, and very end
3 "You've Got to Hide Your Love Away"	First song with outside musician (flute), other than George Martin; written in 12/8 meter
2 "I Need You"	The first time Harrison used a wah-wah pedal to distort the sound of his guitar "I don't need no wah-wah"
3 "Another Girl"	McCartney on lead guitar at end; rhythm guitar chords on the off-beat
3 "You're Going to Lose that Girl"	Starr on bongo drums; the word "you" in the backing vocals barely audible
5 "Ticket to Ride"	First Beatles song over three minutes; McCartney on lead guitar
5 "Act Naturally"	Last of the twenty-four non-original releases, except for the brief "Maggie May"; McCartney only on harmony vocals; Starr on lead vocals

4 "It's Only Love"	Lennon hated the lyrics; lead guitar fed through a Leslie amplifier to give it a different sound
2 "You Like Me Too Much"	Both a piano and an electric piano used; on the intro, the piano is on the left track, and the electric is on the right; the electric plays the chords during the vocals; the piano returns on the instrumental break, along with the only guitar in the song
2 "Tell Me What You See"	Lennon on washboard guitar
5 "I've Just Seen a Face"	No bass guitar; first thirty-two words are without a vocal break, with only "forget" being more than one syllable
4 "Yesterday"	Not released as a single in UK; most-covered song in history, according to *Guinness Book of World Records.*
2 "Dizzy Miss Lizzie"	Last cover of a song written by someone outside the group; prominent rhythm guitar

Album:	Song Rating Average:
Rubber Soul	**2.86**
Rating: Songs:	Comments:
5 "Drive My Car"	As in "Please Please Me," a small lyric difference in Lennon's and McCartney's vocals in last verse; Lennon has only solo vocal with"and baby, I love you;" last real duet until "Two of Us"; single note, rather than chord, rhythm guitar
5 "Norwegian Wood"	First Beatle use of sitar; *Anthology* version bridge has McCartney with a lower, and louder, high harmony which does not sound as good as this version; written in 12/8 meter
3 "You Won't See Me"	Longest song to date at 3:17
5 "Nowhere Man"	First Lennon-McCartney song not written about a boy/ girl relationship
2 "Think for Yourself"	McCartney on fuzz bass
1 "The Word"	Prominent bass line
3 "Michelle"	Reached number one in UK by Overlanders
1 "What Goes On"	First poor song chosen for B-side (of "Nowhere Man"); could have been a reason for the single reaching only number three

3 "Girl"	Sound similar to a drag on a marijuana cigarette in background
3 "I'm Looking through You"	Only song with better version on *Anthology*; the U.S. stereo version has two false guitar intros
2 "In My Life"	Not popular at the time, but now considered hip to like this song; electric piano recorded at half-speed, then sped up to give it a harpsichord sound
2 "Wait"	Split lead vocals, (McCartney on bridge); no rhythm guitar
2 "If I Needed Someone"	Lead guitar patterned after the Byrds' "Bells of Rhymney"
3 "Run for Your Life"	No bridge; "That's the end-uh, little girl"

- *Rubber Soul* had the best album cover

Album:	Song Rating Average:
Revolver	**4.00**
Rating: Songs:	Comments:
5 "Taxman"	No rhythm guitar; Harrison plays off-beat chords during the lyrics and McCartney the lead instrumental part; first of Harrison's great songs, "Declare the pennies on your eyes"
5 "Eleanor Rigby"	One of few songs that deals with death; on the first "Eleanor," backing vocals on only the first two syllables; on final chorus, McCartney double-tracked with one of the voices delayed
4 "I'm Only Sleeping"	Backward guitar recordings; "float upstream;" first ten notes are the same (E)
4 "Love You To"	Title not part of the lyrics; "screw you;" Harrison only
5 "Here, There and Everywhere"	Three-part backing vocals, including McCartney double-tracked
5 "Yellow Submarine"	Written primarily by McCartney, sung by Starr; no bass guitar
5 "She Said She Said"	Only Harrison on background vocals; beat changes from 4/4 to 3/4 at the bridge "When I was a boy"

4 "Good Day Sunshine"	Piano, bass and drums only
4 "And Your Bird Can Sing"	"And your bird can swing" in the last verse, backing vocals on the first verse line only in the last verse; *Anthology* version, as with "Norwegian Wood," has McCartney with a lower, and louder, high harmony
3 "For No One"	Bass, piano, horn and drums only; McCartney and Starr only
4 "Doctor Robert"	Lennon on harmonium; McCartney on high harmony "He's a man you must believe"
3 "I Want to Tell You"	Fade in; McCartney vocal audible only on fade out
4 "Got to Get You into My Life"	First trumpets, saxophones; one note bass line for first eight bars; double drum roll before chorus; reached number seven in 1976; no guitar until 1:49
1 "Tomorrow Never Knows"	First Lennon-McCartney song that did not have the title as part of the lyrics; first song recorded for *Revolver*; first Beatle use of tape loops (McCartney found that by moving the erase and putting a loop on a tape, he could actually saturate the tape with a single noise. It would go round and round and eventually the tape could not absorb any more and he would bring it in and play it, according to George Martin). The distortion of Lennon's vocals was accomplished by his singing through a rotating loudspeaker, and sung through a megaphone. This was only song that was admitted to be about drugs; "float downstream"

- Harrison looks like Keith Richard on the cover with his shag haircut and protruding ears, and Lennon is seen in glasses for the first time.

Lennon is usually listed as the "rhythm guitar" player. Prior to *Sgt. Pepper*, each member primarily played his usual instrument, and all four were on each track, with the exception of "Yesterday." However, after *Revolver*, Lennon and Harrison each played both lead and rhythm guitars. On the noisier songs, both Lennon and Harrison played lead, while on the softer ones, one of them played acoustic. Both also occasionally played bass guitar, and McCartney played guitars. There were also numerous tracks with one, two, or three Beatles missing.

Album:	Song Rating Average:
Sgt. Pepper's Lonely Hearts Club Band	**2.69**
Rating: Songs:	Comments:
4 "Sgt. Pepper"	Split lead vocals, Lennon "It's wonderful to be here;" first song with audience sounds
4 "With a Little Help From My Friends"	Written primarily by McCartney, sung by Starr; bass, piano, drums only
4 "Lucy in the Sky with Diamonds"	Split lead vocals, McCartney sings first line of first chorus; written in 3/4 meter, other than the chorus (4/4)
3 "Getting Better"	George Martin, striking the piano strings, not the keys (the staccato sound)
2 "Fixing a Hole"	Lead guitar double-tracked; "Hey, hey, hey; I'm wrong, I'm right"
1 "She's Leaving Home"	Split lead vocals (concurrently); Beatles played no instruments; vocals doubled so it sounded like a quartet; written in 3/4 meter
1 "Being for the Benefit of Mr. Kite!"	Wurlitzer organ, Hammond organ, and two harmonicas; title not in the lyrics; shifts from 4/4 to 3/4 meter at "waltz" and "Bill"
1 "Within You Without You"	Harrison on Tamboura; title not in lyrics; laughter at the end
3 "When I'm Sixty-Four"	Written by McCartney in 1957; the magical year is 2006
3 "Lovely Rita"	Comb and paper used as an instrument; prominent bass; mouth noises in last part
3 "Good Morning Good Morning"	Horses, chickens, dogs, horses, elephant, and rooster sounds
4 "Reprise"	"1-2-3-4," with Lennon saying "lie" (?) in the background
2 "A Day in the Life"	I could get death threats for this rating. It is a very esoteric, complex song, but the melody is just not that good; two separate songs put together, with the writer being the lead singer; Lennon's voice achieved with a tape echo; title not in the lyrics; "turn you on;" alarm clock sound at 2:18; double- time middle section

Some of the elite will admit that the individual songs on *Sgt. Pepper* are not that great, but will still say that the album as a whole is. It also had all the lyrics on the cover, which was a first, and a dream come true for the elite. It is also a "concept album." What exactly is that? An album is just a collection of individual songs. Whatever is before or after each song does not affect that song.

Lennon said about *Sgt. Pepper*, "It does not go anywhere. All my contributions had nothing to do with the idea of Sgt. Pepper and his band; but it worked because we said it worked."

The only "connection" on the album is that the first two songs do not have a time gap between them, and there is a reprise.

Album:	Song Rating Average:
Magical Mystery Tour	**3.64**
Rating: Songs:	Comments:
4 "Magical Mystery Tour"	Split lead vocals; Lennon sings, "Roll up for the mystery tour"
3 "The Fool on the Hill"	McCartney on recorder (a type of a clarinet); no backing vocals; written in 3/4 meter
1 "Flying"	All four chanting; only other instrumental was "Cry For A Shadow"
1 "Blue Jay Way"	"Don't be long" sung twenty-nine times
2 "Your Mother Should Know"	No lead guitar; prominent instrumentation provided by piano chords
5 "I Am the Walrus"	Lennon's response to Dylan's lyrics. "Dylan got away with murder. I can write this crap, too," meaning much of Dylan's lyrics meant absolutely nothing, but the "experts" tried to read something into them that was not there; "Lucy in the sky"
5 "Hello Goodbye"	Song filmed with Beatles lip-synching; it was banned by the BBC for this reason, because it was against the rules of the British musicians union; title only in background vocals; Harrison only on background vocal "I can stay until it's time to go"
5 "Strawberry Fields Forever"	Two different takes were put together, at 0:59 into the song, where Lennon's vocal wanders during "going to;" after that point, the second take is slowed down, which causes the vocal to have more of a nasal sound; "yeah, yeah, yeah;" the flute-like sound at the beginning is the mellotron

5 "Penny Lane"	Split lead vocals (Lennon "I sit and" and "in summer"); first words are song title
4 "Baby You're a Rich Man"	Two separate songs put together; Lennon on oboe-sounding clavioline; Lennon falsetto lyrics on verses; chorus mainly one note
5 "All You Need Is Love"	Chorus mainly one note; "Yeah, yeah, yeah;" guitar lead only at 1:20; a rare 7/4 tempo

- The elite will downgrade *Magical Mystery Tour* because the last four songs on the second side are a collection of singles.

Album:	Song Rating Average:
Yellow Submarine	**3.17**
Rating: Songs:	Comments:
5 "Yellow Submarine"	See *Revolver*, p. 31
1 "Only a Northern Song"	Written during the *Sgt. Pepper* sessions; discordant instruments, especially during the instrumental break
3 "All Together Now"	1-2-3-4 and 5-6-7-8-9-10; dual lead vocals; Lennon: "Sail the ship"
4 "Hey Bulldog"	Final song written before leaving for India; "Bullfrog" is the lyric used before the last refrains
1 "It's All Too Much"	Too much "too much," as words mentioned thirty-five times, not including fade-out
5 "All You Need is Love"	See *Magical Mystery Tour*

Album:	Song Rating Average:
The Beatles (Disk 1) **(Disc 2)**	**2.88** **1.69** **2.37 (combined average)**
Rating: Songs:	Comments:
5 "Back in the USSR"	Song runs into "Dear Prudence" with no break (start of another "concept album"?); balalaika: three-stringed instrument of Russian origin with a triangular body played by plucking or strumming

5 "Dear Prudence"	McCartney on flugelhorn; first guitar picking by Lennon, picked up from Donovan in India
5 "Glass Onion"	Other songs mentioned in lyrics: "Lady Madonna," "I Am the Walrus," "Strawberry Fields Forever," "Fool on the Hill"; starts with two drumbeats; "Oh yeaaaaaaaaah;" lyrics poked fun at those Lennon felt were over-analyzing his lyrics
5 "Ob-La-Di, Ob-La-Da"	Was Desmond a man or a woman? If there were a single off this album, this would have been it; Marmalade did take it to number one in Britain; peaked at number forty-nine in 1976
1 "Wild Honey Pie"	McCartney alone; title not in the lyrics; the forty-five acoustic guitar notes after "I Love You" belong to this song, not the next
2 "The Continuing Story of Bungalow Bill"	Only song with Yoko Ono solo "Not when he looked so dear;" title not in the lyrics; "Eyes-uh"
4 "While My Guitar Gently Weeps"	Eric Clapton on lead guitar; "diverted," "perverted," "inverted," "alerted"
2 "Happiness Is a Warm Gun"	An extra "down" (error in editing) at 0:57; Lennon's screaming vocals similar to McCartney's on "Oh Darling"
2 "Martha My Dear"	High pitched lyrics on bridge, peaking with "done;" ends with descending bass line
3 "I'm So Tired"	Begins with ascending bass line
2 "Blackbird"	McCartney alone; only instrument is acoustic guitar; bird noises
3 "Piggies"	More animal noises; distorted voice on bridge; Harrison double-tracked on last verse
2 "Rocky Raccoon"	Last song with harmonica and first since "I'm A Loser"
3 "Don't Pass Me By"	Reached number one in Scandinavia; Harrison on violin; Starr on piano; Starr had been talking about this song since 1963
1 "Why Don't We Do It In the Road"	McCartney alone; title mentioned fifteen times in lyrics
2 "I Will"	There is a percussion instrument, starting at 0:41, that sounds like a horse's hooves on a hard surface; bass is McCartney singing "dum"
2 "Julia"	Only song with Lennon alone; acoustic guitar only

(Disk 2)	
5 "Birthday"	Split lead vocals, Lennon: "Yes, we're going to a party, party;" Yoko Ono on background "birthday"
1 "Yer Blues"	Title not in the lyrics; changes from 3/4 to 4/4 time at 2:07 (fittingly, right before the lyrics "rock and roll;" final verse sung into an almost dead microphone)
1 "Mother Nature's Son"	Only McCartney, with session musicians on brass; staccato sounding percussion from 1:00 to 1:21
2 "Everybody's Got Something to Hide Except Me and My Monkey"	Harrison on firebell; title not in lyrics ("for" added); a better title would have been "Come On, Come On"; sounds like an "s" added before some of the "take it easy" verses; lots of "ooh" in the background
2 "Sexy Sadie"	Guitar sounding much like "I Want You" at 2:17
1 "Helter Skelter"	McCartney's raucous vocals similar to "Monkberry Moon Delight" on his *Ram* album
1 "Long Long Long"	The eerie sound at the end is a bottle of wine vibrating
3 "Revolution I"	The "shooby-doo-ah" version; title not in the lyrics; modified and sped up this version for single release
1 "Honey Pie"	For the younger readers: "Now she's hit the big time" is what an old record sounded like
2 "Savoy Truffle"	The horns, which were common for many of Harrison's solo songs, were first heard here
1 "Cry Baby Cry"	"Séance;" split-lead vocals, McCartney: "Can you take me back"
1 "Revolution 9"	Lennon said, "This is the music of the future. You can forget all the rest of the s___ we've done – this is it. Everybody will be making this stuff one day. You don't even have to know how to play a musical instrument to do it!" Yes, there was an instrument used on this song: piano, at the beginning; title not in the lyrics
1 "Good Night"	Written by Lennon, Starr on vocals; only song with harp

- *The Beatles* album starts out as well as any, but falls off after the first four songs, and then crashes after "Birthday." Somehow, a lot of people list this as their favorite. No vocal duets.

Album:	Song Rating Average:
Let It Be	**2.83**
Rating: Songs:	Comments:
5 "Two of Us"	No bass, but the electric guitar plays low notes; first time Lennon and McCartney were unison singers since "Baby's In Black"; unlike many songs with one singer for the verses/chorus and two for the bridge, this one is just the opposite
1 "Dig a Pony"	Starr halts the count-in to blow his nose; McCartney misses falsetto harmony at 2:10; written in 3/4 meter
4 "Across the Universe"	No bass; "Jai guru deva om" means "Yoko, quit commenting on the music, when you really know nothing about it" (not really)
2 "I Me Mine"	Last song recorded, January 3, 1970 (without Lennon); 3/4 (waltz timing)
1 "Dig It"	"Like a Rolling Stone;" all four somehow got songwriting credit; written in 3/4 meter
4 "Let It Be"	Billy Preston does not play on the album version, while Harrison's guitar sounds like an organ; debuted at number six, sixth highest of all time
2 "Maggie Mae"	Lennon with a heavy accent; background vocal sounds neither like Lennon or McCartney; Record and Road say it was McCartney, while ATN say it was Lennon
3 "I've Got a Feeling"	Two separate songs put together, Lennon's "Everybody had a hard year;" split lead vocals, some concurrent, some not; "Wet dream"
2 "The One after 909"	Written by Lennon in 1957, also known as "910;" first duet, along with "Two of Us," since "Drive My Car"
3 "The Long and Winding Road"	Only McCartney and Lennon (bass)
2 "For You Blue"	Title not in lyrics; Lennon on slide steel guitar
5 "Get Back"	Disk credit on single was "Beatles with Billy Preston;" only two chords, fewest since "Love Me Do"; guitar at 1:20 has static (sounds like the record player needle needs to be cleaned)

The last album released, but recorded well before *Abbey Road*. McCartney's solo album (a true solo, as he played all instruments), *McCartney*, was released about the same time.

What is confusing is that McCartney looked very similar on both of these albums, which would lead one to believe the two pictures were taken at about the same time, when actually they were sixteen months apart. He had a beard during the *Let It Be* album, shaved it off for *Abbey Road* and *The Beatles Again*, and then grew it again for the *McCartney* album.

Album:	Song Rating Average:
Abbey Road	**2.53**
Rating: Songs:	Comments:
4 "Come Together"	Chuck Berry took Lennon to court, as he did with Brian Wilson with "Surfing USA," because "Here comes old flat-top" and the opening melody were said to be taken from Berry's "You Can't Catch Me." As compensation, Lennon recorded three Berry songs (he again refused to credit Berry, which led to another lawsuit – not really, on the last part); "1+1+1=3;" last twelve notes of verses the same (F)
4 "Something"	Only Harrison A-side single; second only to "Yesterday" in number of covered versions
1 "Maxwell's Silver Hammer"	Starr on anvil "Bang, bang"
1 "Oh! Darling"	McCartney's screaming "Monkberry Moon Delight" voice on bridge, double-tracked; lots of "ooh" in background; written in 12/8 meter
3 "Octopus's Garden"	Water sounds were made by blowing bubbles in a glass of water, during instrumental break; second song Starr sings about being underwater
1 "I Want You"	Longest song; arpeggio at end lasts 3:08, with an abrupt ending; last words are "she's so;" only lines are "I want you," "It's driving me mad," and "She's so heavy"
5 "Here Comes the Sun"	The word "clear" at 2:24 seems to be an error, because "here" was used in the previous three verses; bridge is "Sun, sun, sun, here it comes" five times
1 "Because"	Only song with three singers throughout; starts with harpsichord arpeggio, with guitar arpeggio added at 0:12; Moog synthesizer at 1:31 to 1:42

2 "You Never Give Me Your Money"	"1-2-3-4-5-6-7;" this song is more of a medley than the album side; first part lasts until 1:10; second (accompanied by a voice change) until 2:14
1 "Sun King"	"Paparazzi," an obscure word at the time, but became trendy a few years ago (as did "diva"); Lennon on multi-tracked vocal
4 "Mean Mr. Mustard"	A "ten bob note" is a British ten schilling bill; starts with drums; McCartney's harmony comes in at 0:26
4 "Polythene Pam"	"Yeah, yeah, yeah;" Liverpool accent
3 "She Came in through the Bathroom Window"	Prominent bass line, especially "Worked at fifty clubs a day;" Harrison said, "A very strange song of Paul's with terrific lyrics, but it's hard to explain what they are all about!"
3 "Golden Slumbers"	Words taken from a Thomas Dekker poem
3 "Carry that Weight"	All four sing on chorus line; "You Never Give Me Your Money" melody starts at 0:24
2 "The End"	Only drum solo; Harrison, McCartney and Lennon all play lead guitar at different times
1 "Her Majesty"	Shortest song; originally between "Mean Mr. Mustard" and "Polythene Pam"; the first chord is from "Mean Mr. Mustard," and there is no chord at the end of the song

Some view the songs from "Because" through "The End" as one song, which has some truth to it, but not much. It is true that "Golden Slumbers/Carry That Weight," "Sun King/Mean Mr. Mustard," "Polythene Pam/She Came in through the Bathroom Window" were recorded at near the same time. The fact that there are no time gaps between the above songs does not make much difference. (All the Moody Blues songs had no gaps between them, and each album was hardly considered one song). One song did contain part of the melody of another song, however.

Album:	Song Rating Average:
Past Masters Volume One	**3.31**
Rating: Songs:	Comments:
4 "Love Me Do"	(1963) Also on "Please Please Me"
4 "From Me to You"	(1963) Falsetto (Lennon) octave leap on vocals; inaudible lead guitar

4 "Thank You Girl"	(1964) More harmonica on The Beatles *Second Album* version; inaudible lead guitar; McCartney sings harmony on second line of verses
4 "She Loves You"	(1963) One of three songs with "Yeah, yeah, yeah" in it; starts with drums, and then chorus
3 "I'll Get You"	(1963) Vocal error at 1:14 where Lennon and McCartney are singing different words; with the first word "imagine" and an "it's easy" in the second line, this song could be called "Pre-Imagine"
5 "I Want to Hold Your Hand"	(1964) Octave leap on vocals "hand"; vocal gaffe at 1:23; lead guitar very light; handclaps; John sings solo on first bridge and with Paul on second
4 "This Boy"	(1964) No drums (but dominant bass) until the bridge; first song not written in 4/4 tempo, with 12/8
2 "Long Tall Sally"	(1964) Part of their live set from the beginning to the end(Candlestick Park)
4 "I Call Your Name"	(1964) Only cover (Mamas and Papas) that was better than the Beatles' version
4 "Slow Down"	(1964) Peaked at only number twenty-five
1 "Matchbox"	(1964) Peaked at only number seventeen; flip-side of "Slow Down"; these two were the only covers released as singles
5 "I Feel Fine"	(1964) First use of feedback with opening bass guitar note; Lennon plays opening guitar riff
2 "She's a Woman"	(1964) No lead guitar until instrumental break; prominent bass line; rhythm guitar sounds on the off-beat; longest song to date at 2:59; first reference to marijuana "turn me on"
2 "Bad Boy"	(1965) Released in United States but not in UK; blues-type lead guitar, playing only between vocal lines; title not in lyrics
1 "Yes It Is"	(1965) Released in 1965 in United States but not UK; on *Anthology*, song returns to *Beatles VI* version after the gibberish lyrics at 1:03
4 "I'm Down"	(1965) Not on any U.S. or UK album; Lennon on Hammond organ, which he played on stage at Shea Stadium

Album:	Song Rating Average:
Past Masters Volume Two	**3.87**
Rating: Songs:	Comments:
5 "Day Tripper"	(1966) Written primarily by Lennon, with McCartney as primary lead singer; split lead vocals, Lennon, "she was a'; prominent use of tambourine; bass line follows lead during verses, which makes it hard to discern; almost inaudible rhythm guitar
5 "We Can Work It Out"	(1966) Lennon on harmonium; Lennon wrote the bridge; prominent use of tambourine; no lead guitar
5 "Paperback Writer"	(1966) Harrison with falsetto; "Frère Jacques" on backup vocals
5 "Rain"	(1966) Starr's best drum work, according to him; Roger McGuinn's favorite Beatles song; best stereo split on vocals on the word "rain," with McCartney on high harmony
5 "Lady Madonna"	(1968) Piano and bass the only instruments until 0:44, then guitar, then saxophones (0:53); Harrison on background vocal "See how they run"
2 "The Inner Light"	(1968) Title not in lyrics; Harrison's last Indian-sounding music
5 "Hey Jude"	(1968) Only the first 3:11 is the regular part of the song; the last four minutes is the "Na-na-na-na"
5 "Revolution"	(1968) Word "revolution" used just once, in the first line; guitar sounded so scratchy that many record buyers (vinyl in those days) tried to return the 45, thinking it was defective
5 "Get Back"	(1969) Also on *Let It Be*
2 "Don't Let Me Down"	(1969) McCartney with high harmony vocals on chorus; Lennon double-tracked on bridge; Lennon's lowest-pitched vocals of any song at 2:28
4 "Ballad of John and Yoko"	(1969) Title not in lyrics; Lennon and McCartney only; bass loudest instrument
1 "Old Brown Shoe"	(1969) A bass as lead-in bridge
4 "Across the Universe"	(1969) Also on *Let It Be* (sounds like ducks flying off the water at the beginning)
4 "Let it Be"	(1969) Also on *Let It Be*
1 "You Know My Name"	(1969) Recorded in 1967; hard to believe this song was chosen for the B-side of "Let it Be."

Chapter Two

Just Give Me Some Truth: Another Side of John Lennon

There are many who idolize John Lennon to this day. The reasoning is probably that since he was a great musician, he was also a great person. Many people seem to have a difficult time separating the person and the music.

John was no saint, and he would probably be surprised at his idolization.

At Paul's birthday party in 1963, John beat up Cavern DJ and longtime friend Bob Wooler, after he suggested that Lennon and Brian Epstein were having a homosexual affair.

Then, in 1964, John traveled alone with Brian. What kind of judgment does that show? If he were that sensitive about being called a homosexual, traveling alone with Epstein was not a good idea. John supposedly became committed to non-violence after this. "That is really nonsense," said Wooler. "Didn't he go berserk with Nillson in the '70s and there were fisticuffs then? I would hate to think that I was the catalyst for "Imagine" because I detest the song."

> Lennon: "Christianity will go. It will vanish and shrink. I needn't argue about that; I am right and will be proved right." Forty years later, there is no conclusive evidence of this.
>
> Lennon: "I do not know which will go first, rock-and-roll or Christianity."

> Lennon: "We are more popular than Jesus now." I am sure that was correct.

This is the comment that got him in trouble, and was the most accurate thing he said. Barabbas would have outpolled Jesus while he was alive. Jesus has never been popular. How many kids would have rather attended church than listened to a Beatles album?

A few months after a mild apology, he was less conciliatory about the "bigger than Christ" comments, and effectively repeated what he had told Maureen Cleave earlier. Why did he apologize in the first place?

Brian Epstein tried to put some ridiculous "spin" (a buzzword not invented yet) on John's comments by saying that he was only concerned about the decline in the church.

December 1967: John takes more than a friendly interest in fellow guest Pattie Harrison, until reprimanded by singer Lulu and reminded that his own wife, Cynthia, is his escort for the evening.

April 1968: He informs Cynthia that he has been unfaithful to her with dozens of women since their marriage.

May 1968: Cynthia finds John and Yoko sitting calmly in dressing gowns in the kitchen of John and Cynthia's home. Yoko is wearing Cynthia's gown. John says, "Oh, hi." He has cheated on his wife for years ("just give me some truth"), and he does not even have the decency to inform her of a new girlfriend.

July 1968: Lennon sues Cynthia for divorce, citing her adultery with Alex Mardas as the cause.

December 1969: Lennon pledges to donate all of his royalties to the peace movement. The promise is discreetly forgotten the next year.

"Imagine no possessions." Why didn't John be the first to set an example?

"Imagine all the people, sharing all the world." Easy to say, but how about actually starting by sharing all that you have, John?

"Imagine all the people, living life in peace." Sounds great, but one first has to imagine human nature entirely changing so that no one feels a need to obtain power and militarily threaten, or terrorize, the freedom of others who are not under that power.

November 1972: Lennon openly seduces another woman in front of Yoko.

January 1974: At the Troubador in Los Angeles, a waitress refuses to serve him any more alcohol, and he says, "Don't you know who I am?" He knocks a man unconscious, assaults his girlfriend, May Pang, wrecks the apartment, and has to deal with a visit from local police officers, replying to reports of gunfire in the house ("peace and love").

Two months later: He is again asked to leave the Troubador, and lashes out at those who are removing him, and reportedly hits a waitress.

March 1974: He attempts to strangle May Pang as she tries to prevent him from drinking. Harry Nilsson loosens his fingers from her neck.

> Julian Lennon: "The only thing he (John) taught me was how not to be a father. He walked out the bloody door and was never around. I would admire him on TV — listen to his words and opinions. But for someone who was praised for peace and love and wasn't able to keep that at home, that is hypocrisy."

John liked to present himself as a "working-class hero" as his "Plastic Ono Band" song indicated.

> Lennon: "It's a song for the revolution. It's like people like me who are working class, who are supposed to be processed into the middle class. It's my experience, and I hope it is a warning to people."

What kind of actual manual labor did John ever perform? He was briefly employed by Scaris and Brick waterworks in Liverpool in 1959, but was soon fired.

No question that his father came from a poor, working-class environment, working as a merchant seaman. However, John lived with his aunt, in a middle-class environment.

> Aunt Mimi: "I get terribly annoyed when he is billed as a street-corner boy. He had a very comfortable home in a good area."

He seemed to resent the fact that the Beatles "sold out" and that he had to act a certain way. However, he was willing to accept the success and money that came with it.

John Lennon was not a bad person, but had his faults like everyone else. He was never rude with autograph-seekers or the news media. He was just not a saint as some have built him up to be.

The Many Faces of John Lennon

© Bettmann/CORBIS

Marijuana Lennon (1965)

© Douglas Kirkland/CORBIS

How I Won the War (1966)

© Hulton-Deutsch Collection/CORBIS

Psychedelic (1967)

© Bettmann/CORBIS

Businessman (1969)

© Hulton-Deutsch Collection/CORBIS

Instant Karma **(1970)**

© Bettmann/CORBIS

Political **(1972)**

© Bettmann/CORBIS

Watergate **(1974)**

© Hulton Archive/Getty Images

No More Moptop **(1966)**

Chapter Three

The Rolling Stones

They were easily the second best group of the era. They were well closer to the Beatles in talent than whoever was third to them. They were the only band to kick out both of its founders. Ian Stewart was not considered hip enough to be in the group, and was asked to be the road manager, session player, and tour pianist, which he accepted. In 1969, Brian Jones, the other founding member, said he was leaving the group because he did not like the direction it was heading. In actuality, three weeks before his death, he was notified by Keith Richards, Mick Jagger, and Charlie Watts that he was out of the group. The rest of the group had known that Jones would not be fit enough to play on the next tour. That might have sent him over the edge. He was drinking heavily, gaining weight, and becoming paranoid when he was still in the group. Jones was the first rock-and-roller of that era to die, even though he was overshadowed by Jimi Hendrix, Janis Joplin and Jim Morrison. He did not directly die of a drug overdose, but neither did Hendrix or Morrison. Watts and Bill Wyman were the only group members to attend his funeral. The circumstances of Jones's death are still cloudy. He was found dead in the bottom of his swimming pool, a "death by misadventure" due to alcohol and other drugs. However, Frank Thorogood, who was living there at the time, was reported to have said on his deathbed in 1993, "I done Brian."

Eric Easton, their co-manager and producer, wanted Jagger out of the band in 1964 because he could not sing, and Jones was amenable. But Andrew Oldham, their manager and publicist, insisted that he stay because of his stage appeal. The producer of one of Britain's television shows on which they performed also urged Oldham to get rid of "that vile looking singer with the tire-tread lips." The sex appeal that Jagger had for many was a complete mystery to everyone else.

Oldham was a marketing genius. He had previously worked for Brian Epstein, promoting the Beatles' *Please Please Me*. Obviously, he had done well with that. He was nineteen when he met them, a year younger than Jones, Jagger and Richards, and was very much in touch with the London trends. He had the foresight to see that the Stones were an appealing stage act. One of his first actions was to sign the group with Decca Records. He knew that organization was looking for redemption after turning down the Beatles.

He knew the group could never compete straight up with the Beatles, so he created a nasty image for them. Watts was ordered to stick out his tongue at newsreel cameras. He changed Keith's last name to Richards, to be associated with Cliff Richard. There was also a rumor that Keith Richard and Little Richard were brothers, but it turned out to be false☺. He encouraged Jagger and Richards to write more music, and promoted Marianne Faithful to sing "As Tears Go By." Jagger was one of the first to dump the coat and tie and perform in a loose sweatshirt and corduroy trousers.

> London Evening Standard, March 21, 1964, said, "This horrible lot have done terrible things to the music scene, set it back (many) years. Just when we'd got our pop singers looking all neat, tidy and cheerful, along come the Stones looking like beatniks. They've wrecked the image of the pop singer of the Sixties. They are a horrible looking bunch, and Mick is indescribable."

This is exactly the publicity that they wanted. Oldham came up with headlines such as "Would you let your daughter marry a Rolling Stone?" "The Rolling Stones, who haven't bathed for a week, arrived here (United States) yesterday," and "Ugliest Group in Britain." On the first UK album, Oldham had all but the Decca logo removed from it, including the group name, to sell the album on the basis of the group picture.

> Ed Sullivan, after the Stones' first appearance on his show, said, "I promise you they will never be back on our show. If things cannot be handled, we'll stop the whole business. We won't book any more rock-and-roll groups and we'll ban teenagers from the theater. Frankly, I did not see the group until the day before the broadcast. I was shocked when I saw them. It took me seventeen years to build this show, and I am not going to have it destroyed in a matter of weeks."

However, this was just a front. Jagger remembered, "Privately, Ed told us it was the wildest, most enthusiastic audience he'd seen any artist get in the history of his show. Got a message a few days later saying, 'Received hundreds of letters from parents complaining about you, but thousands from teenagers saying how much they enjoyed your performance.'" They returned to the show seven months later.

Wallace Scowcroft, president of Britain's National Federation of Hairdressers, said, "The Rolling Stones are the worst. One of them (Jones) looks as if he had got a feather duster on his head." He also offered free haircuts to the next number-one group in the pop charts. He obviously felt understandably threatened by the trend towards long hair and a loss of business.

Most importantly, Oldham got Jagger and Richards to write songs, knowing that they would run out of outside songwriters. Their first song was "As Tears Go By," while "Tell Me" was the first they did themselves. "Tell Me" lasted four minutes and two seconds, which was very long for 1964. Oldham, as with most creative geniuses, was an awful business manager, and negotiated a lousy deal with Decca records. (On the other hand, you want a good business manager to stay away from anything musical or creative.) In 1966, Oldham sold out his interest to Allen Klein, who got them a much better record contract.

The press also hid what was really going on in the group many times. In November 1964, Jones collapsed with alcohol poisoning and exhaustion, but it was said he was in the hospital because of bronchitis.

In May 1965, one of their roadies heard that Jones raped and beat up a girl the prior night. He stormed into Jones's room and broke two of Jones's ribs. (Andrew Oldham said, "Don't mess up his face!") The news story was that Jones fell while practicing karate by the motel pool.

In August 1966, Jones broke his wrist trying to hit another woman. The cause was said to be that he hurt his hand climbing in the mountains.

Jones was easily the best-looking member of the group, even though he did not look the part on the *Between the Buttons* album cover.

"Satisfaction" (June 1965) put them at a new level, and through "Ruby Tuesday" (February 1967), they came close to matching the Beatles in quality of music, achieving four number-one songs and one number-two.

Rock-and-roll bands became more theatrical, and the music less memorable, when the Rolling Stones started wearing makeup in 1968 with their "Jumping Jack Flash" video. They were a darn good band through the *Tattoo You* album in 1981, with the exception of *Black and Blue* in 1976. They should have retired after that. The thirteen years between number-one songs written within the group ("Satisfaction" and "Miss You") is the longest of any group of this era. The Beach Boys had twenty-four years between "I Get Around" and "Kokomo," but the latter was written outside the group.

A group with as much musical talent as they had should not have to go into stage theatrics as they did in the 1970s. However, Jagger is a public relations genius, and the group was one of the few 1960s groups which continued to be a force throughout the 1970s, along with the (disco) Bee Gees, Grateful Dead, Kinks, and Neil Young. Somehow, I cannot picture any other 1960s musician prancing around on stage wearing tights with no shirt. Jagger was a brilliant individual who did not let his drug use interfere with his music.

Jagger and Richards were obviously most of the vocal, stage, and songwriting talent in the group. As with John Lennon and Paul McCartney, their corroboration was better than the sum of the parts. Each of their solo attempts went nowhere.

Definitions:

- Lead Guitar: Loudest, dominant-sounding guitar. Usually, it is played one string at a time with the higher notes. Many times, it is not played during the vocals because of interference.

- Rhythm Guitar: Background guitar, usually played in chords, and almost always during the vocals. It will also often be an acoustic guitar.

Richards is listed as "rhythm guitar" for the band, and Jones, Mick Taylor, and Ron Wood as "lead guitar." The lead guitar is probably a misnomer with this group, as there are few guitar solos. Richards's guitar from "Satisfaction" and forward was the loudest, most dominant guitar, even though it did not have the usual lead characteristics of single-string higher notes. Prior to "Satisfaction," Jones was somewhat of a lead guitarist, even though there were no real lead guitar solos. He probably kept the title after this because of being the group's founder. On hearing Richards's guitar, the average music listener could identify it, but this was not so with Jones's guitar. Richards's guitar has a distinct sound, and his guitars were often only strung with five strings for cleaner fingering.

"I do the bits you can't hear," Jones said. Richards is certainly the main guitar one hears on "*Satisfaction,*" "*19th Nervous Breakdown,*" "*Brown Sugar,*" "Jumpin' Jack Flash," and many others. Jones, when he plays lead guitar, is the high-pitched, one-string-at-a-time guitar or the slide guitar.

Jones was a talented instrumental musician who learned instruments quickly, including autoharp, mellotron, sitar, tamboura, harmonica, dulcimer, marimbas, piano, organ, harpsichord, trumpet, trombone, banjo, kazoo, flute, and slide guitar. His bottleneck slide guitar on "I Wanna Be Your Man" was the first of its kind.

Jones's most notable instrumentals are when he played the recorder and piano on "Ruby Tuesday," slide guitar on "No Expectations" and "Little Red Rooster," mellotron on "2000 Light Years from Home," dulcimer on "Lady Jane" and "I Am Waiting," and sitar on "Paint It Black."

Jones said, "Yes, I will be famous. No, I will not make thirty."

Used by permission of Pennebaker Films

Brian Jones

(Less than a year to live)

The July 1969 Hyde Park concert was previously set up to introduce the new guitarist, Taylor, but it became a tribute concert for Jones, who died two days earlier. "Papa Was a Rolling Stone" was written by one of Jones's children☺.

David Frost, talk show host (1969): "Can you picture yourself at the age of sixty doing what you do now?"

Mick: "Yes, easily." (laughter)
Frost: "Going onstage with a cane?"

Jagger later changed his outlook by saying that he would never be singing "Satisfaction" at age forty, and obviously changed his mind once again, as there is a good chance he will be doing it at age seventy

The longevity of this band easily outdoes any other, with only the Grateful Dead coming close. Jagger, Richards and Watts have been together forty-two years (as of 2005; their last album was *Bridges to Babylon* in 1997). Wyman lasted for thirty years. Their third guitarist, Ron Wood, has lasted thirty years.

Other than the audience screaming, they were the first group to get their audience riled up. Unlike Jim Morison, there was nothing specific they did to incite unruly behavior.

Mick Jagger once said, "We had some very scary moments." He was talking about the female fans. The band members came dangerously close to getting lipstick on their faces, having clothes torn, or even having a piece of their hair cut off.

- Name recall: Mick Jagger, ninety-seven percent; Keith Richard(s), ninety percent; Brian Jones, thirty-one percent; Charlie Watts, twenty-seven percent; Bill Wyman, twenty-one percent.

- The first song in which Jagger did not sing the lead vocal was "Connection," where he and Richards sang in tandem. Richards's first solo vocal part was in "Something Happened to Me Yesterday," singing the line, "He don't know if it's right or wrong." Richards sang the first four lines of "Salt of the Earth." His first time singing an entire song was "You've Got the Silver," and his second time was "Happy."

- There are live songs mixed in on some of the studio albums, including "Route 66," "I'm All Right," "Midnight Rambler," and "I'm Moving On."

- Best bass lines: "19th Nervous Breakdown" (descending part at the end), "Live with Me" (beginning), and "2000 Light Years from Home" (beginning).

- The Rolling Stones had the best guitar riff openings (by Richards) of any group, including "Citadel," "Jumping Jack

Flash," "19th Nervous Breakdown," "Brown Sugar, Happy," and "Satisfaction."

- "Time ... can destroy a woman's face" (Jagger). It has not done much for your face either, Mick, or especially Keith's, for that matter.
- Best songs: 1. "Satisfaction" 2. "19th Nervous Breakdown" 3. "Jumpin' Jack Flash" 4. "Get Off of My Cloud" 5. "Ruby Tuesday"
- Underrated: "Live with Me" and "2000 Man"
- Two of their best songs, "Sympathy for the Devil" and "You Can't Always Get What You Want," were not released as singles.

Year	To Top-Ten Single(s)	Peak	Weeks	RCY	ATR	Gold Album(s)	Sales	Peak	Weeks	RCY
1964	Time Is On My Side	6				The Rolling Stones	Gold	11		53
1965	The Last Time	9				5X12	Gold	3		50
1965	Satisfaction (A)	1	4	1	197	Now	Gold	5		
1965	Get Off Of My Cloud	1	2	13	585					
1965	Paint It, Black	1	2	12	543					
1965	19th Nervous Breakdown (C)	1	3	30						
1966	As Tears Go By	6				December's Children	Gold	4		
1966	Mother's Little Helper	8				Big Hits	Plat 2	3		1966 (15) 1967 (63)

1966	Have You Seen Your Mother, Baby, Standing in the Shadow?	9				Out of Our Heads	Plat	1	3	52
1967	Ruby Tuesday (D)	1	1	15	822	Between the Buttons	Gold	2	4	44
1967						Got Love If You Want It	Gold	6		62
1967						Flowers	Gold	3		75
1968	Jumpin' Jack Flash (E)	3		32		Their Satanic Majesty's Request*	Gold	2	6	87
1969	Honky Tonk Women (F)	1	4	5	166	Beggars' Banquet (H)	Plat	5		86
1971	Brown Sugar (G)	1	2	14	490	Let It Bleed (I)	Plat 2	3		48
1971						Sticky Fingers*	Plat 3	1	4	21
1972						Hot Rocks (J)	Plat 6	4		

All-time single rank #8

At the beginning, lyrics were written by Mick Jagger and the music by Keith Richard(s); it was more mixed in later years.

(A) RS 2; "Hey, hey, hey"

(B) RS 174

(C) Three weeks at number two, all after "Ballad of the Green Berets."

"Nothin' I do don't seem to work." One of only two songs with a bridge portion; the other is *Dance Sister Dance*.

(D) RS 303

(E) RS 124

(F) RS 116

(G) RS 490

Total album sales 63.5 million (eleventh)

*Three-dimensional album

(H) The album cover with the toilet on it was not released until the 1980s.

(I) Both Brian Jones and his replacement, Mick Taylor, played on the album.

After 1971, they obviously continued as a huge band, producing four gold albums, sixteen platinum, and seven number ones. The two biggest-selling albums were *Hot Rocks* (1972) and *Some Girls* (1978), both platinum(6).

(J) On the charts for 243 weeks.

Chapter Four

The Byrds

Ask someone today who was in The Byrds and a typical answer will be, "Wasn't Crosby in that group?" Yes, he was, but he was entirely in the background until the *Fifth Dimension* album. Jim McGuinn was the genius behind this group. However, because David Crosby was a bombastic self-promoter who became famous in a later group, he is certainly the best-known Byrd today.

With Crosby and Gene Clark as songwriters, the Byrds went nowhere. (If you want proof, listen to the *Preflyte* album.) McGuinn had the idea of taking a folk song with a 2/4 or 2/2 beat, and changing it into a rock song with a 4/4 beat.

> McGuinn said, "I started incorporating the beat that they (the Beatles) were doing into the folk songs I was doing in Greenwich Village. And that was really the beginning of what turned into folk rock and the Byrds."

This was first tried with Bob Dylan's "Mr. Tambourine Man" and it met with obvious success, reaching number one. McGuinn also added a Bach-sounding twelve-string guitar to the beginning of the song. The next hit was "Turn, Turn, Turn!" which was also McGuinn's idea (the song previously planned for the band's third single was Dylan's "It's All Over Baby Blue"). This gave the group two number-one songs in three tries. This was the best song ever written. Thank you Pete Seeger (music), McGuinn (arrangement), and Solomon (words).

Unfortunately, that was it for any top-ten songs. McGuinn also masterminded the first "psychedelic rock" song, the complex "Eight Miles High," with help from Clark and Crosby. It included a profound guitar solo in the middle. Clark said he wrote all the lyrics to this song, except, "Rain, gray town, known for its sound," which Crosby added. McGuinn disagrees, and said he contributed to the lyrics. A disagreement on song contributions was also an issue with Lennon and McCartney. On "Norwegian Wood," "In My Life," and "Eleanor Rigby," there were significant disagreements.

The group, unfortunately, headed away from the twelve-string guitar, folk-rock sound, and lost their popularity after 1967. Most musicians feel the need to change music styles to appeal to the elite. (The Beatles did that with tremendous success, but were certainly the exception.) Clark left the Byrds in 1966 and was not replaced. He was the first person to quit a major band. Clark leaving the band was probably the worst decision made in that era. His solo career was one mishap after another. Even though he was a significant songwriter and a lead singer, the band put out two more great albums. The other three became more prolific songwriters, and Chris Hillman and Crosby started to sing solos, Crosby on the third album and Hillman on the fourth. Crosby's voice was more suited to high harmony singer, especially on "Chimes of Freedom," "Eight Miles High," and "Turn! Turn! Turn!" As a lead singer, he was lacking. Crosby was asked to leave in 1967 ("I'll probably feel a whole lot better when you're gone"). McGuinn was the only original member of the group left in 1968 and wrote two notable songs, "Chestnut Mare" and "Ballad of Easy Rider" (with help from Bob Dylan), with the revised group. He also sang a great version of "Wasn't Born to Follow." The band had six more members, after the originals, in seven different combinations.

> McGuinn, on his disappointment over the lack of popularity of his song "5D" ("Fifth Dimension"), said, "It's really painful to think you've got a really hip audience, a mass of them. And so you write this real hip song, "5D," and they don't like it, don't understand it at all, think it must be about dope. "5D" was an ethereal trip into metaphysics, into an almost Moslem submission to Allah, an almighty spirit, free floating, the fifth dimension being that mesh that Einstein theorized about. He proved theoretically, but

> I chose to believe it, that there's an ethereal mesh in the universe, and probably the reason for the speed of light being what it is because of the friction encountered going through that mesh."

The track "Mr. Spaceman" has more to the lyrics than one might think. "We're trying to communicate with those cats out there (in space)," Crosby said on a radio interview. "We don't think that they don't exist. We believe they do exist, and we think that by some stretch of the imagination they can possibly translate what we are saying."

Another song that dealt with aliens was "C.T.A.-102."

> Crosby said, "Signals tell us that you're there. We just want to let you know that we're ready to go out into the universe." There were alien-sounding voices at the end of the song. "They are probably monitoring all the radio and TV, you know. If we get it played enough times, maybe one of them will hear it."

> McGuinn said, "If one of them hears it, and translates it, then maybe they will come and take us for a ride in one of their ships, which is what we want in the first place."

Roger McGuinn was known as "Jim" back then. In 1967, after flirtation with a bizarre religion called Subud (I guess all religions seem bizarre to non-believers), he changed it to "Roger." The founder of Subud, an Indonesian guru named Muhammad Subuh Sumohadiwidjojo, told McGuinn that he should change his name to one beginning with an "R," because it would "vibrate better" in the cosmos. Say what? It would appear that Sumo would have wanted a less mundane name than "Roger," maybe something a little more metaphysical, like Rajneesh or Ramalama.

The group, as with the Rolling Stones, had some distinguished guitar introductions, including "She Don't Care About Time," "Chimes of Freedom," "Mr. Tambourine Man," and "Turn! Turn! Turn!"

They should have released "I'll Feel a Lot Better," "She Don't Care About Time," and "Chimes of Freedom" as A-side singles. "It Won't Be Wrong," "Have You Seen Her Face?" and "Goin' Back" should not have been singles. "Chimes of Freedom" would have been their third Dylan song as a single, and it was somehow frowned upon to use the same songwriter repeatedly, even though it worked for Glen Campbell (Jimmy Webb), the Supremes (Lamont-Dozier-Holland), and Dionne Warwick (David-Bacharach)

The Byrds had four songwriters and lead singers, numbers matched only by the Beatles and the Moody Blues. Individually, McGuinn wrote three songs; Clark, six; Crosby, six; and Hillman, four. There were various songwriting combinations, all of them including McGuinn: McGuinn/Crosby wrote five; McGuinn/Clark wrote three; McGuinn/Hillman wrote two; And Guinn/Clark/Crosby wrote one, "Eight Mile High," though McGuinn said that Crosby only added a line or two. Easily the best known McGuinn/Clark song was "You Showed Me," recorded by the Turtles.

Dave's Beatle friend is George Harrison. The two correspond by phone or letter every two weeks.

He is a teetotaler and non-smoker. He doesn't like to see girls smoke.

Dave drinks a quart of apple juice a day. His favorite food is steak and tacos.

You can write to the Byrds at 9000 Sunset Blvd., Suite 805, Los Angeles 69, Calif.

16 Magazine, April 1966

- Name recall: Dave Crosby, forty-one percent; Jim McGuinn, thirty-four percent; Gene Clark, fourteen percent; Chris Hillman, fourteen percent; Mike Clarke, fourteen percent. (I would guess that Crosby's numbers would be the same as the last three at the time he left the group.)

- If McGuinn played a twelve-string guitar, did Hillman play an eight-string bass? (no)

- Hillman had to straighten out his curly hair to look the part.

- Best songs: 1. "Turn, Turn, Turn!" (best song, period) 2. "Mr. Tambourine Man" 3. "Chimes of Freedom" 4. "So You Want to Be a Rock and Roll Star" (features a guiro, a percussion instrument where a rough surface is scraped with a stick; The Rolling Stones' "Gimme Shelter" also features one (many thanks to Buzz Tremblay for this information).

- Best elite song: "Eight Miles High"

- Underrated: "Born to Rock and Roll" (1973), "She Don't Care About Time" (Clark's best song; not on an album), "Lady Friend" (Crosby's best song, but bombed as a single)

- Worst songs: 1. "Mind Gardens" (truly awful) 2. "If You're Gone" 3. "What's Happening!?"

~~Gene Clark is another artist who feels as Jeff does.~~ Gene wants absolute perfection in every performance he gives. He feels that he owes it to his fans to give the best performance he can and when the Byrds started to flutter their wings instead of flying straight with a performance, Gene decided to go it on his own and has become a very successful song writer and musician. The Byrds of course have had a couple of hit records since Gene left and everything is great for both parties.
60

Tiger Beat, October, 1967

Year	Top-Ten Single(s)	Peak	Weeks	RCY	ATR	Gold Album(s)	Sales	Peak	Weeks	RCY
1965	Mr. Tambourine Man (Dylan) (A)	1	1	19	818					
1965	Turn! Turn! Turn! (B)	1	3	3	311					
1967						Greatest Hits	Plat	6		34

All-time single rank #389

(A) Replaced "I Can't Help Myself" at number one; then "I Can't Help Myself" took the number-one spot back; RS 79

(B) Lyrics from the Bible book of Ecclesiastes, music by Pete

Seeger. It was banned in South Africa because of putting Bible lyrics to a rock beat.

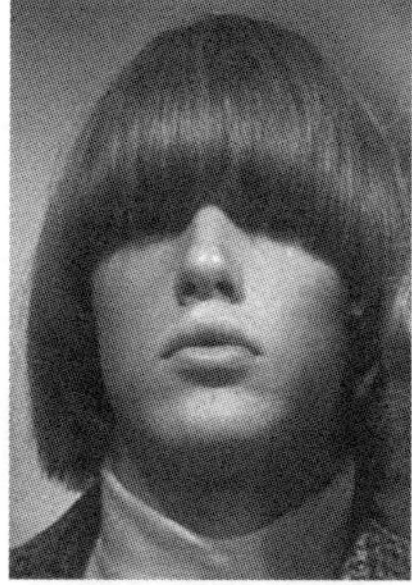

Mike Clarke
Chosen because he looked like one of the Rolling Stones (Jones)

Gene Clark
Sometime Lead Singer and primary songwriter

David Crosby
A very different looking "Dave" Crosby, compared to his later look

Jim McGuinn
The first to wear glasses on stage; lost them while riding a motorcycle

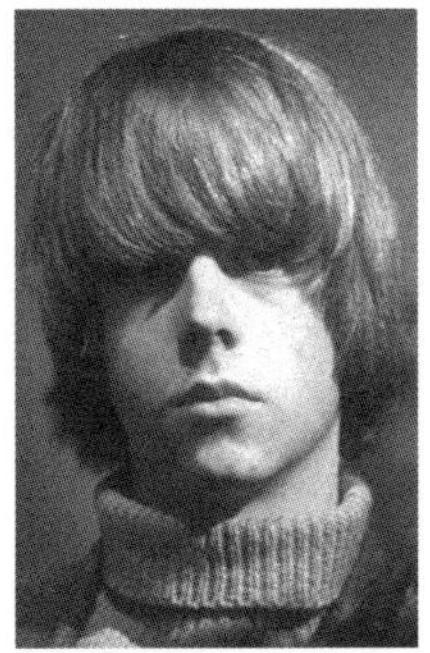

© Hulton=Deutsch Collection/CORBIS

Chris Hillman
Artificially straightened hair

© Elaine Mayes and
Britannia Press

Chris Hillman Again
Naturally curly hair

Chapter Five

The Doors

This gloomy-sounding group was unlike any other. They were the first group to use a keyboard as a prominent instrument. (Other groups, like the Dave Clark Five, the Rascals, and the Animals, used keyboards that were in the background.) They were not into "peace and love" in 1967. Jim Morrison's preferred drug was alcohol. And there were Morrison's black leather pants and wild (sometimes drunken) stage antics, including the indecent exposure charge in Miami during 1969.

Morrison had the best male singing voice of this era, and one of the few low ones. Morrison also sang with eyes closed more than any other singer. (Was he really "into" the songs, or just trying to hide bloodshot eyes?) The songs are usually credited to the Doors, but Morrison and guitarist Robby Krieger were the separate songwriters. The first song Krieger ever wrote was "Light My Fire." This was the first song to have an instrumental section that used both a keyboard (from 1:07 to 3:18) and a guitar (3:18 to 5:33). Even though the song was only slightly longer than Bob Dylan's "Like a Rolling Stone," the single version cut out most of the instrumental section.

Their last album as a quartet, *L.A. Woman*, was one of the few last albums by a group that was outstanding. Even if Morrison had lived, he was probably done working with the group, as he had already moved to Paris. The Miami charges and continued abuse of alcohol had worn him down. He died in Paris of "heart failure" or "natural causes," either of which avoided an autopsy. The evening before he was found dead, he had collapsed at a nightclub, possibly from heroin use. He was bundled up and taken home, where he was placed in a bathtub to resuscitate him. Even after death, Morrison created havoc. There were various attempts by fans to unearth his grave, so a stone block was put over his sealed coffin. Occult and mysticism enthusiasts held orgies, drug parties, and devil worship rites around the grave. This led to the use of security guards, cameras, and lighting.

Somehow, without Morrison, the Doors endured to put out two more albums.

- Name recall: Jim Morrison, ninety-three percent; Ray Manzarek, twenty-seven percent; Robbie Krieger, twenty-one percent; John Densmore, seventeen percent.

- Manzarek, the keyboardist, was eight years older than Krieger, one of the largest age gaps of any group mentioned in this book.

- Manzarek's stage presence was that of his side facing the audience, his head rotating side-to-side with the beat. He played the bass parts with his left hand.

- Morrison graduated from college (UCLA film school in 1965).

- The only non-Morrison lead vocals were on the song "Runnin' Blues" (Krieger sings "All right, look at my shoes, not quite the walking blues, don't fight, too much to lose, can't fight the running blues), and "Close to You" on the live album and "(You Need Meat) Don't Go No Further," both sung by Manzarek.

- Best songs: 1. "Light My Fire" 2. "Touch Me" 3. "Love Her Madly"

- Underrated: "Peace Frog," "Land Ho," and "Ship Of Fools"

- Worst songs: "Horse's Latitudes" (a good song to choose for karaoke), "Been Down So Long," "My Wild Love," and "The Crystal Ship"

- Best elite album: *Strange Days*

- Best elite song: "The End," because it "broke all the rules." It was eleven minutes long and the elite loved the Oedipal-drama lyrics. Paul Rothchild, producer, said during the recording, "This is one of the most important moments in recorded rock-and-roll." The elite loved Morrison because he was somehow considered a poet, rather than a lyricist.

Year	Top-Ten Single(s)	Peak	Weeks	RCY	ATR	Gold Album(s)	Sales	Peak	Weeks	RCY
1967	Light My Fire (Kreiger) (A)	1	3	8	273	The Doors	Plat 2	2	2	1967 (32) 1968 (7)
1968	Hello, I Love You (Morrison)	1	2	11	451	Strange Days (B)	Gold	3		29
1968						Waiting for the Sun (C)	Plat	1	4	68
1969	Touch Me (Kreiger)	3				The Soft Parade	Plat	6		75
1970						Morrison Hotel	Gold	4		79
1970						Absolutely Live (D)	Gold	8		
1971						13	Plat	25		
1971						L.A. Woman	Plat 2	9		42
1972						Weird Scenes Inside the Gold Mine	Gold	55		

All-time single rank #293

(A) RS 35

Total album sales 29.5 million (fifty-third)

(B) None of the group were on the album cover

(C) The song "Waiting for the Sun" was oddly on the *Morrison Hotel* album

(D) "Love Hides," "Build Me a Woman," "Close to You," and "Universal Mind" were not on any studio albums

Chapter Six

Crosby, Stills, Nash, and Young

The group's name is a list, in reverse order, of songwriting talent. This is probably the best group never to have a top-ten single. David Crosby was known as "Dave" with the Byrds, and Stephen Stills as "Steve" with Buffalo Springfield. Their image consultant probably told them that it was not hip to use nicknames, and they would be taken more seriously as musicians using their full names. After all, Van Gogh and DaVinci were not known as "Vince" and "Leo." The group was well known for an incredible blend of voices. Graham Nash's voice is the easiest to pick out because it is the highest and the loudest. Stills' is the second easiest to hear and is usually on the low end. Crosby's voice is the most difficult to hear in the blend, as he is usually in the middle and the softest. On "Helplessly Hoping," the voices can be more easily differentiated:

"They are one person" (Stills)
"They are two alone" (Stills and Nash)
"They are three together" (Stills, Nash, and Crosby; Crosby comes in on the low end.)

In recent concerts, however, Nash and Crosby are reversed on that song. Another example is "Teach Your Children," when Stills and Nash start the lyrics, and Crosby enters on "teach." Even though Crosby sang high harmony (and was easily heard) with the Byrds, Nash was always on the high end with CSNY.

This group started out with three monster albums. They never came close to matching those albums, and their only song in the class of the first albums was "Wasted on the Way," with "Just a Song before I Go" and "Southern Cross" deserving honorable mentions.

The song "4+20" was the only one on the first two albums with one vocalist (Stills) and "Country Girl" is the "Buffalo Springfield" song with only Stills and Young singing together, starting with, "Find out now …"

Having their last names as the group name was a good publicity move. From a survey, twenty-eight percent of people had heard of Crosby, thirty-eight percent of Stills, and seventeen percent of Nash, before the group formed. (Sure, that now seems hard to believe.) Buffalo Springfield was an obscure group, Crosby was in the background during the Byrds' most successful period, and the Hollies (with Graham Nash) were not well known. Allan Clarke was probably the best known of the Hollies, but he was hardly a household name.

Neil Young joining the group was a stroke of genius for both sides. Crosby, Stills and Nash (CSN) needed a first-class guitarist for their stage act, and adding another outstanding songwriter did not hurt. On their first album, Stills played lead guitar, organ, and bass, while Crosby played rhythm guitar. Young's solo career was also given a huge boost. He refused CSN's first offer, but changed his mind when his name would be added to the group name. His first appearance with CSN was July 25, 1969, at Fillmore East in New York City.

Four Way Street was the best live album of the era and included a lot of songs that were not on other albums.

A Neil Young sound-alike was Dewey Bunnell, of the group America. Speaking of America, this group was most similar to Crosby, Stills and Nash — three songwriting guitar players. They never reached the heights of CSN, but were close in 1971-1972, having four songs peaking in the top ten. Obviously, people can name the four members of CSNY (at least their last names), but how many can name just one of the three members of America? Once again, it helps to have your name as part of the group for fame purposes.

David Crosby was the best harmony singer ever and a good songwriter, especially on "Long Time Gone" and "Lady Friend" (the Byrds). However, his talent does not justify his fame. His voice was much more suited to harmony than to lead. He has never written a top-forty single and had almost no solo career. What he did do was be part of two Hall of Fame groups, and added a lot to the harmony vocals of each. Being associated with McGuinn, Stills, Nash, and Young brought him a lot of fame. Having his name as part of CSNY did wonders for him, especially being first on the list. He is also a very outgoing stage presence and his drug arrests have further increased his profile, as have his liver transplant and test tube siring. Is Crosby the only well known musician to actually serve prison time for a drug arrest? It seemed like every single other musical arrestee got off the hook, and Crosby did after his conviction was overturned after a year. That is probably the way it should be. Drug use is a vice, not a crime. What a waste of police time, especially with those results. See p. 295 for more drug arrests that wasted taxpayers' money.

- Best Songs: 1. "Suite: Judy Blue Eyes" (last real words were "be my lady") 2. "Teach Your Children" 3. "Ohio" 4. "Long Time Gone" 5. "Helplessly Hoping"

- Worst Songs: 1. "Lee Shore" 2. "Triad" 3. "Lady of the Island"

- CSNY was the best group never to have a top-ten single during the era. "Woodstock" ("Child of God") peaked at number eleven in 1970.

Year	Top-Ten Single(s)	Peak	Weeks	RCY	ATR	Gold Album(s)	Sales	Peak	Weeks	RCY
1969						Crosby Stills and Nash	Plat 4	6		1969 (35) 1970 (19)
1970						Déjà Vu	Plat 7	1	1	1970 (11) 1971 (50)
1971						Four Way Street	Plat 4	1	1	23

All-time single rank #391

Their next two albums, released in 1974 and 1977, reached platinum(6) and platinum(4), but nothing came close to matching that success after that.

The Second Tier

Chapter Seven

For What It's Worth

The Beach Boys

They were the top U.S. group before the Beatles arrived, even though they had no number-one hits until "I Get Around" in 1964. The Four Seasons or Peter, Paul and Mary were probably the second most successful group. The Beach Boys' biggest hits were bunched into a four-year period, 1963-1966.

Until the *Pet Sounds* album in 1966, the band was a favorite of the proletariat, but not the elite. Why was/is Brian Wilson considered a genius, while many others with similar talent are not? This term was actually orchestrated by the band's publicist, Derek Taylor, around the time of *Pet Sounds*. Being called a "genius" now made Brian acceptable to the elite community, and they now could listen to Beach Boys music out in the open.

Pet Sounds got off to a poor sales start, and was their first album that did not quickly reach gold status. The word on the street was "stay away from the album because it is weird." Because of this, Capitol Records quickly rushed out a *Best Of* package, which quickly did reach gold. When *Pet Sounds* gradually caught on, along with the huge single release, "Good Vibrations," the band was at their musical peak. In a year-end (1966) poll done by the *New Musical Express*, a British newspaper, the Beach Boys were selected as the top "world vocal group."

The intelligentsia loved the album. Paul McCartney called the song, "God Only Knows," the best song ever written.

After 1966, they only had two top-ten songs (1976 and 1987), both written by outside writers. Brian Wilson had "over-expanded" his mind with drugs, and was determined to write a more esoteric type of music. He had been very competitive and he viewed *Pet Sounds* as passing up the Beatles.

When they responded with *Sgt. Pepper*, it might have been enough to put Wilson over the edge. The next album, *Smile*, was supposed to be much more profound than *Pet Sounds*. However, Wilson was not functional, and the album was not released until 2004 (see Wilson's solo career on p. 198). With Brian Wilson over the edge in 1967, the group had lost its songwriter and distinctive falsetto voice.

Brian, like Neil Young in 1974 and John Lennon in 1970, wanted to write for his own interest, rather than the proletariat. Unlike the other two, though, in Brian's case, the rest of the group depended on him for income. They were obviously upset that Brian was writing experimental music and not "keeping with the prior formula." They were losing their meal ticket, but continued on as a successful live band, with occasional moderately successful studio releases.

There are thousands of musicians that wrote music strictly for their own enjoyment. You have probably never heard of any of them. What the smart musicians do is write for their audience at first. Being financially set, they then have the option of writing for themselves. Those albums are going to do well because of name recognition alone. If Wilson's first album were *Smile* (and there were no Beach Boys), Lennon's first were *Plastic Ono Band* (and no Beatles), and Young's were *On the Beach*, it is unlikely these records would have sold at all and they would have mired in obscurity.

This band relied more on vocals than any other group, with the possible exception of the Mamas and the Papas. Brian had the highest voice, and sang lead on "Surfer Girl" and "Don't Worry Baby." As with David Crosby, Brian's voice was more suited to be combined with other voices. His falsettos on "Fun, Fun, Fun," "California Girls," and "Sloop John B" were the best part of the songs. "Do It Again" (1968) was Brian's last falsetto part, and also the last song he wrote for a while.

While being an outstanding vocal group, the Beach Boys were not good musicians, and used session musicians on their albums.

Mike Love sang lead the most, and combined with Brian as separate leads on many of the songs. Al sang lead on "Help Me Rhonda" and "Then I Kissed Her," and Dennis on "Do You Wanna Dance?"

Carl started out with a minor role, singing lead on "Girl Don't Tell Me," "She's Not the Little Girl I Once Knew," and the bridge on "Girls on the Beach." He raised his voice an octave for "Pet Sounds" and started singing more leads after that (coinciding with a reduction of leads from Brian), including "Good Vibrations" and "God Only Knows," and even another different voice on "Wild Honey." Other than Barry Gibb of the Bee Gees, who raised his voice at least an octave for their obnoxious disco music, no one changed his musical voice as much as Carl did.

"Sloop John B" starts with Carl, adds Mike, and then Brian comes in on his best falsetto of any song.

Their personnel changes rival those of the Byrds. When Brian quit the road in late 1964, Glen Campbell became the first road fill-in (many groups in this era had studio fill-ins, but not another one had a road fill-in). Then Bruce Johnston took Campbell's place on both the road and in the studio, though he was not pictured on the *Pet Sounds* album cover (the last pre-1972 Beach Boys album cover that had the members' pictures on it). He might have had the best voice of all of them, but rarely sang on a studio song. He can be heard as the backup on *God Only Knows*, on the song of that title.

Other personnel changes prior to 1983 were Ricky Fataar in, Johnston out; Blondie Chaplin (who sings lead on "Sail On Sailor") in, Dennis out; Fataar out, Chaplin out; Dennis in, Bruce in, Carl out, Carl in, Brian fired (because he was trying to find himself, rather than contributing musically to the group; this does not show a lot of gratitude). Jack Rieley was in to sing lead for one song, "A Day in the Life of a Tree."

- Name recall: Brian Wilson, ninety percent; Mike Love, forty-five percent; Carl Wilson, forty-one percent; Al Jardine, thirty-four percent; Dennis Wilson, twenty-one percent.

- Best songs 1. "Sloop John B" 2. "California Girls" 3. "Fun, Fun, Fun" 4. "Good Vibrations"

- Best elite songs 1. "Good Vibrations" 2. "Don't Worry Baby"

- Underrated: "Do It Again," "Add Some Music to Your Day"

Year	Top-Ten Single(s)	Peak	Weeks	RCY	ATR	Gold Album(s)	Sales	Peak	Weeks	RCY
1964	I Get Around	1	2	10	434	Shut Down II	Gold	13		1964 (29) 1965 (72)
1964	Don't Worry Baby (A)					Little Deuce Coupe	Plat 4	4		42
1964	Fun, Fun, Fun	5				All Summer Long	Gold	4		1964 (49) 1965 (53)
1964						Surfer Girl	Gold	7		58
1965	Help Me Rhonda	1	2	12	532	Concert	Gold	1	4	24
1965	California Girls (B)	3				Today	Gold	4		
1965	Dance, Dance, Dance	8				Summer Days	Gold	2	1	
1966	Barbara Ann	2	2			Pet Sounds (F)	Plat	10		43
1966	Sloop John B (raditional) (C)	3				Best	Plat 2	8		1966 (67) 1967 (83)
1966	Wouldn't It Be Nice	8								
1966	Good Vibrations (D)	1	1	23	803					
1967						Best II	Plat 2	50		

All-time single rank #17. All songs, music by Brian Wilson and some words by Mike Love and Tony Asher

(A) RS 176; B-side to "I Get Around"

(B) RS 71

(C) RS 271

(D) RS 6; the outer-space-sounding instrument was an electrotheremin, which was played like a slide guitar; Mike Love can be seen playing this instrument on a 1967 television broadcast.

Total albums sales twenty million (102nd)

(F)) On "Caroline No," Brian sings all the vocal parts. This song was released as a Brian Wilson single; RS 211

Buffalo Springfield

The chance meeting of Stills and Young in Los Angeles is the stuff of legend. Young and bassist Bruce Palmer had arrived recently, but had little hope of finding Stills, whom Young had met earlier in Canada. Young was driving a hearse, which helped the odds, which sported an Ontario, Canada license plate. Stills happened to be driving the other way with Furay, noticed the car, said, "I'll bet I know who that is," and then made a U-turn to flag the car down.

Buffalo Springfield, a group for less than two years, *had* to be the most poorly marketed and managed group in this era. There was a huge gap between the amount of talent they had and their commercial success. Most people were not familiar with the group at all, except for the single, "For What It's Worth," which reached number six, until Steve (later Stephen) Stills and Neil Young became well known later. Other than Lennon-McCartney and Jagger-Richards, there was no other more talented twosome in a group. If they could have had a public relations guru like Andrew Oldham or Derek Taylor, the group would have been hugely successful.

They only put out three albums. The albums are all great. Richie Furay also was a good songwriter. Stills (his ancestors were in the moonshine business☺) and Furay did most of the vocals, singing in tandem on many songs on the first two albums. Furay sang many of Young's compositions for various reasons. At first, Young's voice was considered "not fit for airplay" and he was also uncomfortable with his voice. As time went on, the vocalist for his songs became a matter of disagreement. Young would want to sing, but would be outvoted by the group. He took a stand on "Mr. Soul" and demanded that he sing his own song, against everyone else's wishes, including those of distinguished record company executive, Ahmet Artegun. It is the only example of one singer-songwriter in a group singing numerous leads for another singer-songwriter's songs. Neil Young is only discernable in the background vocals on "Bluebird," "Special Care," and "Do I Have to Come Right Out and Say It?" He had no vocals at all on the band's best-known song, "For What It's Worth," whose background vocals were performed by Richie Furay and Dewey Martin. When Young did sing, his voice was much lower, and more conventional, than on his solo recordings.

The group did release three singles other than "For What It's Worth" — "Rock and Roll Woman" (peaking at number forty-four), "Burned" (not charting), "Bluebird" (number fifty-eight, though it did reach number two on L.A.'s KHJ list), "Expecting To Fly" (number ninety-eight), and "On The Way Home" (number eighty-two). Why these songs did not rise higher on the charts is an enigma, though poor marketing was certainly a part of it. The first album (the version without "For What It's Worth") peaked at number eighty, the second at number forty-four, and the last at number forty-two. The greatest hits album also peaked at number forty-two. If they had come out with the same exact albums, starting in 1972, it would have been an entirely different outcome. The "marketing" would have been that Stills and Young would have been well known by then because of their other works.

However, the double compilation album *Buffalo Springfield*, released in 1973, reached only 104.

Neil's unreliability plagued the group. He first quit the day before they were scheduled to appear on the Johnny Carson show, and they ended up not appearing. He rejoined, but quit again before Monterey Pop. They did not appear on the film. He quit once more during the making of their last album, and appeared only as a vocalist for "I Am a Child." He rejoined later to make their final tours.

Stills and Young made a huge amount of income in later years and Furay, some. However, Martin and Palmer had no musical future and the sting of being under-marketed hit them the worst. What could have been?

It would be interesting to see what the group's albums sales were during their existence compared to after they split up. Their portion of sales after they split up was significant, as they were for Jimi Hendrix and Buddy Holly.

Were Young's lyrics too cryptic for single airplay? The lyrics of "Mr. Soul," "Broken Arrow," "Flying on the Ground Is Wrong," "Expecting to Fly," "On the Way Home," and "Nowadays Clancy Can't Even Sing" need some type of a translator to be understood:

> "He hung up his eyelids and ran down the hall."
> "Who's seeing eyes through the crack in the floor?"
> "For the thought that I caught that my head is the event of the season."

Here is an incident that might explain the short duration of the band, according to the drummer, Dewey Martin:

> "Things got pretty hot on stage, and when Neil and Steve got into the dressing room, they started swinging at each other with their guitars. It was like two old ladies going at it with their purses."

> Bassist Bruce Palmer said, "Steve was always hard to get along with; Neil was hard to get along with. Steve is brash, egotistical and pushy. Neil is the complete opposite. But the end result is still the same — two spoiled little brats. But instead of screaming and yelling, would just disappear."

The Buffalo Springfield made its debut at The Whisky A Go Go, and they were immediately signed by Charlie Greene and Brian Stone, Sonny and Cher's former mentors. The boys are: Neil Young, lead guitar and singer; Bruce Palmer, bass; Ritchie Furay, guitar, vocals; Dewey Martin, drums; and leader Steve Stills, lead guitar. This group writes all its own material and has terrific stage presence. One of their most outstanding songs is, "Now A Days, Clancy Can't Even Sing."

Teen Set, November 1966

- Best songs: 1. "For What It's Worth" 2. "Broken Arrow"* 3. "Bluebird" 4. "Mr. Soul"
- Best elite song: "For What It's Worth" (because of the lyrics)
- Worst song: "The Hour of Not Quite Rain"
- The opening lyrics of "Broken Arrow" (from "Mr. Soul" [a song within a song]) are sung by Dewey Martin, but it is from the studio, not a live recording, with screaming piped in.

Year	Top-Ten Single(s)	Peak	Weeks	RCY	ATR	Gold Album(s)	Sales	Peak	Weeks	RCY
1967	For What It's Worth (Stills) (A)	6								
(A) RS 63										

Cream

Second only to Jimi Hendrix, Cream was a group of musicians' musicians. Any other musician of this era will rave about the group. Putting it another way, one would never hear,

"Man, I just do not dig that group. They were unimaginative and did not break enough rules."

If you did not dig Cream, you were out of the scene.

Jack Bruce was the lead vocalist on most songs, as well as the primary composer (with Pete Brown writing the lyrics). Eric Clapton sang lead on "Crossroads," "Strange Brew," and part of "Sunshine of Your Love." (Bruce sang lead on the first and third verse lines, and Clapton on the second "I'll soon be with you"; Bruce sang on the first chorus line and Clapton threw in an extra "I've been waiting so long" during the last chorus.)

As with John Entwistle of the Who (another three-piece band), Bruce's bass playing took a more prominent role than most bassists'. He played a six-string bass.

Like Crosby, Stills and Nash, the members of Cream chose each other from previous groups, rather than being a group of friends. However, unlike CSN, they did not previously play in well-known bands. John Mayall's Bluesbreakers and the Graham Bond Organization were/are hardly household names.

Cream was invited to play at Monterey Pop, but their manager, Robert Stigwood, turned it down without them knowing about it.

One of their more memorable songs was their cover of Albert King's "Born Under a Bad Sign," which had the incredibly amusing lyric, "If it wasn't for bad luck, I wouldn't have no luck at all." This song was written by Booker T. Jones and William Bell. Answering the following two questions will tell how well you know this song:

1. How long has Jack Bruce been down? (p. 307)

2. What are his only two friends? (p. 307)

Their decision to split up was made in May 1968, which was midway through a tour. After that tour, they announced a "farewell tour" (which really was, unlike many a Rolling Stones tour). Their last live show was on November 26, 1968. The singles "Crossroads" and "Badge," and the *Goodbye* album were all released in 1969.

Why did the group split up in their prime? A group usually dissolves because of one of these reasons:

1. They have run out of songs or lost their commercial appeal (such as most groups, including the Monkees, Herman's Hermits, the Association).

2. A key member dies or quits (such as the Doors or Lovin' Spoonful).

3. Members clash or want to explore new musical avenues.

Cream certainly fell under the third reason.

- Name recall: Eric Clapton, sixty-nine percent; Ginger Baker, forty-five percent; Jack Bruce, twenty-one percent. Baker's recognition is probably higher than any drummer except Ringo Starr. Bruce's number is surprisingly low, but he was never in another prominent band. This is probably the only group where the primary lead singer and songwriter is the *least* known member of the band.

- Was he glad? Bruce says the word "glad" eighty times in the song "I'm So Glad."

- The song "SWLABR" stood for "She walks like a bearded rainbow."

- Best songs: 1. "White Room" 2. "Sunshine of Your Love"

Year	Top-Ten Single(s)	Peak	Weeks	RCY	ATR	Gold Album(s)	Sales	Peak	Weeks	RCY
1968	Sunshine of Your Love (Clapton-Bruce-Brown) (A)	5				Disraeli Gears	Plat	4		3
1968	White Room (Bruce-Brown) (B)	6				Fresh Cream	Gold	39		32
1968						Wheels of Fire (C)	Gold	1	4	45
1969						Goodbye	Gold	2	2	43
1969						Best	Gold	3		44

(A) RS 65

(B) RS 367

(C) Rare for a number-one album for four weeks not to reach platinum status. The album must have had most of its sales in a brief period.

Clapton (right) is sporting his "Jimi Hendrix Experience" perm

© SUNSET BOULEVARD/CORBIS SYGMA

Eric Clapton

© Henry Diltz/CORBIS

Clapton with David Crosby

Creedence Clearwater Revival

This group was John Fogerty and his backup band. This was one of the few groups in which there were almost no backing or harmony vocals. Despite Fogerty possessing most of the talent in the group, the other three members ruined a good thing.

First, brother Tom Fogerty left for a solo career that went nowhere. There was not much demand for a non-songwriting, non-singing rhythm guitarist. Stu Cook and Doug Clifford had the sense to stay in the group, but became restless playing the role of session musicians in the studio. This led to them writing and singing songs for their last album, *Mardi Gras*. The album sold reasonably well, because most people assumed it would be sung and written by John Fogerty. Moral of this story: Don't bite the hand that feeds you. What were these two thinking about? Did Charlie Watts want a leading role with the Rolling Stones? Steve Boone with Lovin' Spoonful? I am sure John Fogerty was not an easy person to work with, but so what? They caused the breakup of a group that could have gone on longer, and maybe they would have not had to spend their later years doing the oldies circuit.

The group was originally headed up by Tom Fogerty. They were getting nowhere and, as happened with Jim McGuinn and the Byrds, John stepped up and the group took off.

They never did have a number-one song, but had five number-twos (including three in a row), a number-three, and a number-four. The baseball pitcher comparison to this would be Juan Marichal, always second best after Sandy Koufax, Bob Gibson or Tom Seaver, in the Cy Young voting.

Their last album, *Mardi Gras* (1972), reached a peak of twelve on the charts and went platinum, but most people bought this album on the CCR name alone, not knowing what was on it. Three great Fogerty songs, of course, but also polluted with Cook and Clifford songs.

- Name recall: John Fogerty, sixty-nine percent; Tom Fogerty, twenty-one percent; Doug Clifford, seven percent; and Stu Cook, three percent. As with Dennis Wilson of the Beach

Boys and Dave Davies of the Kinks, Tom Fogerty gets some name recall because his well-known brother was in the band.

- Best songs 1. "Bad Moon Risin'" 2. "Have You Ever Seen the Rain?" 3. "Down on the Corner" 4. "Fortunate Son" ("Some people born silver spoon in hand, lord, don't they help themselves. But when the tax man comes to the door, lord, house look like a rummage sale, yeah.") 5. "Who'll Stop the Rain?"

- Best elite song: "Fortunate Son," because it is a protest song

- Underrated: "Lodi," and "Someday Never Comes"

Year	Top-Ten Single(s)	Peak	Weeks	RCY	ATR	Gold Album(s)	Sales	Peak	Weeks	RCY
1968						Creedence Clearwater Revival	Plat	52		
1969	Proud Mary (A)	2	3	18		Bayou Country	Plat 2	4		1969 (4) 1970 (97)
1969	Green River (B)	2	1	27						
1969	Bad Moon Risin' (C)	2	1	31						
1969	Down on the Corner	3		40						
1970	Traveling Band (D)	2	2	25		Willie and the Poor Boys	Plat 2	3		12
1970	Looking out My Back Door (E)	2	1	26		Green River	Plat 3	1	4	29
1970	Who'll Stop The Rain? (F)	9				Cosmos Factory	Plat 4	1	9	1970 (30) 1971 (35)
1970	Up Around the Bend (G)	4								
1971	Have You Ever Seen The Rain?	8				Pendulum	Plat	5		28

1971	Sweet Hitchhiker	6									

All-time single rank #170

All songs written by John Fogerty

(A) Behind "Dizzy;" RS 155

(B) Behind "Sugar, Sugar"

(C) Behind "In The Year 2525;" RS 355

(D) Behind "Bridge Over Troubled Water"

(E) Behind "War"

(F) RS 188

(G) "Get while the getting's good"

Total album sales twenty-two million (ninety-second)

Bob Dylan

He was a true original in both folk and rock music. The A&E Biography segment starts out with "Bob Dylan has simply been himself." Maybe, maybe not. After all, he did change his name, invent stories about his background, and join the folk/protest movement only to further his career. He decided to go that route, rather than rock-and-roll, because no one else in folk/protest was writing their own songs. His lyrics are like no other, and if understood, usually carry a message.

If a current teenager were to listen to an album of his, she would probably wonder "what is the appeal here?" Some also might wonder why he is a household name when he has been only a moderately successful chart topper; he has achieved two number-two songs, and two number-seven. He started writing songs in 1961 and has not stopped, over forty years later. He began as a Woody Guthrie apprentice, down to the Greek sailor's hat, and was ingrained in the left-wing "protest" song movement. Why did Dylan become the only commercial success of all the coffee house folk singers? He obtained a Columbia record contract within eight months of his arrival in New York, which was unheard of in folk music. John Hammond of Columbia records recognized Dylan's songwriting talent and signed him to a contract. Hammond had previously noticed a very positive review in the New York Times. Hammond was ridiculed after Dylan's first album did not sell well. Dylan also signed with a manager, Albert Grossman, who was the only person in the folk area who knew his head from his rear end regarding business. (Business aptitude and folk music aptitude rarely go together. In Frank Zappa's book, he regrets hiring a business manager with an "artistic background.") Grossman knew Dylan's voice was not commercially appealing, so he gave Dylan's most famous song, "Blowin' in the Wind," to Peter, Paul and Mary. That was a brilliant move and it started Dylan on his way to success.

Dylan's earlier work ranges from lighthearted, clever songs like "Bob Dylan's Blues" and "I Shall Be Free," to angry, bitter songs like "Masters of War," where he wishes death for armament makers. (It is government that causes wars, not arms makers. What would have been Nazi Germany's future if the United States and the UK had had no armaments makers?) Another such song is "Ballad of Hollis Brown," who killed himself, his wife, and five children because he could not financially support them. The theme of this song is certainly not one of personal responsibility.

Many of Bob Dylan's songs had complex lyrics, much like Allen Ginsberg's poetry. What made Dylan much more commercially successful is that he wrote tremendous music also, which appealed to the proletariat.

By 1965, he gained the fame he needed to switch to rock-and-roll music. He shocked the folk world by playing electrical instruments and drums ("going electric" is the cliché) at the Newport Folk Festival. Some felt betrayed and booed during his electric music. Some of the folk performers tried to prevent him from playing. Paul Rothchild, who mixed the Dylan set, said,

"On one side you had Pete Seeger and George Wein (concert organizer), the old guard. Pete is backstage, pacifist Pete, with an axe saying 'I'm going to cut the f_____ cables if that act goes onstage.' Eventually, Seeger dashed to his car and rolled up the windows, his hands over his ears." (Later that year, when there was something in it for him, Seeger did not seem to mind the Byrds using "Turn! Turn! Turn!" as a rock-and-roll song.) People had reason to be upset, because they were not hearing the type of music they had expected to hear at a folk festival. However, why people came to his concerts for at least two more years to boo Dylan makes no sense.

Shocking people at Newport was nothing out of character for Dylan. He loved to startle the media with absurd answers to their questions, badmouth the protest movement, and turn to Christianity.

Joe Levy, music editor of *Rolling Stone* magazine said, "People wanted to take Dylan out in the parking lot, they wanted to kill him. People wanted to hit them with bottles. Guys who were on that tour will tell you that they were pelted with bottles. People wanted to kill these guys."

Dylan was through with the "let's hold hands, form a circle, and sing 'We Shall Overcome'" group. His comment, "I would return to the protest movement only if all the people in the world disappeared," left no doubt.

He further irritated the Left at an awards banquet by initially rejecting an award from the Emergency Civil Liberties Committee because he felt no connection with these people "with minks and jewels who had been with the Left in the 1960s." When he was convinced to accept the award, he asked them what they were doing for his friends in Harlem, "some of them junkies, all of them poor."

The meanings of many of Dylan's songs are hard to decipher. Can anyone say what "Just Like Tom Thumb's Blues" is really about? If you have no idea, but want people to think that you are hip, you can always say that it was a Vietnam War protest song; just hope that no one asks you to explain. I am sure Bob is entertained by how some intellectuals attempt to interpret his songs.

Dylan influenced a lot of musicians, and that is why he is such a favorite with the elite. His song "Mr. Tambourine Man" was the beginning of folk rock when played by the Byrds. He also influenced John Lennon, and anyone who influences John Lennon in the field of music is a musical genius. Dylan also influenced Jimi Hendrix. Roger McGuinn said, "Dylan went over to England and met with the Beatles and said, 'You guys don't say anything,' and it really shocked Lennon…and he started writing more intellectual lyrics after that; and by the same token, Dylan started experimenting with music, so the two of them really influenced each other in a profound way." Well said.

He had other changes, like his voice for "Lay, Lady, Lay." He became a Christian in 1979, and was writing almost exclusively Christian-based lyrics. As with the protest gatherings, Dylan was led in this direction by a woman in his life. For someone in the entertainment business to turn to religion is almost unheard of, and if one does so, it is more chic to choose an Eastern religion or a non-traditional domestic religion like Scientology. He quietly quit writing Christian-based lyrics about two years later. He has always appeared to enjoy solitude, and when groups of people try to claim him as their musical spokesman, he turns in the other direction. He almost never used backup singers, or double tracks. (The party going on in the background of "Rainy Day Women" does not count as background vocals!) The only songs of his with a middle-eight (bridge) portion of a song were "I Want You," "Just Like a Woman," and "Watching the River Flow." The Byrds actually added a middle eight to Dylan's "All I Really Want to Do."

He did not put on any airs during interviews, including not using the fake smile or laughter. He was ill at ease, usually puffing intently on a cigarette, which is more refreshing than someone who uses platitudes and puts on a happy face.

Hard to believe, judging from his interviews, but Dylan had considerable personal charm, and had charisma on stage in the league of Sinatra and Presley.

"Subterranean Homesick Blues" and "Maggie's Farm" have almost exactly the same beginning.

- Best Songs: 1. "A Hard Rain's A-Gonna Fall"* 2. "Like a Rolling Stone" 3. "Blowin' in the Wind" 4. "You Ain't Goin' Nowhere"

  * The Rolling Stones' "Gimme Shelter" was written as a response ☺.

Year	Top-Ten Single(s)	Peak	Weeks	RCY	ATR	Gold Album(s)	Sales	Peak	Weeks	RCY
1964						The Times They Are A-Changin'	Gold	20		
						Another Side of Bob Dylan	Gold	43		
1965	Like a Rolling Stone (A)	2	2	29		Bringing It All Back Home	Gold	6		1965 (25) 1966 (61)
1965	Positively Fourth Street (B)	7				Highway 61 Revisited	Plat	3		
1966	Rainy Day Women	2	1			Blonde on Blonde	Plat	9		73
1967						Greatest Hits*	Plat 5	10		1967 (47) 1968 (96)
1968						John Wesley Harding	Plat	2		31
1969	Lay Lady Lay	7				Nashville Skyline	Plat	3		18
1970						Self Portrait	Gold	4		64
1970						New Morning	Gold	7		
1971						Greatest Hits II*	Plat 5	14		
All-time single rank #193 All songs written by Bob Dylan										

(A) RS 1

(B) RS 203

Total album sales 34.5 million (forty-third)

* Easily his best sellers were the greatest hits albums

Jimi Hendrix

(with Experience and Band of Gypsies)

Jimi Hendrix was the ultimate "musician's musician." He is always listed as one of the favorite musicians, if not the favorite, of other musicians of the era. He is the number-one ranked guitarist in the 2003 *Rolling Stone* rankings, and was held in very high regard by other guitarists of his era.

He got his start in New York City and was recognized as a true talent in July 1966 by Chas Chandler, the soon-to-be-ex-bassist of the Animals. (As with Brian Epstein of the Beatles, Chandler had a keen eye for marketable talent.)

Chandler felt that Hendrix would stand out more in England, and he (Chandler) had better connections there. He knew exactly what he was doing, especially considering the fact that Hendrix was neither a vocalist nor a songwriter at the time. (Chandler ended up being a very successful manager, producer, and businessman, one of the few musicians to move on successfully to another career.) He linked Hendrix with bassist Noel Redding and drummer Mitch Mitchell, and the group was called the Jimi Hendrix Experience. Redding and Mitchell permed their hair, so all three had the same hairstyles. "Hey Joe," "Purple Haze," and "The Wind Cries Mary" all reached the top ten in England, along with a very successful album, *Are You Experienced?* The album was released in the United States in August 1967, two months after the band played at the Monterey Pop Festival, and was their biggest-selling album.

Hendrix was a true gentleman (at least offstage) and this,

unfortunately, might have cost him his life. He rarely said "no" to anyone, and was always a pushover for all the sycophants that hung around him. He never used a bodyguard. He struggled in finding a permanent lineup of accompanying musicians. He first replaced Redding and Mitchell with Billy Cox and Buddy Miles, respectively. Later, Mitchell replaced Miles. Hendrix felt continual pressure from his record company and struggled endlessly trying to complete a fourth album. He also had the most grueling road schedule of anyone of that era. It has been said that "the system" killed Hendrix, but he had a choice in the matter. He could have chosen to isolate himself more, as Bob Dylan, the Beatles, Brian Wilson, and others chose to do when being overwhelmed.

The first instance of Hendrix setting his guitar on fire was not at Monterey, but actually three months earlier in London, where he was treated for burns afterwards.

Hendrix had the unique ability to play what sounded like both a lead and rhythm guitar at once on his guitar. He also used extensive feedback and wah-wah pedals.

His only single release in the United States was "All Along the Watchtower" (Bob Dylan), which peaked at number twenty.

Hendrix was mostly around white people, even his audience, and was criticized for this by some. When asked about racial matters, he would say, "I'm only a musician." When black militant leaders spoke with him, they did not like that he favored nonviolence. He also said, "I don't feel black. It's the Indian part that I pay most attention to." (His maternal grandmother was a full-blooded Cherokee, and his paternal grandmother was half Indian).

When author Sharon Lawrence first spoke to Hendrix's father after his death, he said, "Would you be knowing how much money there is?" It sounds to me like he did not have a great relationship with his father.

Peter Noone said of Jimi Hendrix, "I saw Hendrix, and I thought it was time to quit." First of all, Noone's band, Herman's Hermits, were already done by then. It was time for them to quit because they had run out of other writers' material. Secondly, he is somehow implying that Hendrix and the Hermits played the same type of music, which is obviously not true.

As in the deaths of Jim Morrison and Brian Jones, there were mysterious circumstances surrounding Hendrix's death. In the early morning of his death, he had his girlfriend drive him to "see some people" and then pick him up about an hour later. Hendrix went to sleep at 7 a.m., after taking nine Vesperax sleeping pills. The friend tried to wake him at 10:20, but was not able to, and she called an ambulance. It did not arrive for one hour and Hendrix, still alive, was seated upright in the back seat with no head support. He died from vomit inhalation sometime during the twenty-five-minute ride to the hospital. There have been thirty-six albums of his music released since his death.

Currently everyone's losing their minds to a tall, thin ugly man, who is a phenominal guitar player with a gravel voice, called JIMI HENDRIX. With his group THE EXPERIENCE, they are the hippies favourite. Jimi, who is American, was found by the ANIMALS on their last trip over. Now CHAS CHANDLER, who since his split with the group, has been taking up record production has made a great version of **Hey Joe** which swept Jimi to success here.

Jimi did his first big London date at the **Bag Of Nails** club in London. What a scene it turned out to be! One of the really raving evenings. I turned up early to be safe—which was just as well. By 11:30 pm, and Jimi's first set, the place was packed and the temperature was rising—literally. PETE TOWNSHEND, musical brain behind the WHO and lead guitarist and songwriter in the group, sat transfixed for the first five minutes of Jimi's act, then went mad, leaping about. Joining him was good looking ERIC CLAPTON, famous guitarist with the CREAM.

Teen, June 1967

- Best songs: 1. "Purple Haze" 2. "If Six Was Nine" 3. "Foxey Lady"

Year	Top-Ten Single(s)	Peak	Weeks	RCY	ATR	Gold Album(s)	Sales	Peak	Weeks	RCY
1968						Are You Experienced?	Plat 4	5		1968 (1) 1969 (71)
1968						Axis	Plat	3		22
1968						Smash Hits	Plat 2	6		67
1969						Electric Ladyland	Plat 2	1	2	99
1970						Band of Gypsies	Plat 2	5		34
1971						Cry of Love	Plat	3		29
1971						Rainbow Bridge	Gold	15		
1972						Hendrix in the West	Gold	12		
Total album sales twenty million (102nd)										
Hendrix has sold twenty-five albums since 1971, including two platinum and five gold										

The Mamas and the Papas

They were known, foremost, for their tremendous vocal arrangements. The Mamas and the Papas was one of the few groups (along with the Who) where the only real songwriter rarely sang a lead. John Phillips sang lead on "Meditation Mama," "Straight Shooter," "Hey Girl," and parts of "Safe in My Garden" and "Too Late." Cass Elliott was certainly the best-known person in the group, as she had the best stage presence and had a solo career, which was certainly more successful than Phillips's.

Phillips's songwriting was in continual decline. His best songs were on the first album. The second and third albums were a step down, but there were still no "skip-over" songs. The fourth album contained four "skip-over" songs: "Gemini Child," "Mansions," "Too Late," and "Rooms." By the time *People Like Us*, their fifth and final album, came out, his pen was completely dry, which showed in his solo career. One exception to this was "Kokomo," written in 1987 for the Beach Boys.

When John Phillips asked Michelle Phillips to join the previous group, she thought it was funny. John then said, "You're going to sing, because it costs too much to keep you on the road."

Cass was the last to join the group. According to Michelle's sister Russell, John would not let Cass in because she was too fat. However, Nick Venet from Capitol Records would not record them without her (they signed with Dunhill Records soon after that).

Michelle was briefly dismissed from the group, at John's insistence, during the recording of *The Mamas and the Papas*. According to her look-alike replacement, Jill Gibson, Michelle only sang on two of the twelve tracks. At their first concert with Gibson, Michelle was not noticed as missing until Gibson was introduced after a few songs.

"Dream A Little Dream of Me" was a single released by "Mama Cass with the Mamas and the Papas" soon before the group disbanded in 1968. It was marketed as Elliott's debut "solo" single.

- The most recognizable singing voice was Cass's, followed by Denny Doherty's, Michelle's, and then John's. Most people would not recognize John's voice if heard solo.

- They were the only group to do a cover of a Beatles's song ("I Call Your Name") that was better than the Beatles' version.

- John Phillips was one of the few musicians with organizational skills enough to produce the Monterey Pop Festival. This type of festival had never been done before. He was also the tallest musician of the era and the first one to wear a hat on stage. He only played acoustic guitar, never electric.

- The only group to feature a toilet on an album cover. The Rolling Stones *Beggar's Banquet* "toilet" cover was nixed by Decca Records and did not appear until the 1980s.

- Four of their nine albums were greatest hits albums.

- Best Songs: 1. "California Dreaming" 2. "Monday, Monday" 3. "Creeque Alley"

- Underrrated: 1. "Safe in My Garden" 2. "Midnight Voyage"

~~ager, ANDREW LOOG OLDHAM~~ . . . Beautiful MICHELLE, of the above-mentioned M & Ps, is no longer with the group. Her replacement is another lovely named JILL GIBSON (who used to be JAN's girl). You can bet that former MAMA MICH has plently of offers to star on her own . . . JAN, by the way, is much improved after his serious car accident. You can write to him at 321 S. Beverly Dr., Beverly Hills, Calif. . . . New REMAINS drummer, N. D. SMART II, made the BEATLES tour with the group . . . Surprise! When a leading British pop mag ran a poll to find out who the English kiddies' fave singer was, it came out like this: SCOTT (of the WALKER BROS.): 12,500; Paul McCartney: 3,000; Mick Jagger: 1,500!

16 Magazine, October 1966

Year	Top-Ten Single(s)	Peak	Weeks	RCY	ATR	Gold Album(s)	Sales	Peak	Weeks	RCY
1966	California Dreaming* (A)	4				If You Can Believe Your Eyes and Ears	Gold	1	1	1966 (6) 1967 (25)
1966	Monday Monday*	1	3	5	315	The Mamas and The Papas	Gold	4		
1966	I Saw Her Again* (B)	5								
1966	Words of Love	5								

1967	Dedicated to the One I Love (C)	2	3	21		Deliver	Gold	2	7	24
1967	Creeque Alley* (D)	5								28
1968						Farewell	Gold	5		17

All-time single rank #252

* Written by John Phillips

(A) RS 89; featured a flute

(B) The first "I saw her" at 2:43 is an error that was left in.

Features a flute.

(C) Lead singer is Michelle Phillips, singing with a very low-volume voice.

(D) "Good vibrations"

Simon and Garfunkel

The brainy duo. They were friends since grade school and began playing music together as high school juniors. Paul Simon graduated from college and started law school. Art Garfunkel received a master's degree in mathematics. In this era, a college graduate in the music arena was rare, and a master's degree in mathematics was about as rare someone who supported the Vietnam War.

Their first song, "Hey Schoolgirl," was performed on American Bandstand. Their first album, *Wednesday Morning, 3 AM*, featured folk songs and was released in 1964. Because this album did not sell much, they split up, and Simon moved to England. About a year later, in November 1965, their producer added an electric guitar, bass, and drums to "The Sound of Silence" and released it as a single. Even though neither liked the changes (they found out about them after the re-release), the song soon reached number one, and the duo decided to give it another go. If they would have had to approve the release of the new version, it probably would not have occurred.

Like the Beatles, they went out on top. Their final album, *Bridge over Troubled Water*, was easily their best. It was the best album, period, by anyone other than the Beatles.

Each album they released was a huge seller (platinum), and the albums after the first and through *Greatest Hits* lasted on the charts an incredible 143, 145, 66, 85, and 127 weeks consecutively. This does not even include *The Graduate* soundtrack, which lasted 69 weeks. In comparison, no Beatles album was on the charts for more than seventy-seven weeks before *Sgt. Pepper* (175 weeks, their longest).

Simon was an excellent songwriter and clever lyricist, but his voice had no resonance. Garfunkel had most of the vocal talent and should have been used on more leads. Simon has said in later years that he regrets not having the vocal on "Bridge Over Troubled Water," but that would have been a huge mistake. There is a live version of him singing the song, and it does not compare well to the original

- Best songs: 1. "Mrs. Robinson" 2. "Bridge over Troubled Water" 3. "Cecilia"

- Underrated: "April Come She Will," "The Only Living Boy in New York"

- Worst songs: "So Long Frank Lloyd Wright," "Blessed"

- They went out at their peak of popularity with a number-one album and number-one and number-four singles.

Year	Top-Ten Single(s)	Peak	Weeks	RCY	ATR	Gold Album(s)	Sales	Peak	Weeks	RCY
1966	Sounds of Silence (A)	1	2	14	594	Sounds of Silence (D)	Plat 3	21		1966 (50) 1968 (25)
1966	Homeward Bound	6				Wednesday Morning, 3 AM (E)	Plat	30		90
1966	I Am a Rock (B)	3								
1967						Parsley Sage Rosemary and Thyme (F)	Plat 3	4		1967 (33) 1968 (8)
1968	Mrs. Robinson(C)	1	3	8	338					1968 (11) 1969 (96)
1969	The Boxer (D)	7				Bookends (G)	Plat 2	1	7	
1970	Bridge over Troubled Water (E)	1	6	1	85	Bridge over Troubled Water	Plat 13	1	10	1970 (1) 1971 (55)
1970	Cecilia	4								

All-time single rank #130

All songs written by Paul Simon

(A) RS 156

(B) Song ends with a bridge.

(C) "Jesus loves you" "Hey, hey, hey"

(D) RS 105

(E) One of the few songs of the era featuring a piano as the lead instrument. Others are "After the Gold Rush," by Neil Young, and "Let It Be, Hey Jude," "Lady Madonna," and "Hey Bulldog," by the Beatles. RS 47

Total album sales 37.5 million (thirty-third)

(E) This album sold well, retroactively, after *Sounds of Silence*, though it was released two years earlier.

(F) The lyric "Lenny Bruce" is in two songs on this album

(G) The elite's favorite album of the duo

The Who

The angry group. Pete Townshend was angry as a child and he is angry to this day. When Townshend and Roger Daltry met in 1961, Daltry believed that Townshend's volatile temper was caused by the fact that Townshend had never worked as a laborer, but attended a "soft" art school instead. (Townshend was hardly alone in this matter, as many British rockers attended art school before their music careers. However, I know of none in the United States who did.)

> Keith Moon said of the band members, "We really have absolutely nothing in common, apart from music."
>
> Daltry concurred, "We're not mates at all."
>
> Townshend offered this opinion, "Roger is not a very good singer at all."
>
> So much for the myth that a band has to have "chemistry."

Daltry did most of the singing, but Townshend was the soloist on "Legal Matter." He also sings the "Don't cry. Don't raise your eyes. It's only teenage wasteland" part on "Baba O'Riley," and the beginning of "I'm a Boy" (Daltry comes in on "My name is Bill and I'm a head case").

Townshend's guitar work was more chord-oriented than single-string as with most lead guitarists, which certainly facilitated his windmill method. There were also few guitar solos. Because of this, John Entwistle's bass had to take more of a lead role; a good example of this is "Substitute," where, except for the opening guitar, the bass is the lead instrument.

Daltry and Townshend were always antagonistic toward each other, unlike alliances such as Lennon-McCartney and Jagger-Richard. Daltry often used his fists, especially with Townshend, to get his way, even onstage. Daltry, being a sheet-metal worker, could probably have beaten up anyone in any other group also, with the exception of Gene Clark of the Byrds.

In late 1964, the Who entertained much of the audience with Townshend smashing his guitar and Moon kicking over his drums. Back then, the group couldn't afford to destroy its instruments. They would be paid $140 per performance, and Townshend would smash guitars worth $560 and amplifiers worth even more. Moon's drum damage could usually be repaired. At one time, the group was in debt for $168,000. Part of this was because they concentrated on live performances more than recordings, though the latter are much more profitable. There were also huge bills for hotel damage. They finally made it above water financially after the *Tommy* album release in 1969. (To convert the above dollar amounts to 2004, multiply by five).

The Who was the last British Invasion band to make it big in the United States. Their first three UK singles, "I Can't Explain," "Anyway, Anyhow, Anywhere," and "My Generation" did not break the top forty in the United States. Their first success in the U.S. market did *not* start after their Monterey Pop appearance, but with the single, "Happy Jack," which was released two months before and reached number twenty-four. This group was not identified with one or two big hits, but was more of an album group.

The Who was not the typical 1967 psychedelic band. Their hair was relatively short. The only member who had any sympathy with hippie ideals was Townshend. Moon hated hippies and his preferred drug was alcohol.

They were very different in their spending habits. Entwistle and Daltry lived well within their means. Townshend felt guilty about having grown so wealthy and donated to charities, including a Meher Baba center (Baba did not speak from 1925 until his death in 1969. One of the reasons given was that he grew weary of large phone bills☺). Moon lived on the edge, of course.

When Keith Moon died in 1978, there were the usual platitudes about him not being replaceable, insinuating that they would not carry on as a band, in respect to him. He was replaced soon after, of course.

Does anyone know how Pete is coming along with his book on child abuse?

- Best songs: 1. "I Can't Explain" 2. "Won't Get Fooled Again" ("Meet the new boss, same as the old boss" is an incredible lyric. Examples of this where the "new boss" was the same (or worse) than the "old boss" are: Old boss, King Louis XIV, new boss, Napoleon; Czar Nick II and Josef Stalin; Fulgencio Bastista and Fidel Castro; Samoza and Daniel Ortega; Mr. Jones and Napoleon (Animal Farm) 3. "Substitute"

Year	Top-Ten Single(s)	Peak	Weeks	RCY	ATR	Gold Album(s)	Sales	Peak	Weeks	RCY
1967	I Can See for Miles (Townsend) (A)	9								
1969						Tommy	Plat 2	4		1969 (34) 1970 (60) 1971 (67)
1970						Live at Leeds	Plat 2	4		42
1971						Who's Next	Plat 3	4		
1971						Meaty Beaty Big and Bouncy	Plat	11		

All-time singles rank #174

All songs written by Pete Townshend, guitarist

(A) RS 258

Total album sales 20 million (102nd)
After 1971, the band achieved six platinum and three gold albums.

Post 1971, there were three gold and five platinum albums, the last being in 1983. The latest six albums released have not broken the top one hundred.

Neil Young

His first album, Neil Young, which was released after Buffalo Springfield, but before his association with Crosby, Stills, and Nash, topped out at only number 196 on the charts. His career started to take off with his second album, Everyone Knows This Is Nowhere, which was the forty-fifth ranked album in 1970, propelled by his CSN fame. His next album, After the Gold Rush, was ranked number twenty in 1971. Harvest was easily his best selling album. Again, it certainly helped Young, in the fame category, to have his name added to the CSNY group name. Harvest (as Lennon's Imagine) was the one album that Young did with the mass audience in mind. Interestingly, when he toured after Harvest, he did not play any of the songs on that album, or any other album. Time Fades Away was his next album, which was comprised of his latest-tour-only songs. On the Beach was a huge disappointment, especially being the first studio album after Harvest. The first song, "Walk On," was among his best, but the rest of the album was music that appealed to him more than his listeners. Over a long career, he wrote many good songs after that, but no albums that would come close to matching After the Gold Rush and Harvest. Suprisingly, of the eleven singles he released, only three made the Top Forty: "Heart of Gold" (1), "Old Man" (31), and "Only Love Can Break Your Heart (33).

Two of his best songs, "Sugar Mountain" and "Ohio" were never on any studio albums. He is not on the Woodstock film because he refused to be filmed.

As was the case when he was with Buffalo Springfield, many of Young's song meanings are next to impossible to understand. Can anyone translate "After the Gold Rush" or "Last Trip to Tulsa"?

Young is "walleyed" — when his left eye is looking directly forward, his right eye looks to the right. This can most easily be seen on the early Buffalo Springfield photos and on the inside cover of the *Everybody Knows This Is Nowhere* album. The same was true with George Harrison (see his picture on *The Beatles [White Album]).*

- Three charting singles, including "Only Love Can Break Your Heart," which peaked at number thirty-three (1970); "Heart of Gold," which was at number one for one week (1972) and number 728 all time (RS 297); and "Old Man," which peaked at number thirty-one (1972), all of which were written by Young.

- He has played all different types of music for the past thirty years, and was hassled by his record company for not making albums that had commercial appeal.

- Best songs: 1. "Heart of Gold" 2. "Comes a Time" 3. "Cinnamon Girl" 4. "Walk On"

Year	Top-Ten Single(s)	Peak	Weeks	RCY	ATR	Gold Album(s)	Sales	Peak	Weeks	RCY
1970						Everybody Knows This Is Nowhere	Plat	34		45
1971						After the Gold Rush	Plat 2	8		20
1972	Heart of Gold	1	1			Harvest	Plat 4	1	2	

After 1971, he achieved five platinum albums and eleven gold. The biggest seller was *Harvest* at platinum 4, followed by *Harvest Moon* at platinum 2. In later years, he had five platinum and nine gold albums.

The Third Tier

Chapter Eight

The Beat Goes On

Animals (and Eric Burdon and the Animals)

- Best songs: 1. "House of the Rising Sun" 2. "We Gotta Get Out of This Place"

Year	Top-Ten Single(s)	Peak	Weeks	RCY	ATR	Gold Album(s)	Sales	Peak	Weeks	RCY
1964	House of the Rising Sun (Price) (A)	1	3	6	317					
1966						Best	Gold	6		1966 (13) 1967 (20)
1967	San Franciscan Nights	9								
1967	See See Rider	10								
All-time single rank # 212 (A) Written in the 1920s, but because the copyright had expired, Alan Price assumed authorship										

Association

The Association was voted the number-one group of 1967 by Bill Gavin Radio-Record Congress. The Beatles had won the prior three years. For its fiftieth anniversary, BMI, a performing rights organization, announced that the only two songs to receive over five million plays were "Yesterday" and "Never My Love." The Association might have been the last group to appear in coats and ties (at the Monterey Pop Festival). The band had six members, all singing and playing instruments. Like the Monkees, they were a hugely successful group for the two years 1966-1967. Not being in the Monterey Pop video cost the Association a lot of publicity, and the group quickly fell out of fashion in the increasing counterculture of the late 1960s.

- Name recognition: Jim Yester, ten percent Terry Kirkman, seven percent; Gary Alexander, zero percent; Russ Giguere, zero percent; Brian Cole, zero percent; Ted Bluechel, zero percent.

- Best song: "Everything That Touches You"

Year	Top-Ten Single(s)	Peak	Weeks	RCY	ATR	Gold Album(s)	Sales	Peak	Weeks	RCY
1966	Along Comes Mary (Almer)	7				And Then along Comes The Association	Gold	5		
1966	Cherish (Kirkman)	1	8	8	352					
1967	Windy Friedman	1	4	3	193	Inside Out	Gold	8		77
All-time single rank # 350 Group members Bluechel and Yester also wrote songs.										

Badfinger

Pete Ham and Roger McGuinn, of The Byrds, are the two most underrated musicians of the era. Badfinger had three songwriters: Ham, Tom Evans, and Joey Molland. Ham's and Evans's voices sounded very much alike. On "Without You," Ham starts out, and Evans comes in on "I can't live, if living is without you."

Ham and Evans wrote "Without You," which became a number-one hit for Harry Nillson in 1972.

Problems with management and finances plagued the group, which led to the suicides of Ham in 1975 and Evans in 1983.

- Best song: "No Matter What"

Year	Top-Ten Single(s)	Peak	Weeks	RCY	ATR	Gold Album(s)	Sales	Peak	Weeks	RCY
1970	Come and Get It	7								
1970	No Matter What*	8								
1971	Day after Day*	4								
* Written by Pete Ham, lead guitar and vocalist.										

Dave Clark Five

Dave Clark was the drummer and the lead singer had the very original name of Mike Smith, even though most of the songs featured four concurrent vocalists. They had a huge year in 1964, but regressed fairly quickly over the next few years. They remained a group, with no turnover, until 1970.

- A current buzzword is "front man" which has replaced the term "lead singer." He is called this because he is "out front" on the stage. However, this term did not fit the Dave Clark

Five. The "front man" in this group was the drummer, Clark. The lead singer, Smith, was the "back man," on keyboards.

- Very loud group, especially with the saxophone. They wrote more of their own songs than any other group in 1964. A rare group with no lineup changes. Clark produced all the records

- Best song: "Catch Us if You Can"

Year	Top-Ten Single(s)	Peak	Weeks	RCY	ATR	Gold Album(s)	Sales	Peak	Weeks	RCY
1964	Glad All Over	6				Glad All Over	Gold	3		34
1964	Bits and Pieces	4								
1964	Can't You See that She's Mine	4								
1964	Because	3								
1965	Over and Over	1	1	21	891					
1965	I Like It Like That	7								
1965	Catch Us if You Can	4								
1966						Greatest Hits	Gold	9		47
1967	You've Got What It Takes	7								
All-time single rank #125 Songs written by Dave Clark, along with either Lenny Davidson, Mike Smith, or Danny Paxton										

Donovan

Donovan was a writer of some peculiar lyrics, including "electrical banana," "oh so lah-dee-dah," "first there is a mountain, then there is no mountain, then there is." Some great music, but most of his songs make no sense. As with Bob Dylan, he used his own voice for backup/harmony vocals.

- Best songs: 1. "Colours" 2. "Jennifer Juniper" 3. "Atlantis"
- Worst song: "Hurdy Gurdy Man"

Year	Top-Ten Single(s)	Peak	Weeks	RCY	ATR	Gold Album(s)	Sales	Peak	Weeks	RCY
1966	Sunshine Superman	1	1	26	817					
1966	Mellow Yellow (A)	2	3	29						
1968	Hurdy Gurdy Man	5				A Gift from a Flower to a Garden	Gold	19		
1969	Atlantis	7				Greatest Hits	Plat	4		9
All-time single rank #274 All songs written by Donovan Leitch										

Herman's Hermits

- Name recall: Peter Noone, twenty-four percent; Lek Leckenby, zero percent; Keith Hopwood, zero percent; Karl Green, zero percent; Bean Whitwam, zero percent.
- Best songs: 1. "I'm in to Something Good" 2. "She's a Must to Avoid" 3. "Leaning on a Lamppost"
- Worst songs: "Dandy," "This Door Swings Both Ways"

Year	Top-Ten Single(s)	Peak	Weeks	RCY	ATR	Gold Album(s)	Sales	Peak	Weeks	RCY
1965	Can't You Hear My Heartbeat	2	5	28		Introducing Herman's Hermits	Gold	2	4	9
1965	Mrs. Brown You've Got A Lovely Daughter	1		4	344	Herman's Hermits on Tour	Gold	2	6	13
1965	I'm Henry the Eighth I Am	1		23	898	Best (A)	Gold	5		
1965	Just a Little Bit Better	7								
1966	A Must to Avoid	8				Best II	Gold	20		1966 (21) 1967 (69)
1966	Listen People	3								
1966	Leaning on a Lamppost	9								
1966	Dandy	5								
1967	There's a Kind of Hush	4				There's a Kind of Hush	Gold	13		59
All-time single rank #128 Wrote none of their own songs (A)Probably the only "best" album released in a group's first year of existence. The band released three greatest hits albums and only five non- compilation albums.										

Jefferson Airplane

This group was the most successful of the San Francisco bands, and had the required house in Haight-Ashbury. Their appearance at Monterey Pop and their appearance in the film were catalysts.

Grace Slick, being the female lead singer and having a high-profile personality, was easily the most famous person in the band, though she was not an original member. She replaced Signe Anderson, who left to have a baby. Paul Kantner was probably the second best known, though he was not a primary singer or songwriter. Original drummer Skip Spence was previously a guitarist, and left for Moby Grape to play the guitar again. Marty Balin (real name Martyn Jerald Buchwald) was the group's founder and male vocalist. Jack Cassidy played bass and Jorma Kaukonen, lead guitar. Spencer Dryden replaced Spence on drums.

- Best songs: 1. "Somebody to Love" 2. "Volunteers"

Year	Top-Ten Single(s)	Peak	Weeks	RCY	ATR	Gold Album(s)	Sales	Peak	Weeks	RCY
1967	Somebody to Love (A)	5				Surrealistic Pillow	Gold	3		22
1967	White Rabbit (Grace Slick) (B)	5								
1968						Crown of Creation	Gold	6		
1969						Volunteers	Gold	13		76
1971						Worst	Plat	13		48
1971						Blows against the Empire	Gold	20		
1971						Bark	Gold	11		

(A) Written by Darby Slick, lead guitarist of Great Society, and brother-in-law of Grace Slick. He was disappointed in the Jefferson Airplane because he believed them to be too commercial. RS 274

(B) RS 478

The group, including its incarnations as Jefferson Starship and Starship, had nine gold and four platinum albums after 1971.

Jethro Tull

This group was dominated by one individual more than any other. The group could have easily been called Ian Anderson, as there was a lot of turnover with the other group members, with the exception of Martin Barre (guitar). Anderson was also one of the few musicians who had an aptitude for business and investments.

Year	Top-Ten Single(s)	Peak	Weeks	RCY	ATR	Gold Album(s)	Sales	Peak	Weeks	RCY
1969						Stand Up	Gold	20		
1970						Benefit	Gold	11		
1971						Aqualung (A)	Plat 3	7		33

Ian Anderson, lead vocalist and flute (it was rare when he was able to do both at the same time), was the songwriter.

Group had ten gold and one platinum after 1971

(A) No skip-over songs. The elite called it a concept album, but Anderson described it as just "a bunch of songs." "Hymn 43" peaked at only number ninety-one, and "Locomotive Breath" was released as a single in 1976, reaching only number sixty-two.

Kinks

Along with the Rolling Stones and the Beach Boys, the only 1960s group to have a top-ten hit in the 1980s ("Come Dancing" in 1983). They had top-forty songs in 1964-1966, 1970, 1978 and 1983, but nothing in-between. Their music took a large turn after their first two similar-sounding hits, "You Really Got Me" and "All Day and All of the Night," into more introspective, acoustic songs. From a 1980 film of them live, they certainly had changed with the time. Ray Davies was not playing guitar and strutting around on stage, doing a Mick Jagger imitation. Dave Davies performed the "guitar on the knees while bending back" routine. The talent in the group was dominated by Ray. He had various singing voices, ranging from macho ("You Really Got Me") to effeminate ("Celluloid Heroes") to punk-angry ("I'm Not Like Everybody Else"). He was the best lyricist of the era, and poked fun at English lifestyles. The Davies brothers would often fight on stage.

"You Really Got Me" was the first song to feature a guitar riff throughout the song. It also features a scream right before the chaotic-sounding instrumental break. "All Day and All of the Night," the follow-up single, has a similar guitar riff and instrumental break. Their next single, "Tired of Waiting for You," had an entirely different sound, and the only successive single that even remotely sounded like the first two was "Till the End of the Day."

- Name recall: Ray Davies, thirty-one percent; Dave Davies, twenty-one percent; Pete Quaife, zero percent; Mick Avory, zero percent."

- Best Songs: 1. "You've Really Got Me" 2. "Lola" 3. "Apeman" 4. "A Well Respected Man"

- The elite's favorite album was *The Village Green Preservation Society* (1968). It was a concept album which railed against progress.

Year	Top-Ten Single(s)	Peak	Weeks	RCY	ATR	Gold Album(s)	Sales	Peak	Weeks	RCY
1964	You Really Got Me (A)	7								
1965	All Day and All of the Night	7								
1966						Greatest Hits	Gold	9		
1965	Tired of Waiting for You	6								

1970	Lola (B)	9								
All-time single rank # 204 All songs written by Ray Davies, rhythm guitar (A) RS 82 (B) This song had a very expensive word in it. BBC radio would consider the term "Coca Cola" to be advertising, and would have banned it. Thus, Ray Davies flew round-trip from New York to London (six thousand miles) to change "Coca" to "cherry." Maybe a telephone call would have been less expensive and time consuming. RS 422										

Led Zeppelin

The Yardbirds disbanded in July 1968. Because of concert obligations, Jimmy Page formed the New Yardbirds. He asked Robert Plant to join in August 1968, and in September, the group added John Paul Jones, a session bassist, and John Bonham. In October, the name was changed to Led Zeppelin. They were one of the best managed groups, right from the beginning. Page (along with Paul McCartney and Mick Jagger) had an organizational talent that most musicians lack. He did not take drugs, other than occasional alcohol. Peter Grant was an outstanding manager.

They had difficulty finding tour venues at first. They played for £150 at Surrey University as their first date. One early review said "the most exciting sound to be heard since the early days of Hendrix or Cream." However, most criticized them for being too loud, and called them the "heavy music group." Page got complete control of production, cover art, scheduling, publishing, and concerts. Grant negotiated a $200,000 advance from Atlantic Records, easily the highest royalty rate at the time and said to be five times the Beatles' cut.

The band's strategy on their first U.S. tour was to play as many concerts as possible that paid fees from $200 to $1,500 per night (the Yardbirds received $2,500). They opened for Iron Butterfly and MC5, other "heavy music" groups. Even though the first tour was a huge success, there was some question about whether Page still wanted Plant in the group.

Rolling Stone magazine ridiculed the highly successful *Led Zeppelin II.*

- Name recall: Robert Plant, fifty-five percent; Jimmy Page, fifty-one percent; John Bonham, twenty-one percent; John Paul Jones, seventeen percent.

- Six single releases, but only one top-ten — "Whole Lotta Love" (4). They were one of the few bands that did well from the beginning without releasing a single (there were none on the first album) and also refused to appear on television.

- Best songs: 1. "Whole Lotta Love" 2. "Black Dog" 3. "Rock and Roll"

- Best elite song: "Stairway to Heaven" (fifty-two-second instrumental intro; acoustic guitar and flute only through 2:17; drums and bass start at 4:19; the famous Led Zeppelin heavy metal starts at 5:54)

Year	Top-Ten Single(s)	Peak	Weeks	RCY	ATR	Gold Album(s)	Sales	Peak	Weeks	RCY
1969	Whole Lotta Love (A)	4				Led Zeppelin	Plat 8	10		5
1970						II	Plat 12	1	7	2
1970						III	Plat 6	1	4	94
1971						IV (B)	Plat 22	2	4	

All-time single rank #597

(A) "I've been droolin'" RS 75

Total album sales 106 million (third)

(B) The album actually had no title, but four symbols

Fifteen of their sixteen albums reached platinum, with an average of 7.1

Lovin' Spoonful

- Name recall: John Sebastian, forty-one percent; Zal Yanofsky, seven percent; Joe Butler, three percent; Steve Boone, three percent.

- John Sebastian, who had most of the talent in the group, was the first to leave. As would be expected, the group did not last long after that. Sebastian was the first one to wear circular wire-rimmed glasses.

- Best song: "You Didn't Have to Be So Nice"

- Underrated: "Rain on the Roof"

Year	Top-Ten Single(s)	Peak	Weeks	RCY	ATR	Gold Album(s)	Sales	Peak	Weeks	RCY
1965	Do You Believe In Magic? (A)	9								
1965	You Didn't Have to Be So Nice	10								
1966	Summer in the City (B)	1	3	7	347					
1966	Daydream	2	2	32						
1966	Did You Ever Have to Make up Your Mind?	2	2	34						
1967	Rain on the Roof	10				Best	Gold	3		23
1968	Nashville Cats	8								

All-time single rank #294

Songs written by John Sebastian

(A) RS 216

(B) RS 393; no lead guitar, which gives the song a unique sound during the instrumental break.

© Henry Diltz/CORBIS

Lovin' Spoonful

This picture is similar to the one on their "Best" album.However, on that picture, they all four appear to be the same height.

Monkees

Why were the Monkees negatively singled out as not playing instruments on their first few albums? This was fairly commonplace. The Beach Boys, Herman's Hermits, Simon and Garfunkel, Sonny and Cher, the Righteous Brothers, the Mamas and the Papas, among others, used studio musicians. The 1970s version of the Monkees was Three Dog Night. They neither played instruments nor wrote their own songs. Yes, on some of their albums there were four instrumentalists pictured as part of the band. Okay, if the Monkees had shown studio musicians on their album covers, would all have been forgiven?

On their television show, where they certainly were not playing the instruments, why was Davy Jones only playing a tambourine? Why was Peter Tork only allowed to sing a few obscure songs, including "Auntie Grizelda?" It would make sense that if someone beat out hundreds of other competitors for the job, he would be a good enough singer to have some major lead vocals. It would make sense that they were hired for their acting and singing voices.

They had great outside songwriters and good vocals, and were the second most popular group behind the Beatles for about a year. Of course, when they insisted on playing their own instruments and writing more songs, they lost their popularity (see CCR). Tork actually paid $160,000 to get out of the group. Maybe Tork planned on teaming up with Tom Fogerty to form another super group ☺. Why would he audition for the group in the first place if he wanted to do his own thing? These four would have been unknown in the music business if it were not for the Monkees, except Mike (later Michael, of course) Nesmith's writing of "A Different Drum."

There was quite a period of time when it was certainly not chic to admit you ever liked the group, and the albums were hidden or thrown away. However, over time, that sentiment disappeared, and the group did fairly well with a reunion tour in the 1980s.

- The best-selling album group of 1967.
- Best songs: 1. "I'm a Believer" 2. "Girl I Knew Somewhere"

Year	Top-Ten Single(s)	Peak	Weeks	RCY	ATR	Gold Album(s)	Sales	Peak	Weeks	RCY
1966	I'm a Believer	1	7	1	52	The Monkees	Plat 5	1	13	2
1966	Last Train to Clarksville	1	1	20	685	More of the Monkees	Plat 5	1	18	1
1967	Daydream Believer	1	4	2	182	Headquarters	Plat 2	1	1	45
1967	A Little Bit Me, A Little Bit You	2	1	31						
1967	Pleasant Valley Sunday	3		35						
1968	Valleri	3				Pisces	Plat	1	5	52
1968						Birds	Plat	3		54
All-time single rank #152 Mike Nesmith wrote some of their songs, but none of the above										

The Moody Blues

Their lead singer for their first top-ten single, "Go Now," was Denny Laine. By the time of their next charting single, two-and-a-half years later, Laine was no longer in the group. They had five songwriters (listed in order of talent): Justin Hayward, John Lodge, Ray Thomas, Mike Pinder, and Graeme Edge. The first four were also lead vocalists.

From *Legend of a Mind*, "Timothy Leary's Dead." This was amazingly prophesied twenty-eight years before the actual event ☺.

- Best songs: 1. "Question" 2. "Story in Your Eyes" 3. "Lovely to See You" 4. "Tuesday Afternoon"

- Worst songs: "Have You Heard," "Melancholy Man," "When You're a Free Man" (all written by Pinder)

Year	Top-Ten Single(s)	Peak	Weeks	RCY	ATR	Gold Album(s)	Sales	Peak	Weeks	RCY
1965	Go Now	10								
1968						Days of Future Passed	Plat	3		
1968						In Search of The Lost Chord	Gold	23		
1969						On The Threshhold of a Dream	Plat	20		1969 (41) 1970 (78)
1970						To Our Children's Children's Children	Gold	14		37
1970						A Question of Balance	Plat	3		62
1971						Every Good Boy Deserves Favour	Gold	2	3	

1972	Nights in White Satin (A)	2	2							

(A) Written four years earlier, on the *Days of Future Passed* album

All-time single rank #186

Three platinum and four gold albums after 1971. Surprisingly, *Seventh Soujourn* (1972), which was number one for five weeks, only reached gold status.

Paul Revere and The Raiders

- Best songs: 1. "Kicks" 2. "Ups and Downs" 3. "Indian Reservation"
- Revere's real name is Paul Revere Dick
- Had a number-thirty-eight song in 1961
- Were first "Paul Revere and the Raiders," then "Paul Revere and the Raiders featuring Mark Lindsay," then back to the original, then "The Raiders"

THE RAIDERS

Take the case of **Jim Valley**, ex-Raider and his two buddies **Smitty** and **Phil "Fang" Volk.** Jim felt that he had to express himself musically and that the Raiders as a group were not sounding the way Jim felt he had to sound. Jim has an idea about Love and Beauty and he feels that his idea of universal Love should be expressed. The Raiders weren't doing this in their music and Jim left because he had to spread his feeling about this great and beautiful belief.

Smitty and Fang left because they felt that they could do better on their own. They loved working with the Raiders, but neither one was getting the recognition from other professionals in the business that he deserved.

Tiger Beat, October 1967

Year	Top-Ten Single(s)	Peak	Weeks	RCY	ATR	Gold Album(s)	Sales	Peak	Weeks	RCY
1966	Kicks (A)	4				Just Like Us	Gold	5		35
1966	Hungry (B)	6				Midnight Ride	Gold	9		78
1966						The Spirit Of 1967	Gold	9		54
1967	Good Thing*	4				Greatest Hits	Gold	9		57
1967	Him or Me, What's It Going to Be*	5								
1971	Indian Reservation (C)	1	1	15	669					

All-time single rank #145

* Written by Mark Lindsay, vocals, and Terry Melcher

(A) They had the audacity to release an anti-drug song. Many of the hip radio stations refused to play it. "Magic carpet ride"

(B) "I can almost taste it"

(C) The group name had changed to The Raiders. Song sung by

Freddy Weller, after Mark Lindsay had left the group.

Peter, Paul and Mary

- They were the best-selling album group of 1962-1963

Year	Top-Ten Single(s)	Peak	Weeks	RCY	ATR	Gold Album(s)	Sales	Peak	Weeks	RCY
1965						In Concert	Gold	4		11
1965						A Song Will Rise	Gold	8		

1965						See What Tomorrow Brings	Gold	11		
1967	I Dig Rock and Roll Music (A)	9				Album 1700	Plat	15		
1969	Leaving on a Jet Plane (B)	1	1	13	640	Peter, Paul, and Mommy	Gold	12		
1970						Ten Years Together (Best)	Plat 2	15		100

All-time single rank #214

(A) Written by Paul Stookey-Mason-Dixon. Mason and Dixon had previously come up with a "line".

(B) One of the few groups to have a number-one single on last release.

Sonny and Cher

They were the odd couple. Cher had the lower voice and was taller than Sonny. Their voices sounded very much the same.

Bono did not fit the typical profile of a songwriter, as he did not play an instrument and was somewhat of an entertainer. He also wrote "Needles and Pins" (with Jack Nitzsche) for the Searchers.

Both released solo songs while still performing as a duo. Cher released "All I Really Want to Do" and "Bang Bang," along with five other songs, prior to 1968 because she was under contract with Imperial Records, while the duo was under contract with Atco. Bono's singles were "Laugh at Me" and "The Revolution Kind."

- Best songs: 1. "I Got You Babe" 2. "The Beat Goes On"

Year	Top-Ten Single(s)	Peak	Weeks	RCY	ATR	Gold Album(s)	Sales	Peak	Weeks	RCY
1965	I Got You Babe (A)	1	3	5	346					
1965	Baby Don't Go	8								

1965	Laugh at Me	10								
1966						Look at Us	Gold	2	5	63
1967	The Beat Goes On (B)	6								
1971	All I Ever Need Is You	7				Live	Gold	35		
1972	A Cowboy's Work Is Never Done	8				All I Ever Need Is You	Gold	14		

All-time single rank #232

All songs written by Sonny Bono

(A) RS 444

(B) "Electrically, they keep a baseball score"

Steppenwolf

- Name recall: John Kay, thirty-four percent; Michael Monarch, three percent; Rushton Moreve, three percent; Goldie McJohn, three percent; Jerry Edmonton, three percent.

Year	Top-Ten Single(s)	Peak	Weeks	RCY	ATR	Gold Album(s)	Sales	Peak	Weeks	RCY
1968	Born to Be Wild (A)	2		20		Steppenwolf	Gold	6		1968 (39) 1969 (60)
1968	Magic Carpet Ride*	3		36						
1969	Rock Me*	10				The Second	Gold	3		40
1970						Monster	Gold	17		62

1970						Live	Gold	7		38
1970						Seven	Gold	19		
1971						Greatest Hits	Gold	24		58
All-time singles rank #396 * Written by John Kay, lead singer (A) RS 129; "Get your motor running;" written by Mars Bonfire										

The Supremes

- They were the most successful group, looking at *both* the pop and rhythm and blues charts.
- Best songs: 1. "You Can't Hurry Love" 2. "Love Child"

Year	Top-Ten Single(s)	Peak	Weeks	RCY	ATR	Gold Album(s)	Sales	Peak	Weeks	RCY
1964	Where Did Our Love Go (A)	1	2	12	442					
1964	Baby Love (B)	1	4	4	212					
1964	Come See about Me	1	2	11	441					
1965	Stop! in the Name of Love	1	2	11	494					
1965	Back in My Arms Again	1	1	25	922					
1965	I Hear a Symphony	1	2	14	591					
1966	My World Is Empty without You	5								

1966	Love Is Like an Itching in My Heart	9								
1966	You Can't Hurry Love	1	2	9	492					
1966	You Keep Me Hanging On	1	2	14	588					
1967	Love Is Here and Now You're Gone (C)	1	1	14	820	Greatest Hits	Plat 2	5		5
1967	The Happening	1	1	17	896					
1967	Reflections	2	2	27						
1967	In and Out of Love	9								
1968	Love Child	1	2	9	388					
1969	I'm Gonna Make You Love Me*	2	2			Supremes Join The Temptations	Gold	2	1	
1969	Someday We'll Be Together	1	1	15	671	TCB	Gold	1	1	
1970	Stoned Love	7								

All-time single rank #25

* With the *Temptations*

Wrote no songs

(A) RS 472

(B) RS 324

(C) RS 339

Three Dog Night

They had three singers who sounded similar. On the song "Celebrate," the first singer is Danny Hutton. Chuck Negron is next with "Satin and lace, isn't it a pity," and then Cory Wells with "Sitting alone, sitting on a pillow." They were the 1970s version of the Monkees.

- Best song: "Shambala" (1974)

Year	Top-Ten Single(s)	Peak	Weeks	RCY	ATR	Gold Album(s)	Sales	Peak	Weeks	RCY
1969	One	5				Three Dog Night	Gold	11		12
1969	Easy to Be Hard	4				Suitable for Framing	Gold	16		51
1969	Eli's Coming	10				Captured Live at the Forum	Gold	6		10
1970	Mama Told Me Not to Come (A)	1	2	12		It Ain't Easy	Gold	8		35
1971	Joy To The World (B)	1	6	1	81	Naturally	Gold	14		12
1971	Liar	7				Greatest Hits	Gold	5		14
1971	Old Fashioned Love Song	4				Harmony	Gold	6		

All-time single rank #92

Wrote none of the above songs

(A) "I seen a lot of things I ain't *never* seen before"

(B) "I never understood a single word he said"

The Turtles

- Name recall: Howard Kaylan, ten percent; Mark Volman, seven percent; Al Nichol, three percent; Jim Tucker, zero percent; Chuck Portz, zero percent; Don Murray, zero percent.

- Best song: 1. "You Baby" 2. "Elenore"

- Underrated: "Can I Get to Know You Better?"

Year	Top-Ten Single(s)	Peak	Weeks	RCY	ATR	Gold Album(s)	Sales	Peak	Weeks	RCY
1965	It Ain't Me Babe	8								
1967	Happy Together	1	3	9	281					
1967	She'd Rather Be with Me	3								
1968	Elenore (Kaylan)	6				Greatest Hits	Gold	7		80
1969	You Showed Me	6								
All-time single rank #298										

Yardbirds

The Yardbirds were a group, like Buffalo Springfield, that became famous retroactively, with later fame by Eric Clapton, Jimmy Page, and to a lesser degree, Jeff Beck. How many people know their lead singer was bongo-playing Keith Relf? (He was about as famous as the lead singer of the Ventures☺). None of the above guitarists were in the original group. Clapton replaced the original guitarist, Anthony Topham, in late 1963. Clapton left in March 1965, and was not the guitarist on their first hit, "For Your Love." Clapton despised the song. Page was asked to join at that point, but he recommended

Beck. Page did join the group in August 1966, replacing Paul Samwell-Smith. Page had been the top session guitarist in England, playing for the Who, the Kinks, and Them. Page and Beck were co-lead guitarists, but Beck was soon kicked out of the group. The Yardbirds released five albums, reaching number ninety-six, number fifty-three, number fifty-two, number twenty-eight, and number eighty.

They were the first group to have long instrumental sections and free-form soloing. The group was grossly mismanaged and did not make any money on touring until Page joined the group and Peter Grant became their manager. They had a somewhat gloomy sound, especially on "Still I'm Sad" and "Heart Full of Soul." Some of their songs were written by Relf, Samwell-Smith, and McCarty.

If someone mentions he likes the Yardbirds because Clapton and Page were in the group, ask him exactly which songs he likes with these guitarists in them. It was Beck who played on their five most recognizable songs (in chronological order): "For Your Love," "Heart Full of Soul," "I'm a Man," "Shapes of Things," and "Over Under Sideways Down." None of the lead guitarists wrote any of these songs. Clapton had just left before "For Your Love," and Page joined after "Over Under."

Page was with the group for two years (until it disbanded), but that was a period of no commercial success. Both Clapton and Page were virtually unknown when they left the group. Beck and Page were co-lead guitarists for only three months, and only three songs were recorded with both of them. When Page joined, it was considered a possibility by some (years later, of course), that this could have been the best group of all. Two skillful lead guitarists are, by themselves, not going to make a great group, at least commercially. The Beatles had nothing to worry about.

In July 1968, when the group split up, who would have thought that it would someday be elected to the Hall of Fame? Did it get in because of the work that Beck, Page, and Clapton did with the group, or what they did later in their careers? I would say the latter.

The same question could be asked about Buffalo Springfield,

even though their music was much better than that of the Yardbirds. In May 1968, did anyone expect the group to end up in the Hall of Fame? Was it Stephen Stills's and Neil Young's work in the group, or after the group, that was the deciding factor? I would say what they did in the group. These are the only two groups in this book with dual lead guitarists, and this situation did not last long with either group.

- "Heart Full of Soul" had some of the greatest harmonies of any song, with the title line featuring one voice ascending and the other one descending.

Year	Top-Ten Single(s)	Peak	Weeks	RCY	ATR	Gold Album(s)	Sales	Peak	Weeks	RCY
1965	Heart Full of Soul	9								
1965	For Your Love	6								

© George Stroud/Hulton Archive/Getty Images

Yardbirds

One of the few Yardbirds pictures with both Beck (second from the left) and Page (middle). The lead singer Relf (right) also wore his shades on stage, and was probably the first to do so

The Fourth Tier

Chapter Nine

Groovin'

The Band

They had the same five members for the group's ten-year existence. The group's name came from being Bob Dylan's "band."

- Name recognition: Robbie Robertson, thirty-one percent; Rick Danko, twenty-one percent; LeVon Helm, twenty-one percent; Richard Manuel, ten percent; Garth Hudson, seven percent.

- Best song: "The Weight" (Robertson). RS 41. "'No' was all he said." The first three verse groups are sung by Helm, the fourth by Manuel ("Crazy Chester" at 2:38), then the last by both Helm and Manuel.

Year	Top Ten Single(s)	Peak	Weeks	RCY	ATR	Gold Album(s)	Sales	Peak	Weeks	RCY
1968						Music from the Big Pink	Gold	30		
1969						The Band	Plat	9		
1970						Stage Fright	Gold	5		
Primary songwriter was Robbie Robertson										

Bee Gees

This is a group that achieved moderate success during the era, probably similar to Paul Revere and the Raiders. The two lead singers were Barry and Robin Gibb, while Barry did most of the songwriting. Barry had the breathy voice (and later the repugnant falsetto during their disco era), and sang lead on "Holiday" and "To Love Sombody"; Robin had the vibrato voice and sang on "I Started a Joke" and "Massachusetts." On "How Can You Mend a Broken Heart?" Robin started at the verse, and Barry at the chorus. It was later, during the disco era, that the group had most of its success.

- Best song: "I Started a Joke"

Year	Top Ten Single(s)	Peak	Weeks	RCY	ATR	Gold Album(s)	Sales	Peak	Weeks	RCY
1968	I've Gotta Get a Message to You	8								
1969	I Started a Joke	6				Best	Gold			59
1971	Lonely Days	3								
1971	How Can You Mend a Broken Heart	1	4	4	178					

All-time single rank #15

Primary songwriter was Barry Gibb, with the other two on some songs.

Post-1971, they had twelve top-ten songs, including eight at number one.

Total album sales 25.5 million (sixty-fifth)

Blood Sweat and Tears

Al Kooper was replaced as lead vocalist and primary songwriter by David Clayton-Thomas in 1969. With Kooper, the group was getting nowhere. Their first album peaked at number forty-seven (though it did eventually reach gold status) and charted no singles. The elite preferred the jazz-oriented, Kooper-led group.

Year	Top Ten Single(s)	Peak	Weeks	RCY	ATR	Gold Album(s)	Sales	Peak	Weeks	RCY
1968						Child Is Father to the Man	Gold	47		
1969	You've Made Me So Very Happy (Gordy-Holloway-Holloway-Wilson)	2	3			Blood Sweat and Tears	Plat 4	1	7	1969 (3) 1970 (13)
1969	Spinning Wheel (Clayton-Thomas)	2	3							
1969	And When I Die (Nyro)	2	1							
1970						Blood Sweat and Tears III	Gold	1	2	43
1971						Blood Sweat and Tears IV	Gold	10		92
1972						Greatest Hits	Plat 2	19		
All-time single rank #492										

Bread

Year	Top Ten Single(s)	Peak	Weeks	RCY	ATR	Gold Album(s)	Sales	Peak	Weeks	RCY
1970	Make It with You (A)	1	1	18		On the Waters	Gold	12		
1970	It Don't Matter to Me	10								

1971	If	4				Manna	Gold	21		
1971	Baby I'm a Want You	3								

All-time single rank #281

All songs written by David Gates, vocalist, guitar

(A) Three weeks at number two, behind "Close to You.". Soft rock was very "in" at the time.

James Brown

Year	Top Ten Single(s)	Peak	Weeks	RCY	ATR	Gold Album(s)	Sales	Peak	Weeks	RCY
1965	Papa's Got a Brand New Bag (A)	8								
1965	I Got You (I Feel Good) (B)	3								
1966	It's a Man's Man's Man's World (C)	7								
1967	Cold Sweat	7								
1968	I Got the Feeling	6								

All-time singles unit sales rank #6

All songs written by Brown

(A) RS 72

(B) RS 78

(C) RS 123

Fifty-one albums, including one gold (1974)

Glen Campbell

- Best songs: 1. "Try a Little Kindness" 2. "Galveston"

Year	Top Ten Single(s)	Peak	Weeks	RCY	ATR	Gold Album(s)	Sales	Peak	Weeks	RCY
1967						By The Time I Get to Phoenix	Plat	15		1967 (12) 1969 (91)
1968						Gentle on My Mind	Plat	5		33
1968						Hey Little One	Gold	26		48
1969						Bobbie Gentry and Glen Campbell	Gold	11		38
1969	Wichita Lineman (Webb) (A)	3				Wichita Lineman	Plat 2	1	5	19
1969	Galveston (Webb)	4				Galveston	Plat	2	1	28
1969						Live	Gold	13		
1970						Try a Little Kindness	Gold	12		93
1971						Greatest Hits	Plat	39		

All-time single rank #76

Wrote none of his songs

(A) RS 192; this song was not about a football player.

The Carpenters

Year	Top Ten Single(s)	Peak	Weeks	RCY	ATR	Gold Album(s)	Sales	Peak	Weeks	RCY
1970	Close to You	1	4			Close to You	Plat 2	2	1	3
1970	We've Only Just Begun	2	4			Carpenters	Plat 4	2	2	39
1971	For All We Know	3								
1971	Rainy Days and Mondays	2	2							
1971	Superstar	2	2							
1972	Hurting Each Other	2	2							
All-time singles sales rank #60										

Johnny Cash

Year	Top Ten Single(s)	Peak	Weeks	RCY	ATR	Gold Album(s)	Sales	Peak	Weeks	RCY
1964						I Walk the Line	Gold	53		
1967						Greatest Hits	Plat 2	82		
1969	A Boy Named Sue	2	3			Folsom Prison	Plat 2	13		1969 (6) 1970 (87)
1969						San Quentin	Plat 2	1	4	
1970						Hello, I'm Johnny Cash	Gold	6		54

1970						The World of Johnny Cash	Gold	54		
1970						Johnny Cash Show	Gold	44		
1971						Greatest Hits	Plat	94		

Petula Clark

Year	Top Ten Single(s)	Peak	Weeks	RCY	ATR	Gold Album(s)	Sales	Peak	Weeks	RCY
1964	Downtown*	1	2							
1965	I Know a Place*	3								
1966	My Love*	1	2							
1966	I Couldn't Live without Your Love	9								
1967	This Is My Song	3								
1967	Don't Sleep in the Subway*	5								

All-time single rank #154

* Written by Tony Hatch

Fourteen'albums, but no gold. Top peak position was twenty-one.

Judy Collins

Year	Top Ten Single(s)	Peak	Weeks	RCY	ATR	Gold Album(s)	Sales	Peak	Weeks	RCY
1967						In My Life	Gold	46		
1968	Both Sides Now	8				Wildflowers	Gold	5		
1970						Whales and Nightingales	Gold	17		

Neil Diamond

Year	Top Ten Single(s)	Peak	Weeks	RCY	ATR	Gold Album(s)	Sales	Peak	Weeks	RCY
1969	Sweet Caroline	4				Brother Love's Traveling Salvation Show	Gold	82		
1969	Holly Holy	6								
1970	Holly Holy	1	1			Touching You Touching Me	Gold	30		
1970						Gold	Plat 2	10		
1971	I Am I Said	4				Stones	Gold	11		

All-time singles rank #24

After 1971 he had eighteen platinum albums and eleven gold. He is ranked number eleven on *Billboard's* all-time album sales rank, but was not in the top 105 on RIAA.

Jose Feliciano

Year	Top Ten Single(s)	Peak	Weeks	RCY	ATR	Gold Album(s)	Sales	Peak	Weeks	RCY
1968	Light My Fire	3				Feliciano!	Gold	2	3	1968 (82) 1969 (85)
1969						10 to 23	Gold	16		65
1970						Alive, Alive-O!	Gold	29		

Fifth Dimension

Year	Top Ten Single(s)	Peak	Weeks	RCY	ATR	Gold Album(s)	Sales	Peak	Weeks	RCY
1967	Up, Up and Away	7								
1968	Stoned Soul Picnic	3								
1969	Aquarius/ Let the Sunshine In	1	6	1	78					
1969	Wedding Bell Blues	1	3	8	298					
1970	One Less Bell to Answer	2	2	23						
All-time single rank #82										

The Four Tops

Year	Top Ten Single(s)	Peak	Weeks	RCY	ATR	Gold Album(s)	Sales	Peak	Weeks	RCY
1965	I Can't Help Myself (A)	1	2	7						
1965	It's the Same Old Song	5								
1966	Reach Out I'll Be There (B)	1	2	11						
1967	Bernadette	4								
1967	Standing in the Shadows Of Love (C)	6								
All-time single rank #49 (A) RS 415 (B) RS 206 (C) RS 464										

Marvin Gaye

Year	Top Ten Single(s)	Peak	Weeks	RCY	ATR	Gold Album(s)	Sales	Peak	Weeks	RCY
1965	How Sweet It Is to Be Loved by You	6								
1965	I'll Be Doggone (Robinson-Moore-Tarplin)	8								
1965	Ain't That Peculiar (Robinson-Moore-Tarplin-Rogers)	8								

1967	Your Precious Love (Ashford-Simpson)	5									
1967	If I Could Build My Whole World around You (Fuqua-Bristol-Bullock)	10									
1968	Ain't Nothing Like the Real Thing	8									
1968	You're All I Need to Get By	7									
1968	I Heard It through the Grapevine (A)	1	7	2							
1969	Too Busy Thinking About My Baby	4									
1969	That's the Way Love Is	7									
1971	What's Going On (B)	2	2	19							
1971	Mercy Mercy	4									
1971	Inner City Blues	9									

All-time single rank #12

All songs written by Gaye unless otherwise noted

(A) RS 80

(B) RS 4

Grass Roots

Like the Association and their ensemble singing style, the individual members of Grass Roots were mostly anonymous.

- Best song: 1. "Temptation Eyes" 2. "Lovin' Things"

Year	Top Ten Single(s)	Peak	Weeks	RCY	ATR	Gold Album(s)	Sales	Peak	Weeks	RCY
1967	Let's Live for Today	8								
1968	Midnight Confessions	5				Golden Grass	Gold	25		48
1971	Sooner or Later	9				16 Greatest Hits	Gold	58		
All-time single rank #233 Wrote none of their songs. On the *16 Greatest Hits* album, there are twelve different sets of songwriters, including Barri-Sloan twice.										

Grateful Dead

They only had one album that peaked in the top ten (*In the Dark*, 1987), but had six platinum albums, and eleven gold. Good sales, and low peak positions, indicate that the albums sold over a long time period. Their success was especially in their live concerts, and they are thought to be the highest-grossing band ever (records sales *and* concerts). The concerts lasted up to six hours and contained as few as six songs. (They really "pushed the envelope" on the two-and-one-half-minute song). They started out as a local cult band, but quickly outgrew that label. Most fans acquired a taste for the group over time.

This is one group that really was not interested in commercial success, and found that their live playing was better than in the studio. They were deeply in debt until the mid-1970s. On the three part harmonies, Jerry Garcia sang the melody (low), Phil Lesh the high harmony, and Bob Weir in the middle. Some of their songs were mixed versions of live and studio. With the addition of Mickey Hart, the group had six members, all playing instruments.

The original lineup was comprised of Jerry Garcia, Bob Weir, Phil Lesh, Ron McKernan, and Bill Kreutzman. All but McKernan stayed on until 1995. Mickey Hart was added as a second drummer in 1968. Hart left the group between 1971 and 1974. Garcia, Weir, and Lesh were band mates for thirty years, second only to the Rolling Stones threesome in consecutive years together. The life insurance policy for a Grateful Dead keyboardist is excessive, as their first three died.

Jerry Garcia was in the army for nine months at age of seventeen. It appeared that Garcia had his right index finger bent while picking the guitar, but he was actually missing part of it.

Year	Top Ten Single(s)	Peak	Weeks	RCY	ATR	Gold Album(s)	Sales	Peak	Weeks	RCY
1967						Grateful Dead	Gold	73		
1969						Aoxomoxia	Gold	73		
1970						Live Dead	Gold	64		
1970						Workingman's Dead	Plat	27		
1970						American Beauty	Plat 2	30		
Only one charting single, "Touch of Gray" (1987), which peaked at number nine. Music written primarily by Garcia and, to a lesser degree, by Phil Lesh; lyrics by Robert Hunter.										

Guess Who

Year	Top Ten Single(s)	Peak	Weeks	RCY	ATR	Gold Album(s)	Sales	Peak	Weeks	RCY
1969	These Eyes	5								
1969	Laughing	10								
1970	No Time	5				American Woman	Gold	9		17
1970	American Woman	1	1	8	297	Share the Land	Gold	14		
1971						Best	Gold	12		31
All-time single rank #188 Songs written by Burton Cummings, vocals, and Randy Bachman, lead guitar										

Hollies

Naming some of the pop people he likes and dislikes, George said he digs the **Hollies** among others—"but not **Graham Nash.**"

"What's wrong with him?" we asked.

"Oh, he's a johnny-come-lately to the hip scene," George replied. "He should have been one with us long time ago."

Although he didn't explain this curious comment, we figured out what he probably meant. Before Graham repented and changed his ways to keep cool, he was hung up on money-making commercialism and gung-ho success. Hip is a state of mind based on a new culture of universal love, sharing of gifts, turned-on creative force and rejection of ancient hates, prejudices, pressures and ego games.

"Don't judge the Way of Hip by the bummer elements in the movement," advises **Johnny Rivers.**

Tiger Beat, Febuary 1966

- Best songs: 1. "Long Dark Road" 2. "Carrie-Anne"

Year	Top Ten Single(s)	Peak	Weeks	RCY	ATR	Gold Album(s)	Sales	Peak	Weeks	RCY
1966	Bus Stop	5								
1966	Stop Stop Stop*	7								
1967	Carrie Ann*	9								
1970	He Ain't Heavy, He's My Brother	7								
All-time single rank #128										
* Written by Graham Nash, Allan Clarke, and Tony Hicks. Hicks was the one who looked like one of the Gibb brothers.										

Iron Butterfly

This group was sometimes inaccurately considered a one-hit wonder. In reality, they had four top-twenty albums. It was considered very trendy to buy the *In-A-Gadda-Da-Vida* album, rather than the single, to get the longer version. This is a rare instance where a brief-stardom group's album was a much bigger seller than the single. The elite have a difficult time rating "In-A-Gadda-Da-Vida." They like the fact that it "broke all the rules," being seventeen minutes long, but they disliked the simple-minded lyrics. They were not able to tie the lyrics into a war protest song, even though some claimed the title translated as "spend money on jobs and education, not war"☺.

Year	Top Ten Single(s)	Peak	Weeks	RCY	ATR	Gold Album(s)	Sales	Peak	Weeks	RCY
1968	In-A-Gadda-Da-Vida (A)	30				In-A-Gadda-Da-Vida	Plat 4	4		1968 (85) 1969 (1) 1970 (16)
1969						Ball	Gold	3		

(A) Length 2:52; Doug Ingle, lead vocals and keyboard

Jackson Five

Year	Top Ten Single(s)	Peak	Weeks	RCY	ATR	Gold Album(s)	Sales	Peak	Weeks	RCY
1970	I Want You Back (A)	1	1	19	665					
1970	ABC	1	2	13	445					
1970	The Love You Have	1	2	14	446					
1970	I'll Be There	1	5	2	107					
1971	Mama's Pearl	2	3	25						
1971	Never Can Say Goodbye	2	3	20						

All-time single rank #55

Group members wrote none of the above songs. Early songs were written by "The Corporation," who turned out to be Freddie Perren, Fonzo Mizell, Deke Richards, and Barry Gordy.

(A) RS 120

Tommy James and the Shondells

Year	Top Ten Single(s)	Peak	Weeks	RCY	ATR	Gold Album(s)	Sales	Peak	Weeks	RCY
1966	Hanky Panky	1	2		589					
1967	I Think We're Alone Now	4	2		589					
1968	Mony Mony	3	2		589					
1969	Crimson and Clover*	1	2	10	389					
1969	Sweet Cherry Wine	7								
1969	Crystal Blue Persuasion*	2	3							
1971	Draggin' the Line*	4								
All-time single rank #83 * Partial songwriting credit to James										

Jan and Dean

Year	Top Ten Single(s)	Peak	Weeks	RCY	ATR	Gold Album(s)	Sales	Peak	Weeks	RCY
1964	Dead Man's Curve	8								
1964	Little Old Lady from Pasadena	3								
All-time single rank #162 Songs written by Jan Berry Their number-one song was "Surf City" (1963), which was number 534, all time.										

Elton John

Elton John had great timing. He was releasing music in 1970 and 1971, but was still obscure. He came into his own in 1972 (the year the music died), when all the good music and groups had disappeared.

Year	Top Ten Single(s)	Peak	Weeks	RCY	ATR	Gold Album(s)	Sales	Peak	Weeks	RCY
1970	Your Song (A)	8				Elton John	Gold	4		30
1971						Tumbleweed Connection	Plat	5		24
1971						Friends	Plat	5		

All-time single rank #3

Words by Bernie Taupin, music by Elton John

After 1971, John had twenty-six top-ten songs, including ten number-ones.

(A) RS 136

Total album sales 67.5 million (ninth)

After 1971, he had twenty-two platinum albums and seven gold albums. The top seller was *Greatest Hits*, at platinum 15.

Janis Joplin

(with Big Brother and the Holding Company, Cosmic Blues Band, and Full Tilt Boogie Band)

Year	Top Ten Single(s)	Peak	Weeks	RCY	ATR	Gold Album(s)	Sales	Peak	Weeks	RCY
1968						Cheap Thrills	Plat 3	1	8	57
1969						I Got Dem Old Kozmic Blues Again Mama	Plat	5		
1971	Me and Bobby McGee (A)*	1	2	13	498	Pearl	Plat 4	1	9	4

(A) RS 148

* Written by Kris Kristofferson

Greatest Hits (1973) achieved platinum 7

Carole King

Carole King and Neil Diamond had the biggest successes moving from a songwriter only, to a singer.

Year	Top Ten Single(s)	Peak	Weeks	RCY	ATR	Gold Album(s)	Sales	Peak	Weeks	RCY
1971	It's Too Late (A)	1	5	3	115	Tapestry	Plat 10	1	15	2

All-time single rank #254

Songs written by King

(A) RS 469

She had two platinum and five gold albums after 1971.

Gary Lewis and the Playboys

Year	Top Ten Single(s)	Peak	Weeks	RCY	ATR	Gold Album(s)	Sales	Peak	Weeks	RCY
1965	This Diamond Ring**	1	2	10	450					
1965	Count Me In	2	2	31						
1965	Save Your Heart for Me	2	1	33						
1965	Everybody Loves a Clown*	4								
1966	She's Just My Style	3				Greatest Hits	Gold	10		
1966	Sure Gonna Miss Her*	9								
1966	Green Grass	8								
All-time singles unit rank #234 * Written by Gary Lewis- Snuff Garrett-Leon Russell **Written by Al Kooper										

Joni Mitchell

Joni's best song was "Both Sides Now." Her version was great, and she should not have turned it over to Judy Collins. She was easily the most talented female of the era. CSNY's version of "Woodstock," though, was much better than hers.

Year	Top Ten Single(s)	Peak	Weeks	RCY	ATR	Gold Album(s)	Sales	Peak	Weeks	RCY
1969						Clouds	Gold	31		

1970						Ladies of the Canyon	Plat	27		55
1971						Blue	Plat	15		87
She had five gold albums and one platinum after 1971. Her ten albums after 1976 did not reach gold.										

Elvis Presley

Presley was prominent in the mid- to late-1950s (and he was huge (in girth, that is) in the mid-1970s), but he was not a major player during 1964-1971. He was the first white singer to sing rhythm and blues. White rhythm and blues then became called rock-and-roll. Only the Beatles matched Presley's onstage charisma. Even though he never gave an intelligent interview, and was certainly not an intellectual, he was a favorite of many elites because he was a pioneer. People who are extreme Beatles fans are rarely Presley fans, or vice versa.

- He released 104 albums in all, including twenty-five gold and twenty-seven platinum, and nine that reached number one. Forty-two of these albums were released after his death. There was only one album over platinum (3) — *Elvis' Golden Records* (1958) — at platinum (8).

- Presley had an average sales amount per album (106) of 1.13 million, while the Beatles (forty-six albums) averaged 3.62 million.

Year	Top Ten Single(s)	Peak	Weeks	RCY	ATR	Gold Album(s)	Sales	Peak	Weeks	RCY
1964						Roustabout	Gold	1	1	
1965	Crying in the Chapel	3				Girl Happy	Gold	8		

1967						How Great Thou Art	Plat 2	18		
1968						Gold Records Volume 4	Gold	22		
1969	In the Ghetto (Mac Davis)	3				Elvis Sings Flaming Star	Gold	96		
1969	Suspicious Minds (Mark James) (A)	1	1	16	869	From Elvis in Memphis	Gold	13		
1970	Don't Cry Daddy	6				Let's Be Friends	Gold	105		
1970	The Wonder of You	9				On Stage	Plat	13		
1970						That's the Way it Is	Gold	21		
1971						Elvis Country	Gold	12		
1971						You'll Never Walk Alone	Plat	69		
1972						Elvis Now	Gold	43		

All-time single rank #1

Presley wrote no songs, though he did receive some songwriting credits

(A) RS 91

Total album sales 117.5 million (second)

Gary Puckett and The Union Gap

Year	Top Ten Single(s)	Peak	Weeks	RCY	ATR	Gold Album(s)	Sales	Peak	Weeks	RCY
1968	Woman, Woman	4				Young Girl	Gold	21		71
1968	Young Girl	2	3							

1968	Lady Willpower	2	2							
1968	Over You	7								
1969	This Girl Is a Woman Now	9								
1970						Greatest Hits	Plat	50		

(Young) Rascals

Year	Top Ten Single(s)	Peak	Weeks	RCY	ATR	Gold Album(s)	Sales	Peak	Weeks	RCY
1966	Good Lovin' (A)	1	1	24	804	Young Rascals	Gold	15		76
1967	Groovin' (B)	1	4	6	201					
1967						Groovin'	Gold	5		89
1968	Beautiful Morning	3				Greatest Hits	Gold	1		1968 (56) 1969 (61)
1968	People Got to Be Free	1	5	5	126	Collections	Gold	14		15
1969						Freedom Suite	Gold	17		

All-time single rank #164

Songs by Felix Cavaliere, keyboards, and some with Dino Dinelli, drums

(A) The words "good lovin'" are never said, but rather something like "gula." "Doctor, Mr. M.D., can you tell me what's ailing me? He said 'yeah, yeah, yeah, yeah.'" I think I would get a second opinion!

(B) Number one for two weeks, then number two, behind "Respect," then number one again for two weeks

Righteous Brothers

In March 1968, Bill Medley quit the group for a solo career. That is not surprising, but the band continuing with the same name is. A two-man band with a new singer would be hard pressed to keep the same name. Bobby Hatfield teamed up with Jimmy Walker. Medley soon came to his senses, and returned. In the interim, the band should have been called the "Righteous Brother."

On a related subject, Diana Ross temporarily left the Supremes in October 1969, and the group was re-named the New Supremes.

Year	Top Ten Single(s)	Peak	Weeks	RCY	ATR	Gold Album(s)	Sales	Peak	Weeks	RCY
1965	You've Lost That Loving Feeling	1	2	8	432					
1965	Unchained Melody	4								
1966	Ebb Tide	5				Soul and Inspiration	Gold	7		
1966	Soul and Inspiration	1	3	4	314					
1967						Greatest Hits	Gold	21		
All-time single rank #147 They wrote none of their songs										

Johnny Rivers

- Best song: "Summer Rain" ("And the jukebox kept playing 'Sgt. Pepper's Lonely Hearts Club Band.'" It is questionable whether a jukebox has ever been on a beach, and played an album rather than a single.)

Year	Top Ten Single(s)	Peak	Weeks	RCY	ATR	Gold Album(s)	Sales	Peak	Weeks	RCY
1964	Memphis	2	2							
1964	Mountain of Love	9								
1965	Seventh Son	9								
1966	Secret Agent Man	3				Soul and Inspiration	Gold	7		
1966	Poor Side of Town (Johnny Rivers-Lou Adler)	1	1	21	799					
1967	Baby, I Need Your Loving	3				Greatest Hits	Gold	21		
All-time single rank #107										

Tommy Roe

Tommy Roe probably had the largest differential between single and album success. He also had a number-one song in 1962, "Sheila," thus having seven years between number-one hits.

Year	Top Ten Single(s)	Peak	Weeks	RCY	ATR	Gold Album(s)	Sales	Peak	Weeks	RCY
1966	Sweet Pea	3								
1966	Hooray for Hazel	8								
1969	Dizzy	1	4	7	192					

1969	Jam Up Jelly Tight	8								

All-time single rank #200

All songs written by Roe

Kenny Rogers (and the First Edition)

Kenny Rogers was a minor player during this era, but he became huge from 1977-1983, while writing his own music.

Year	Top Ten Single(s)	Peak	Weeks	RCY	ATR	Gold Album(s)	Sales	Peak	Weeks	RCY
1968	Just Dropped In (To See What Condition My Condition Was in)	5								
1969	Ruby, Don't Take Your Love to Town	6								
1971						Greatest Hits	Plat	57		

All-time single rank #40

Total album sales 50.5 million (twenty-first)

He released thirty albums after the *Greatest Hits* album, including six gold and eighteen platinum. His second *Greatest Hits* was number one for two weeks and was platinum(12)

Santana

Carlos Santana was the only prominent musician of the era born in Mexico. Lead singer of the group was Gregg Rolie, not Santana.

Year	Top Ten Single(s)	Peak	Weeks	RCY	ATR	Gold Album(s)	Sales	Peak	Weeks	RCY
1970	Evil Ways (Santana)	9				Santana	Plat 2	4		1970 (5) 1971 (78)
1970	Black Magic Woman	4				Abraxas	Plat 5	1	6	5
1971						III	Plat 4	1	5	
Total album sales 43.5 million (twenty-eighth)										

Sly and the Family Stone

Sly and the Family Stone had various lead singers on each song, including the amazing "all together now" voice on "You Can Make It if You Try."

- Best songs: 1. "Everyday People" 2. "Dance to the Music"

Year	Top Ten Single(s)	Peak	Weeks	RCY	ATR	Gold Album(s)	Sales	Peak	Weeks	RCY
1968	Dance to the Music (A)	8								
1969	Everyday People (B)	1	4	6		Stand	Gold	13		25
1969	Hot Fun in the Summertime (C)	2		24						
1969	Thank You Falettinme Be Mice Elf Agin (D)	1	2							
1971						Greatest Hits	Plat 5	2		9

1971	Family Affair (E)	1	3			There's a Riot Going On	Plat	1	2	

All-time single rank #191

Songs written by Sylvester "Sly" Stone

(A) "boom-lacka-lacka-lacka"; RS 223

(B) RS 145

(C) RS 247

(D) RS 402

(E) RS 138

Cat Stevens

- Best songs: 1. "Moonshadow" 2. "Father and Son"

Year	Top Ten Single(s)	Peak	Weeks	RCY	ATR	Gold Album(s)	Sales	Peak	Weeks	RCY
1971	Peace Train (Stevens)	7				Tea for the Tillerman	Plat 3	8		8
						Mona Bone Jakon	Gold	164		
						Teaser and the Firecat	Plat 3	2	1	

All-time singles unit sales rank #356

James Taylor

Year	Top Ten Single(s)	Peak	Weeks	RCY	ATR	Gold Album(s)	Sales	Peak	Weeks	RCY
1970	Fire and Rain (Taylor) (A)	3				Sweet Baby James	Plat 3	3		15 1971 (7)

1971	You've Got a Friend (Carole King)	1	1	17	729	Mud Slide Slim	Plat 2	2	4	27

All-time single rank #171

(A) RS 227

Total album sales 30.5 million (fifty-first)

Post 1971, Taylor had nine platinum albums, the highest being *Greatest Hits* (11), and three gold.

Temptations

Year	Top Ten Single(s)	Peak	Weeks	RCY	ATR	Gold Album(s)	Sales	Peak	Weeks	RCY
1965	My Girl (A)	1	1	17	731					
1967	All I Need	8				Greatest Hits	Plat 2	5		15
1967	You're My Everything	6								
1968	I Wish It Would Rain	4								
1969	Cloud Nine	6				With Diana Ross And The Supremes	Gold	2	1	
1969	I'm Gonna Make You Love Me	2				TCB	Gold	101		
1969						Cloud Nine	Gold	4		

1969						Puzzle People	Gold	5		
1970						Psychedelic Shack	Gold	9		
1970						Greatest Hits II	Gold	15		
1971						Sky's the Limit	Gold	16		

All-time single rank #121

Wrote no songs

(A) RS 88

B.J. Thomas

Year	Top Ten Single(s)	Peak	Weeks	RCY	ATR	Gold Album(s)	Sales	Peak	Weeks	RCY
1966	I'm So Lonesome I Could Cry (Hank Williams)	8								
1969	Hooked on a Feeling (Mark James)	5								
1970	Raindrops Keep Falling on My Head (Burt Bacharach) (A)	1	4	3	148	Raindrops Keep Falling on My Head	Gold	12		20

1970	I Just Can't Help Believing (Barry Mann)	9								
All-time single rank #142 (A) How many syllables in the word "me" at 2:22? I count at least ten.										

Ventures

Year	Top Ten Single(s)	Peak	Weeks	RCY	ATR	Gold Album(s)	Sales	Peak	Weeks	RCY
1964	Walk Don't Run '64	8								
1967	Tell Her No					Greatest Hits	Gold	59		
1969	Hawaii Five-O	4				Hawaii Five-O	Gold	11		
All-time single rank #470 Released thirty-eight albums										

Dionne Warwick

Year	Top Ten Single(s)	Peak	Weeks	RCY	ATR	Gold Album(s)	Sales	Peak	Weeks	RCY
1964	Anyone Who Had a Heart*	8								
1964	Walk on By* (A)	6								
1966	Message to Michael (Jackson)*	8								
1967						Here Where There Is Love	Gold	18		

1968	Valley of the Dolls	2	4	16		Valley of the Dolls	Gold	6		40
1968	I Say a Little Prayer*	4								
1968	Do You Know the Way to San Jose*	10								
1970	This Girl's in Love with You*	7				Greatest Motion Picture Hits	Gold	31		
1971	I'll Never Fall in Love Again*	5								
1972						Dionne Warwick Story	Gold	48		
All-time single rank #30 * Written by Hal David and Burt Bacharach										

Zombies

The Zombies released five singles, three of which reached number six or better and the last two being four years apart.

Year	Top Ten Single(s)	Peak	Weeks	RCY	ATR	Gold Album(s)	Sales	Peak	Weeks	RCY
1964	She' Not There	2	1							
1965	Tell Her No	6								
1969	Time of the Season (A)	3								
Songs written by Ron Argent, keyboards (A) "Who's your daddy?" "Ahhhhhhhhhhhhhhhhhhhh"										

Chapter Ten

Mad Dogs and Englishmen: The Others

Herp Alpert

(and the Tijuana Brass)

Year	Top Ten Single(s)	Peak	Weeks	RCY	ATR	Gold Album(s)	Sales	Peak	Weeks	RCY
1965	Taste of Honey	7				South of the Border	Gold	6		1965 (94) 1966 (11) 1967 (34)
1966						Going Places	Gold	1	6	1966 (3) 1967 (9) 1968 (62)
1966						Whipped Cream and Other Delights	Gold	1	8	1966 (1) 1967 (8)
1966						What Now My Love	Gold	1	9	1966 (5) 1967 (11)
1967						S.R.O.	Gold	2	6	7
1967						Sounds Like	Gold	1	1	43

1968	This Guy's in Love with You	1	4			Ninth	Gold	4		
1968						The Beat of the Brass	Gold	1	2	
All-time single sales rank #79										

Black Sabbath

Year	Top Ten Single(s)	Peak	Weeks	RCY	ATR	Gold Album(s)	Sales	Peak	Weeks	RCY
1970						Black Sabbath	Plat	23		
1971						Paranoid	Plat 4	12		
1971						Master of Reality	Plat 2	8		

Chicago

- Another anonymous band, regarding individuals in the group.

Year	Top Ten Single(s)	Peak	Weeks	RCY	ATR	Gold Album(s)	Sales	Peak	Weeks	RCY
1970						Chicago Transit Authority (A)	Plat 2	17		1970 (3) 1971 (15)
1971	Make Me Smile	9				Chicago II	Gold	4		19
1970	25 or 6 to 4	4								
1971	Does Anybody Know What Time It Is?	4				Chicago III	Plat	2	2	10

1971	Beginnings	7				Carnegie Hall	Plat	3		

All-time single rank #22

Songs written by Robert Lamm, keyboards

(A) This was the group's original name until being hassled by the actual CTA. They had fourteen post-1971 top ten songs, including three at number one.

Total album sales 37 million (thirty-fourth)

The group had twelve post-1971 platinum albums and four gold.

Eric Clapton

He had previously been in the Yardbirds, John Mayall's Bluesbreakers, Cream, Blind Faith, and Delaney and Bonnie.

Year	Top Ten Single(s)	Peak	Weeks	RCY	ATR	Gold Album(s)	Sales	Peak	Weeks	RCY
1970						Layla	Gold	16		
1972						History of Eric Clapton	Gold	6		

All-time single rank #108

He had five top-ten, post-1971 singles, including one at number one

Total album sales 38.5 million (thirty-second)

He had twelve post-1971 platinum albums and ten gold

Joe Cocker

Year	Top Ten Single(s)	Peak	Weeks	RCY	ATR	Gold Album(s)	Sales	Peak	Weeks	RCY
1969						With A Little Help From My Friends	Gold	35		
1969						Joe Cocker	Gold	11		
1970						Mad Dogs and Englishmen	Gold	2		
All-time single rank #257										

Four Seasons

Year	Top Ten Single(s)	Peak	Weeks	RCY	ATR	Gold Album(s)	Sales	Peak	Weeks	RCY
1964	Dawn (Go Away)*	3								
1964	Ronnie*	6								
1964	Rag Doll*	1	2	16						
1965	Let's Hang On*	3								
1966	Working My Way Back to You*	9				Greatest Hits	Gold	10		41
1966	I've Got You under My Skin (Cole Porter)	9								
1967	C'mon Maryanne*	9				Greatest Hits II	Gold	22		46

All-time single rank #31

Three number-one songs in 1962-1963

* Written by Bob Gaudio, keyboards

Aretha Franklin

Year	Top Ten Single(s)	Peak	Weeks	RCY	ATR	Gold Album(s)	Sales	Peak	Weeks	RCY
1967	I Never Loved a Man The Way I Love You	9				I Never Loved a Man The Way I Love You	Gold	2	3	26
1967	Respect	1	2	11						
1967	Baby I Love You	4								
1967	(You Make Me Feel Like) A Natural Woman	8								
1968	Chain of Fools	2		22		Aretha: Lady Soul	Gold	2	2	
1968	Since You've Been Gone	5				Aretha Now	Gold	3		
1968	Think	7								
1968	The House that Jack Built	6								
1971	Bridge over Troubled Water	6				Live at the Fillmore West	Gold	67		

1971	Spanish Harlem	2								
1971	Rock Steady (Franklin)	9								
1972						Young, Gifted and Black	Gold	11		
All-time single rank #10 Post-1971 she had six gold and three platinum										

Grand Funk (Railroad)

Year	Top Ten Single(s)	Peak	Weeks	RCY	ATR	Gold Album(s)	Sales	Peak	Weeks	RCY
1970						On Time	Gold	27		68
1970						Closer to Home	Plat 2	6		1970 (65) 1971 (100)
1971						Live	Plat 2	5		16
1971						Survival	Plat	6		37
1971						E Pluribus Funk	Plat	5		
All-time single rank #217 Group had four post-1971 top-ten songs, including two number-ones.										

Arlo Guthrie

Year	Top Ten Single(s)	Peak	Weeks	RCY	ATR	Gold Album(s)	Sales	Peak	Weeks	RCY
1967						Alice's Restaurant	Plat	17		

Engelbert Humperdinck

Year	Top Ten Single(s)	Peak	Weeks	RCY	ATR	Gold Album(s)	Sales	Peak	Weeks	RCY
1967	Release Me	4				Release Me	Gold	7		65
1968						The Last Waltz	Gold	10		
1968						A Man without Love	Gold	12		
1969						Engelbert	Gold	12		
1970						Engelbert Humperdinck	Gold	8		
1970						We Made It Happen	Gold	19		
1971						Sweetheart	Gold	22		
1971						Another Time	Gold	25		
All-time singles rank # 267										

Tom Jones

Year	Top Ten Single(s)	Peak	Weeks	RCY	ATR	Gold Album(s)	Sales	Peak	Weeks	RCY
1965	It's Not Unusual	10								
1965	What's New Pussycat	3								
1968						Green Grass of Home	Gold	65		
1968						Fever Zone	Gold	14		

1969	I'll Never Fall in Love Again	6				Help Yourself	Gold	5		
1969						Live!	Gold	13		
1969						This Is	Gold	4		
1969						Live in Las Vegas	Gold	3		
1970	Without Love	5				Tom	Gold	6		
1970	She's a Lady	2	1			I (Who Have Nothing)	Gold	23		
1971						She's a Lady	Gold	17		
						Live at Caesar's Palace	Gold	43		

All-time single rank #97

None of the songs were written by Jones

Lettermen

Year	Top Ten Single(s)	Peak	Weeks	RCY	ATR	Gold Album(s)	Sales	Peak	Weeks	RCY
1967						Best	Gold	17		
1968	Going Out of My Head	7				Live	Gold	10		
1968						Going Out of My Head	Gold	13		
1969						Hurt So Bad	Gold	17		

All-time singles rank #330

Dean Martin

Year	Top Ten Single(s)	Peak	Weeks	RCY	ATR	Gold Album(s)	Sales	Peak	Weeks	RCY
1964	Everybody Loves Somebody Sometime	1	1	9	724	Everybody Loves Somebody Sometime	Gold	2	4	1964 (59) 1965 (44)
1964	The Door Is Still Open to My Heart	6				Dream with Dean	Gold	15		
1964						The Door Is Still Open to My Heart	Gold	9		
1965						Hits Again	Gold	13		59
1965						I'm the One Who Loves You	Gold	12		
1966						Houston	Gold	11		79
1966						Somewhere There's a Someone	Gold	40		65
1967						Welcome to My World	Gold	20		
1968						Greatest Hits	Gold	26		
1968						Greatest Hits II	Gold	83		
1969						Gentle on My Mind	Gold	14		
All-time single rank #109										

Van Morrison

Year	Top Ten Single(s)	Peak	Weeks	RCY	ATR	Gold Album(s)	Sales	Peak	Weeks	RCY
1967	Brown Eyed Girl (Morrison) (A)	10								
1970	Domino (Morrison)	9				Moondance	Plat 3	20		
1971						Tupelo Honey	Gold	27		
(A) RS 109 Twenty-eight album releases after 1971, including one platinum and three gold										

Donny Osmond

Year	Top Ten Single(s)	Peak	Weeks	RCY	ATR	Gold Album(s)	Sales	Peak	Weeks	RCY
1971	Sweet And Innocent	7				Donny Osmond	Gold	13		
1971	Go Away Little Girl (Goffin/ King)	1	3			To You with Love, Donny	Gold	12		
1971	Hey Girl	9								
1972	Puppy Love (Paul Anka)	3								
All-time single rank #176										

Partridge Family

Year	Top Ten Single(s)	Peak	Weeks	RCY	ATR	Gold Album(s)	Sales	Peak	Weeks	RCY
1970	I Think I Love You (Tony Romeo)	1	3	6	248					
1971	Doesn't Somebody Want to Be Wanted	6				Album	Gold	4		6
1971	I'll Meet You Halfway	9				Up to Date	Gold	3		
1971						Sound Magazine	Gold	9		

All-time single rank #553

Singles released reached 1,6,9,13,29,28,39, in that order

Pink Floyd

Year	Top Ten Single(s)	Peak	Weeks	RCY	ATR	Gold Album(s)	Sales	Peak	Weeks	RCY
1970						Ummagumma	Plat	74		
1971						Atom Heart Mother	Gold	55		
1971						Meddle	Plat 2	70		

Total album sales 73.5 million (seventh)

They had huge success after 1971, with eleven platinum albums and one gold. *The Dark Side of the Moon* was only number one for one week, but reached platinum 15 because it stayed on the charts for over fourteen years. *The Wall* was number one for fifteen weeks and reached platinum 23.

Bobby Sherman

Year	Top Ten Single(s)	Peak	Weeks	RCY	ATR	Gold Album(s)	Sales	Peak	Weeks	RCY
1969	Little Woman	3								
1969	La La La (If I Had You)	9								
1970	Easy Come Easy Go	9				Bobby Sherman	Gold	11		
1970	Julie, Do Ya Love Me?	5				Here Comes Bobby	Gold	10		
1970						With Love, Bobby	Gold	21		
All-time sales rank #531 Sherman and *Shindig* host, Jimmy O'Neill, had the same hairstyle (very un-hip).										

Frank Sinatra

Year	Top Ten Single(s)	Peak	Weeks	RCY	ATR	Gold Album(s)	Sales	Peak	Weeks	RCY
1966	Strangers in the Night (Bert Kaempert)	1	1	25	811	September of My Years	Gold	5		
1966	That's Life	4				A Man And His Music	Gold	5		
1966						Strangers in the Night	Plat	1	1	
1966						At the Sands	Gold	9		
1967						That's Life	Gold	6		
1968						Greatest Hits	Plat 2	55		

1969						Cycles	Gold	18		
1969						My Way	Gold	11		

All-time singles rank #130

Total album sales 25.5 million (sixty-sixth)

Sinatra had eleven greatest hits albums, titled *This Is Sinatra, This is Sinatra II, All the Way, Frank Sinatra's Greatest Hits, Frank Sinatra's Greatest Hits II, The Capitol Years, Sinatra Reprise – the Very Good Years, Sinatra 80th – All the Best, The Capitol Collectors' Series, The Best of the Capitol Years,* and *The Very Best of Frank Sinatra*

Nancy Sinatra

Year	Top Ten Single(s)	Peak	Weeks	RCY	ATR	Gold Album(s)	Sales	Peak	Weeks	RCY
1966	These Boots Are Made for Walking (Lee Hazlewood)	1	1	22		Boots	Gold	5		
1966	How Does That Grab You Darling?	7								
1967	Something Stupid (with Frank) (Carson Parks)	1	4	5						
1968						Nancy and Lee (Hazlewood)	Gold	13		

All-time single rank #242

Wrote none of her songs

All-time album unit sales rank #424

Barbra Streisand

Year	Top Ten Single(s)	Peak	Weeks	RCY	ATR	Gold Album(s)	Sales	Peak	Weeks	RCY
1964						The Third Album	Gold	5		1965 (49)
1964						Funny Girl	Gold	2	3	
1965						People	Gold	1	5	1965 (19) 1966 (55)
1965						My Name Is Barbra	Gold	2	3	1965 (14) 1966 (40)
1965						Color Me Barbra	Gold	3		1965 (14) 1966 (9)
1968						Funny Girl	Plat	12		
1968						A Happening in Central Park	Gold	30		
1970						Greatest Hits	Plat 2	32		
1971						Stoney End	Plat	10		
All-time album sales rank #8										

Traffic

Year	Top Ten Single(s)	Peak	Weeks	RCY	ATR	Gold Album(s)	Sales	Peak	Weeks	RCY
1970						John Barleycorn Must Die	Gold	5		
1971						The Low Spark of High Heeled Boys	Plat	7		

Vanilla Fudge

Year	Top Ten Single(s)	Peak	Weeks	RCY	ATR	Gold Album(s)	Sales	Peak	Weeks	RCY
1968	You Keep Me Hanging On	6				Vanilla Fudge	Gold	6		9

Andy Williams

Year	Top Ten Single(s)	Peak	Weeks	RCY	ATR	Gold Album(s)	Sales	Peak	Weeks	RCY
1964						The Wonderful World of Andy Williams	Gold	9		67
1964						The Academy Award Winning "Call Me Irresponsible"	Gold	5		
1964						The Great Songs from "My Fair Lady"	Gold	5		
1965						Dear Heart	Gold	4		8

Musical Miscellany

Chapter Eleven

Flash in the Pan Groups and Solo Careers

This chapter discusses groups who had brief successes, other chart-topping singles, solo careers, and top-selling albums.

Kingsmen

Singles: "Louie, Louie" (1963-4) peaked at number two for six weeks; twenty-first ranked single for 1963; 949th for all time; written by Richard Berry (number two for two straight weeks, then number three, and then number two for four more straight weeks; it was kept from the top position by the forgettable "Dominique" and "There I've Said It Again").

The words to "Louie, Louie" are almost impossible to understand and are rumored to be obscene. No question that this added significantly to the sales of the single. There was probably a leak somewhere that the lyrics were obscene; otherwise no one would have realized it. This was the most ingenious marketing scheme ever. The FBI tried to track down the writer, R&B singer Richard Berry, the Kingsmen, and various record "suits." They were never able to determine the actual lyrics used.

To this day, the Kingsmen insist they said nothing lewd, despite the obvious mistake at the end of the instrumental, where Jack Ely started to sing the last verse one bar too soon, and can be heard yelling something in the background. Ely also said that he sang far away from the microphone, which caused the fuzzy sound, and that the notoriety was initiated by the record company.

This makes a lot of sense after listening to the song again. The words sound much more like the official version seen below, especially the word "rose" instead of "bone." The lyrics rumor was a sham.

The official lyrics are in plain print, and one of the many alternative versions is in parentheses.

> CHORUS: "Louie, Louie, oh no. Me gotta go. Aye-yi-yi, I said. Louie Louie, oh baby. Me gotta go."
> "Fine little girl waits for me. Catch a ship across the sea. Sail that ship about, all alone. Never know if I make it home.
>
> CHORUS
>
> "Three nights and days, I sail the sea." (Every night and day, I play with my thing.) "Think of girl, constantly." (I f___ you girl, oh, all the way.) "Oh that ship, I dream she's there. (On my bed, I'll lay her there.) "I smell the rose in her hair." (I feel my bone, ah, in her hair.)
>
> CHORUS
>
> "See Jamaica, the moon above." (Hey lovemaker, now hold my thing.) "It won't be long, me see my love." (It won't take long, so leave it alone.) "Take her in my arms again." (Hey, senorita, I'm hot as hell.) "Tell her I'll never leave again." (I told her I'd never lay her again.)
>
> CHORUS

The "see" of "see Jamaica" comes in one line too early and is repeated.

By the time the song became a hit, lead singer Jack Ely had left the group, and when they appeared on television, Lynn Easton mimed Ely's vocals.

Paul Revere and the Raiders released "Louie, Louie" at the same time the Kingsmen did, but their version, a superior one musically, did not chart. The "marketing" of their competition did them in.

Don McLean

Don McLean is questionably in this "brief period" section, because he was ranked number 567 on the all-time single selling list, having seven charting singles. He and Barry Sadler were the only two whose albums also reached number one. However, McLean also had a second charting single from the same album, "Vincent," which reached number twelve. After his *American Pie* album, so much more was expected of him. For a baseball comparison, see Vida Blue.

How much money does a musician make when his single reaches number one? McLean said it made him an instant millionaire. When asked, "What does the song mean to you?" he replied, "It meant that I never had to work another day in my life."

Albums: *American Pie* (1971), number one for seven weeks; platinum

Singles: "American Pie" (1971), number one for four weeks; third bestseller for 1972; number 163 best single seller of all time; the first part of the song was on side one, and the rest on the flip side. The song was too long (8:27) to put on one side. This was easily the best song *not* included in the *Rolling Stone* top five hundred.

Zager and Evans

Single: "In the Year 2525" (1969); number one for six weeks; second-ranked song for 1969; number eighty-seven best single seller of all time; Denny Zager and Rick Evans; released regionally in 1968; easily the most successful song of any one-hit groups; no other charting singles. The album reached only number thirty.

(Bill Cosby's albums were not music, but he was a top album seller during this era, achieving six platinum albums and two gold between 1964 and 1969.)

Other Number-one Singles

Number in parentheses is the rank for the entire year; the number in boldface is the all-time ranking. Songwriter is in brackets

1964

Bobby Vinton: "There! I've Said It Again", four weeks (3) **(199)** [Vinton]

Louis Armstrong: "Hello, Dolly!" one week (17) **(614)** [Jerry Herman]

Dixie Cups: "Chapel of Love," **(342)** three weeks

Peter and Gordon: "World without Love," one week (7) **(732)** [McCartney]

Roy Orbison: "Oh, Pretty Woman," three weeks (5) **(296)**[Orbison]

Manfred Mann: "Do Wah Diddy Diddy," two weeks (13) **(448)**

Shangri-Las: "Leader of The Pack," one week (23) **(920)**

Lorne Green (Ben Cartwright): "Ringo," one week (21) **(819)** [even though it was not about Ringo Starr, the title probably increased sales]

Bobby Vinton: "Mr. Lonely," one week (18) **(679)** [Vinton-Allen]

1965

Freddy and the Dreamers: "I'm Telling You Now," two weeks (15) **(593)** [Brian Garrity]

Mindbenders: "Game of Love," one week (24) **(921)**

Barry McGuire: "Eve of Destruction," one week (20) ["don't forget to say grace;" when you return, it's the same old place"] **(821)**

1966

Lou Christie: “Lightning Strikes,” one week (27) **(892)** [Christie]

Percy Sledge: “When a Man Loves a Woman,” three weeks (13) **(587)** [Calvin Lewis, Andrew Wright]

Troggs: “Wild Thing,” two weeks (10) **(495)** [Chip Taylor]

? and the Mysterians: “96 Tears,” one week (19) **(684)** [Rudy Martinez is “?”]

New Vaudeville Band: “Winchester Cathedral,” three weeks (3) **(266)**

1967

Buckinghams: “Kind of a Drag,” two weeks (12) **(541)** [James Holvay]

Bobbie Gentry: “Ode to Billy Joe,” four weeks (4) **(194)**; RS 412 [Billie Joe took the plunge off the Tallahatchie Bridge on June 3, 1967]* [Gentry]

Box Tops: “The Letter,” four weeks (7) **(208)**; RS 363; “air-o-plane” [Barry McGuire sound-alike] [Wayne Carson Thompson]

Lulu: “To Sir with Love,” five weeks (1) **(123)**

Strawberry Alarm Clock: “Incense and Peppermints,” one week (13) **(678)**

John Fred and His Playboy Band: “Judy in Disguise (with Glasses)”, two weeks (12) **(478)** [John Fred and Andrew Bernard, saxophone]

*“Ode to Billy Joe” and another story-telling song, “Harper Valley PTA” (see next page), were the only big hits for either of the two female singers. Both of their albums reached gold status, with Gentry’s peaking at number one for two weeks. Both singers were from the South. Riley’s lyrics had a full “country music” twang to it, while Gentry’s twang was slight. Gentry wrote “*Ode*” and played the guitar.

1968

Lemon Pipers: "Green Tambourine," one week (15) **(806)**
Paul Mauriat: "Love Is Blue," five weeks (3) **(114)**

Otis Redding: "(Sitting On) The Dock Of The Bay," four weeks (6) **(165)** RS 28 [Redding]

Bobby Goldsboro: "Honey," five weeks (4) **(121)** [Goldsboro]

Archie Bell and The Drells: "Tighten Up," two weeks (10). RS 265 **(439)**[Archie Bell-Billy Butler]

Herb Alpert: "This Guy's In Love With You," four weeks (7) **(211)**

Hugh Masakela: "Grazing In The Grass," two weeks (13) **(542)** [Masakela]

Jeannie Riley: "Harper Valley PTA," one week (14) **(686)** (moved from number eighty-one to number seven in one week, the largest jump of the era) [Tom T. Hall]

1969

Henry Mancini: "Love Theme From Romeo and Juliet," two weeks (12) **(488)**

Archies: "Sugar, Sugar," four weeks (4) **(156)**

Steam: "Na Na Hey Hey Kiss Him Goodbye," two weeks (11) **(477)**

1970

Shocking Blue: "Venus," one week (20) **(682)** [Robbie Van Leeuwen, lead singer]; also the same title as a number-one Frankie Avalon song in 1959

Ray Stevens: "Everything Is Beautiful," one week (16) **(573)** [Stevens]

Edwin Starr: "War," three weeks (9) **(303)**

1971

Tony Orlando and Dawn: "Knock Three Times," three weeks (6) **(249)**

Osmonds: "One Bad Apple," three weeks (4) **(127)**

Honey Cone: "Want Ads," one week (16) **(723)**

Donny Osmond: "Go Away Little Girl," three weeks (8) **(278)** [Osmond]

Rod Stewart: "Maggie May," five weeks (2) **(109)** [Stewart]

Isaac "Purple" Hayes: "Theme from Shaft," two weeks (12) **(447)** [Hayes]

Melanie: "Brand New Key," three weeks (7) **(265)** [Melanie Saka]

Other Great Songs of the Era That Are Not Mentioned Elsewhere in the Book

"You've Got Your Troubles," Fortunes (1965)
"You Were On My Mind," We Five (1965)
"I Ain't Marching Anymore," Phil Ochs (1965)
"Keep on Dancing," the Gentrys (1965) [best false ending]
"You're The One," Vogues (1965)
"No Matter What Shape," T-Bones (1965)
"I Fought the Law," Bobby Fuller Four (1966)
"Red Rubber Ball," Cyrkle (1966)
"Come On Down To My Boat," Every Mother's Son (1967)
"Itchycoo Park," Small Faces (1967)
"Western Union," Five Americans (1967)
"Fire," Arthur Brown (1968) ["I am the god of hell fire"]
"Sky Pilot," the Animals (1968)
"Bottle of Wine," Fireballs (1968)
"Do It Again," Beach Boys (1968)
"Abraham, Martin and John," Dion (1968) [his only top-ten song in the era, but nine prior to 1964]

"Good Morning Starshine," Oliver [real name William Oliver Swofford] (1969)
"Going Up the Country," Canned Heat (1969) [featured a flute]
"Ride, Captain, Ride," Blues Image (1970). I still have of two of their albums. *Open* is an outstanding album.
"Hitchin' a Ride," Vanity Fare (1970)
"Green Eyed Lady," Sugarloaf (1970)
"Arizona," Mark Lindsay (1970)
"Montego Bay," Bobby Bloom (1971)
"Sunshine," Jonathan Edwards (1971)
"Signs," Five Man Electrical Band (1971)

The Best Songs That Went Nowhere On the Singles Charts

"The Weight," the Band (reached only 63)
"Lucky Man," Emerson, Lake and Palmer (48 and 51; two tries)
"Long Dark Road," the Hollies (26)
"So You Want To Be a Rock and Roll Star," the Byrds (29)
"Fifth Dimension," the Byrds (44)
"Ballad of Easy Rider," the Byrds (65)
"Break On Through," the Doors (did not chart)

Some Groups With Top-Ten Songs Not Listed Elsewhere

American Breed
Blues Magoos
Johnny Cash
Chad and Jeremy (can anyone distinguish between these two and Peter and Gordon?)
Classics IV
Arthur Conley
Count Five
Cuff Links
Georgie Fame
Flying Machine
Gerry and the Pacemakers

Norman Greenbaum
Hamilton, Joe Frank and Reynolds
Happenings
Bobby Hebb
Mary Hopkin
Bryan Hyland (number-one song in 1960, number-three in 1962, number-three in 1970)
Ides of March
Keith
Bob Lind
Jay and the Americans
Jay and the Techniques (did Jay change groups?)
Left Banke
Gordon Lightfoot
Lobo
Los Bravos
Mitch Ryder and the Detroit Wheels
Roger Miller
1910 Fruitgum Company
Ocean
Ohio Express
O'Kaysions
Royal Guardsmen
Crispian St. Peters
Sam and Dave
Searchers
Dusty Springfield
Vanilla Fudge
Mason Williams
Stevie Wonder

1964-1972 Album Sales of Four Million or More:

1. *Led Zeppelin IV* (22 million)
2. *The Beatles* (19)
3. *Led Zeppelin II* (12)
3. *Abbey Road* (12)

5. *Sgt. Pepper* (11)
6. *Tapestry* (10)
6. *Led Zeppelin* (10)
8. *Bridge Over Troubled Water* (8)
9. *Déjà vu* (7)
10. *All Things Must Pass* (6)
10. *Led Zeppelin III* (6)
10. *Magical Mystery Tour* (6)
10. *Rubber Soul* (6)
14. *More of the Monkees* (5)
14. *The Monkees* (5)
14. *Revolver* (5)
14. *Meet the Beatles* (5)
18. *Crosby, Stills and Nash* (4)
18. *Blood, Sweat and Tears* (4)
18. *In-A-Gadda-Da-Vida* (4)
18. *Are You Experienced?* (4)
18. *Hard Day's Night* (4)
18. *Four Way Street* (4)
18. *Cosmo's Factory* (4)
18. *Let It Be* (4)

Solo Careers from Previous Members of Groups:

(Number in boldface is all-time ranking.)

Animals
Eric Burdon (and sometimes War)

Five albums peaking at 18, 82, 81, 171, 140.

Beach Boys
Brian Wilson

Two albums peaking at 54, 88. The album *Smile*, recorded in 1968, was not released until 2004. It was hard to smile after listening to that album. The elite, of course, loved it because it was a "concept" album. However, it should have remained in the vaults. The three good songs on it had already been released (Capitol Records was not stupid): "Good Vibrations," "Heroes and Villains," and "Surf's Up." The rest of the album is not worth listening to.

Carl Wilson

One album, which peaked at 185.

Dennis Wilson

One album, which peaked at 96.

The Beatles

John Lennon

After the Beatles, John Lennon's music declined even further. *Plastic Ono Band* was Lennon trying to "find himself." He wanted to stay as far away from Beatles-type music as possible. The album reached "only" number six, compared to number one for both Paul McCartney's and George Harrison's solo efforts.

Once someone associates a voice with good songs, he will tend to overrate that same voice singing songs that are not as good. *Imagine* was almost up to Beatles standards, but the other albums after that were not much, until *Starting Over*.

John Lennon's (a.k.a. John Lennon and Yoko Ono, Plastic Ono Band) *Live Peace in Toronto* (1970) peaked at number ten and went gold. *Plastic Ono Band* (1971) peaked at number six and went gold. *Imagine* (1971) peaked at number one for a week and went platinum (2). After that, Lennon had seven gold albums and three platinum.

Two number-one singles ("Whatever Gets You through the Night" **(932)** and "(Just Like) Starting Over" **(97)**, and others peaking at numbers two and three ("Imagine"), three, five, nine and ten. All-time single sales rank number 134.

Paul McCartney

McCartney's solo career was mediocre after *McCartney* and *Ram*, although he easily had the most commercially successful solo career, with 25 million in album sales (sixty-ninth all time).

Paul McCartney's (a.k.a Paul and Linda McCartney, Wings, Paul McCartney and Wings) total album sales were 25 million (sixty-ninth). *McCartney* (1970) peaked at number one for three weeks and reached platinum(2) (no singles from this album; "Another Day" was not on any album). *Ram* (1971) peaked at number two and reached platinum. McCartney had seven gold albums and twelve platinum albums after 1971.

Nine number-one singles, including: "Band on the Run" **(782)**, "Coming Up" **(247),** "Ebony and Ivory" **(50)**, "Listen to What the Man Said" **(812)**, "My Love" **(188)**, "Say Say Say" **(71)**, "Silly Love Songs" **(108)**, "Uncle Albert/Admiral Halsey" **(805)**, "With a Little Luck" **(482)** and also other singles peaking at three, three, five, five, six, seven, and ten (three times). All-time single sales rank is number nineteen.

<u>George Harrison</u>

Harrison had the best solo album of all with *All Things Must Pass*, even though most of the songs drag on too long and the third disk is atrocious. Harrison never came close to matching that album.

All Things Must Pass album (1970) peaked at number one for seven weeks and reached platinum(5). The gold album, *Concert for Bangla Desh* (1972), peaked at number two for six weeks. The only other platinum album was *Cloud Nine* (1987). *Living in the Material World* peaked at number one for five weeks, but only reached gold status.

Three number-one singles ("My Sweet Lord" **(181)**, "Give Me Love," and "Got My Mind Set on You") and also a number-two and a number-ten. All-time single sales rank number 221.

<u>Ringo Starr</u>

Ringo Starr became a better songwriter on his own and was surprisingly successful, due in part to voice association and name recognition.

One gold album (1974) and one platinum (1973).

Two number-one singles ("Photograph" **(880)**, "You're Sixteen" **(797)**, and also three, four, five, six, eight and nine. All-time single sales rank number 316.

Yoko Ono

Released three solo albums from 1971-1973, peaking at 182, 199, and 193. She did have a platinum (3) album in 1980 (*Double Fantasy* with seven of her songs and seven of Lennon's). With records, it was much more difficult to skip over songs than it is with compact discs☺.

Bee Gees

Barry Gibb

Released one album, which peaked at seventy-two.

Blood Sweat and Tears

David Clayton-Thomas

Two albums peaking at 159 (prior to BST) and 184.

Buffalo Springfield

Richie Furay

One album that peaked at 130.

Steve Stills

See Crosby Stills Nash Young

Neil Young

See separate listing

Bread

David Gates

Three albums, which peaked at 107, 102, and 165.

Byrds

Roger McGuinn

Four albums that peaked at 137, 92, 165, and 44.

Gene Clark

One album that peaked at 144.

Chris Hillman

Two albums that peaked at 152 and 188

Chicago

Peter "Et" Cetera

Released five albums, including one platinum.

Cream

Jack Bruce

Six albums, peaking at 55, 160, 153, 182, 37, and 109.

Eric Clapton

See separate entry

Creedence Clearwater Revival

John Fogerty

Released six albums, including one platinum and three golds. Fogerty's single career has been good, but he never matched his best songs with the group. He is not as well known as he should be because he has never been high profile. His first two solo albums were under the name of the Blue Ridge Rangers. Fogerty is on a musical par with John Sebastian, but Sebastian was higher profile with his hip Woodstock speech and his single, "Welcome Back." Sebastian also dominated his group, but unlike Fogerty, was the first to leave. Without the singer-songwriter, the band quickly dissolved.

Tom Fogerty

Released one album that peaked at 180. Once again, what was he thinking about, leaving the group?

Crosby Stills Nash and Young

Neil Young

See separate entry.

David Crosby:

Released three albums, including one gold, and other two peaking at 104 and 133.

Graham Nash

Four albums, including one gold, and others peaking at 34, 117, and 136.

Stephen Stills

Ten albums, including three gold, and others peaking at 26, 18, 42, 31, 127, 83, and 75.

Doors

Ray Manzarek

Released one album, which peaked at 150.

Fifth Dimension

Marilyn McCoo and Billy Davis, Jr.

Three albums, including one gold. Single "You Don't Have to Be a Star (to Be in My Show)" peaked at number one.

Grateful Dead

Jerry Garcia

Ten albums peaking at 35, 49, 42, 114, 100, 97, 135, 81, 137, and 194.

Bob Weir

Two albums peaking at 68 and 69.

Mickey Hart

One album, which peaked at 190.

Guess Who

Burton Cummings

Two albums that peaked at 30 and 51.

Hollies

Graham Nash

See Crosby Stills Nash Young

Jackson Five

Michael Jackson

Forty-six single releases, including thirteen number-ones; all-time single sales ranking number seven; fifteen albums, including platinums (7, 26, 8, 7, 7, and 1). Total albums sales of 58.5 million (fifteenth).

Jermaine Jackson

Seventeen single releases, including two number-nines; all-time single sales ranking number 322; two gold albums; all-time album sales ranking number 417.

Jefferson Airplane

Grace Slick

Three albums peaking at 127, 32, and 48.

Marty Balin

Two albums peaking at 35 and 156; one single reaching eight.

Jorma Kaukonen:

One album peaking at 163.

Led Zeppelin

Jimmy Page

Had three gold albums and one platinum.

Robert Plant

Had four golds and four platinums, which included all of his albums.

Lovin' Spoonful

John Sebastian

Five albums with peaks of 20, 129, 75, 93, and 76. His single, "Welcome Back," reached number one **(813).**

The Mamas and the Papas

John Phillips

Released one album (1970), which peaked at 181.

Cass Elliott

Released five albums, which peaked at 87, 91, 169, 49, and 194.

Moody Blues

Justin Hayward

Two albums, peaking at 37 and 166.

John Lodge

One album peaking at 121.

Ray Thomas

Two albums, peaking at 68 and 147.

Monkees

Davy Jones

Released an album in 1967 that reached only 185.

Mike Nesmith

Released three albums, which reached 143, 159, and 151.

Peter, Paul, and Mary

Mary Travers

Five albums peaking at 71, 157, 169, 200, and 186.

Paul Revere and The Raiders

Freddy Weller

One album, which peaked at number 144.

Mark Lindsay

Three albums, peaking at 36, 82, and 180. Single, "Arizona," reached ten.

Pink Floyd

David Gilmour

Two gold albums.

Syd Barrett

One album, which peaked at 153.

Roger Waters

Five albums, including one gold, and others that peaked at 50, 56, 21, and 136.

Nick Mason

Two albums, peaking at 170 and 154.

Righteous Brothers

Bill Medley

Two albums, peaking at 188 and 152.

Rolling Stones

Mick Jagger

Had three albums releases, including one gold and one platinum.

Keith Richards

Released two albums, including one gold.

Ron Wood

Three releases, peaking at 118, 155, and 164.

Bill Wyman

Two releases, peaking at 99 and 166

Simon and Garfunkel

Paul Simon

Five gold albums and six platinum. Single, "Fifty Ways to Leave Your Lover," peaked at number one for three weeks (**351**). Other singles peaked at 2, 2, 2, 6, and 9. All-time single sales rank number 180.

Art Garfunkel

Six album releases, including two gold and one platinum; not a good peak trend at 5, 7, 19, 67, 113, and 134. One single, "All I Know," that peaked at number nine.

Sonny and Cher

Cher

Five gold albums and three platinum (first in 1987).

Four number-one singles ("Half Breed" [**471**], "Gypsies, Tramps and Thieves" [**427**], "Believe" [**139**] and "Dark Lady" [**881**]) and also peaks of 2, 6, 7, 8, and 8.

Steppenwolf

John Kay

Two albums, peaking at 113 and 200

The Supremes

Diana Ross

Three gold and two platinum. Four number-one singles ("Ain't No Mountain High Enough," "Endless Love," "Mahogany," "Touch Me in the Morning," "Love Hangover"), and also 5, 7, 8, 9, 10, and 10. All-time single sales rank of number 35.

The Temptations

Eddie Kendricks

Nine album releases peaking at 80, 131, 16, 30, 108, 63, 38, 144, and 180. One single ("Keep on Truckin'") reached number one and another, number two.

David Ruffin

Six albums, peaking at 31, 148, 178, 160, 31, and 51. Two singles reached number nine.

Dennis Edwards

One album, which peaked at 48.

The Who

Roger Daltry

Seven albums, peaking at 45, 28, 46, 22, 185, 102, and 42.

Keith Moon

One album, which peaked at number 155.

Pete Townshend

Nine albums, including one gold and one platinum; others peaked at 69, 45, 26, 35, 98, 198, 58, and 118.

John Entwistle

Five albums, peaking at 126, 138, 174, 192, and 71.

Yardbirds

Eric Clapton

See separate listing.

Jimmy Page

See Led Zeppelin.

Jeff Beck

Five gold albums and two platinum.

Soloists who didn't chart:

Here are some other individuals who left groups, released singles, but could not get anything on the charts:

Peter Tork (Monkees), Ronnie Bond (Troggs), Reg Presley (Troggs), Chris Britten (Troggs), Robin Gibb (Bee Gees), Maurice Gibb (Bee Gees), and Allan Clarke (Hollies).

Generally, solo work by group members was hugely disappointing. Low name recall was a large negative. Also, many group members have a highly inflated view of their talent.

Songwriters' talent is similar to an oil well, in that there is a limited number of good songs for each writer. Also, there is a need for musicians to change, which means writing different music than they did in their old group, which almost always meant lower sales.

Chapter Twelve

Lists, Ratings, and R&B

This chapter is an opinionated almanac of lists and other fun, miscellaneous information, such as the Rock and Roll Hall of Fame, a list of who is still touring, and a look at the music festivals that helped shape this musical era.

Some Fun with Trivia and Ratings

Good Weeks …

The best week of music for the top-ten songs was the week ending on September 11, 1965 (song peak is in parentheses):

1. "Help!"
2. "Like a Rolling Stone" (2)
3. "Eve of Destruction" (1)
4. "You Were on My Mind" (3)
5. "California Girls" (3)
6. "Unchained Melody" (4)
7. "I Got You Babe" (1)
8. "Papa's Got a Brand New Bag" (8)
9. "It Ain't Me Babe" (8)
10. "The "In" Crowd" (5)

Second place was the week ending on March 19, 1966:

1. "Ballad of the Green Berets"

2. "19th Nervous Breakdown" (2)
3. "These Boots Are Made For Walking" (1)
4. "Nowhere Man" (3)
5. "Elusive Butterfly" (5)
6. "Listen People" (3)
7. "California Dreaming" (4)
8. "Homeward Bound" (5)
9. "I Fought the Law" (9)
10. "Daydream" (2)

Bad Weeks …

In comparison, the worst week was the week ending on February 20, 1971:

1. "One Bad Apple"
2. "Knock Three Times" (2)
3. "Rose Garden" (3)
4. "I Hear You Knocking" (4)
5. "If You Could Read My Mind" (5)
6. "Mama's Pearl" (2)
7. "Groove Me" (6)
8. "Sweet Mary" (7)
9. "Mr. Bojangles" (9)
10. "Lonely Days" (3)

Second place was the week ending on January 27, 1968:

1. "Judy in Disguise (with Glasses)"
2. "Chain of Fools" (2)
3. "Green Tambourine" (1)
4. "Woman, Woman" (4)
5. "Bend Me, Shape Me" (5)
6. "Hello, Goodbye" (1)
7. "Spooky" (3)
8. "Daydream Believer" (1)
9. "I Heard It through the Grapevine" (2)
10. "If I Could Build My Whole World around You" (10)

These last two are better than anything in 1972, a typical week being the one ending on July 29:

1. "Alone Again (Naturally)"
2. "Brandy (You're a Fine Girl)"
3. "Too Late to Turn Back Now"
4. "(If Loving You Is Wrong) I Don't Want to Be Right"
5. "Daddy, Don't You Walk So Fast"
6. "Where Is the Love?"
7. "School's Out"
8. "How Do You Do"
9. "Lean on Me"
10. "Long Cool Woman (in a Black Dress)"

Even these songs were "Beatlesque" compared to the following 1973-1979 hit songs:

"Sailing," "You Make Me Feel Dancing" (should be "You Make Me Feel Like Turning Off the Radio"), "Minute By Minute," "Staving Alive," "I Am Woman," "Brother Louie," "Seasons In The Sun," "Billy Don't Be A Hero," "Rock Your Baby," "Can't Get Enough Of Your Love," "Rock Me Gently," "That's The Way I Like It," "Fly Robin Fly," "Shake Your Booty," "Disco Duck," "Muscrat Love," "Night Fever," "Shadow Dancing," "Shake Your Groove Thing," "Don't Go Breaking My Heart," and "Dream Weaver."

Best instrumental song openings:

1. "I Feel Fine," Beatles
2. "Day Tripper," Beatles
3. "Jumping Jack Flash," Rolling Stones
4. "Satisfaction," Rolling Stones
5. "She Don't Care about Time," Byrds
6. "No Matter What," Badfinger
7. "Wah Wah," George Harrison
8. "Norwegian Wood," Beatles
9. "To Susan on the West Coast Waiting," Donovan
10. "19th Nervous Breakdown," Rolling Stones
11. "Mr. Tambourine Man," Byrds

12. "Brown Sugar," Rolling Stones
13. "Venus," Shocking Blue

Most bizarre song titles:

1. "(You Need Meat) Don't Go No Further," Doors
2. "Rainy Day Women #12 and 35," Bob Dylan
3. "Nowadays Clancy Can't Even Sing," Buffalo Springfield
4. "In-A-Gadda-Da-Vida," Iron Butterfly
5. "Everybody Has Something to Hide Except Me and My Monkey," Beatles
6. "Hurdy Gurdy Man," Donovan
7. "Celebration of the Lizard," Doors
8. "Thank You Falettinme Be Mice Elf Agin," Sly and the Family Stone
9. "Cowgirl in the Sand," Neil Young
10. "SWALBR," Cream
11. "Peace Frog," Doors
12. "Do Wah Diddy Diddy," Manfred Mann

Longest song titles:

1. "The Anaheim, Azuza and Cucamonga Sewing Circle, Book Review and Timing Association"
2. "Just Dropped In (to See What Condition My Condition Was In)" [contains lyrics "eight miles high"]
3. "Everybody's Got Something to Hide Except Me and My Monkey"
4. "Have You Seen Your Mother, Baby, Standing in the Shadow"

Shortest song titles:

1. "If"
2. "War"
3. "One"

Novelty Songs

1. "Ringo" (Lorne Greene) 1964
2. "The Name Game" (Shirley Ellis) 1965
3. "Wooly Bully" (Sam the Sham and The Pharaohs) 1965; stayed on the charts for fifteen weeks
4. "They're Coming to Take Me Away, Ha Ha" (Napoleon XIV) 1966
5. "Snoopy vs. The Red Baron" (Royal Guardsmen) 1966 (four weeks at number two, behind "I'm a Believer")
6. "Na Na Hey Hey Kiss Him Goodbye" (Steam) 1969

Best lyrics:

(Not cryptic, no hidden political messages, just entertaining):

1. "First I Look at the Purse," Contours ("I don't care if she waddles like a duck")
2. "Leopard Skin Pillbox Hat," Bob Dylan
3. "So You Want to Be a Rock and Roll Star," Byrds
4. "Sympathy for the Devil," Rolling Stones
5. "Money," Lovin' Spoonful

Best singing voices:

1. Judith Durham (Seekers)
2. Cass Elliott
3. Jim Morrison
4. Art Garfunkel
5. Karen Carpenter

Most distinctive singing voices:

1. John Fogerty
2. Robert Plant
3. Al Wilson (Canned Heat)
4. Neil Young
5. Bob Dylan

6. Cass Elliott
7. John Kay

Late bloomers as songwriters:

1. George Harrison (who came into his own with "Taxman" in 1966; who ever would have thought that he would be the best songwriter on the Beatles' last album?)
2. Rick Nelson
3. Jagger-Richards (who took a year to start writing songs at all and two years to start writing prolifically)
4. Howard Kaylan (who wrote "Elenore," the Turtles' second-to-last hit)
5. Jim McGuinn (whose first prominent composition was "Eight Miles High")
6. Ringo Starr (whose first composition was in 1968).

Groups most dominated by a talented individual:

1. Jethro Tull: Ian Anderson
2. Creedence Clearwater Revival: John Fogerty
3. Jimi Hendrix Experience: Jimi Hendrix
4. Lovin' Spoonful: John Sebastian

Best Non-Beatle Albums

1. *Bridge Over Troubled Water* (Simon and Garfunkel)
2. *If You Can Believe Your Eyes and Ears* (Mamas and Papas)
3. *Crosby Stills and Nash*
4. *Déjà vu* (Crosby, Stills, Nash and Young)
5. *American Pie* (Don McLean)

Songs renamed with correct grammar:

1. "Bobby McGee and I"
2. "It Is Not I, Woman"

3. "A Hard Rain Is Going To Fall"
4. "It Does Not Come Easy"
5. "(I Cannot Get Any) Satisfaction"
6. "I Have You, Babe"
7. "Isn't That A Shame"
8. "It Does Not Matter To Me"
9. "You Are Not Going Anywhere"
10. I Am Not Going To Work On Maggie's Farm Any More

Most well-known session musicians:

- The Beatles were the most famous session musicians, backing Tony Sheridan in 1961.

Klaus Voorman (bass)
Hal Blaine (drums)
Larry Knechtel (keyboards)
Joe Osborne (bass)
Leon Russell (bass, guitar, keyboards)
Glen Campbell (guitar, banjo)
Al Kooper (keyboards)

And in the UK

Nicky Hopkins (piano)
Jimmy Page (guitar)

Kooper played organ on Bob Dylan's "Like a Rolling Stone," even though he had never played organ before. He also played French horn, piano, and organ on "You Can't Always Get What You Want," and rhythm guitar on Hendrix's "Electric Ladyland."

Instrumentalists:

(Those whose primary instrument was other than the mundane guitar-bass-drums)

Autoharp: John Sebastian

Flute: Ian Anderson (Jethro Tull), Ray Thomas (Moody Blues)

Keyboards: Ray Manzarek (Doors), Alan Price (Animals), Felix Cavaliere (Rascals), Steve Winwood (Traffic), Mike Smith (Dave Clark 5), Paul Revere (Raiders), Leslie Maguire (Gerry and the Pacemakers), Garth Hudson (Band) and Richard Manuel (Band). Maguire and Manuel were the only piano players (very un-hip), and the Band was the only group with two keyboard players.

Saxophone: Mark Lindsay, Denis Payton

Bass guitar lead singers: Paul McCartney, Brian Wilson, Jack Bruce

Keyboard lead singers: Felix Cavaliere, (Rascals), Mike Smith (Dave Clark Five)

Best-Looking Individuals:

("Got to be good looking, 'cause he's so hard to see")

1. Dave Clark
2. Linda Ronstadt
3. Paul McCartney
4. Sam Cooke
5. Michelle Phillips
6. Dave Davies
7. Petula Clark

Ugliest Individuals:

("A pretty face you may not possess")

1. Janis Joplin

2. Robin Gibb
3. Keith Richards (either his gaunt 1971 look, with rotted-out teeth, or his current look, which resembles an iguana)
4. Howard Kaylan
5. Bobby Goldsboro
6. Jerry Garcia
7. Joe Cocker
8. Don McLean
9. Leon Russell (at the Bangladesh benefit only; he looked like he just rose from a coffin; his skin-tight tank top did not help his appearance, either)

Best-looking groups:

1. Dave Clark Five
2. Beatles
3. Monkees
4. Beach Boys
5. Paul Revere and the Raiders

Ugliest groups:

1. Canned Heat (pictured at the Monterey Pop)

Used by permission of Pennebaker Films

Henry Vestine

Used by permission of Pennebaker Films

Frank Cook

Used by permission of Pennebaker Films

Larry Taylor

Used by permission of Pennebaker Films

Al Wilson

Had a distinctive falsetto voice.

He died in September 1970, the second casualty of the era.

Used by permission of Pennebaker Films

Bob Hite

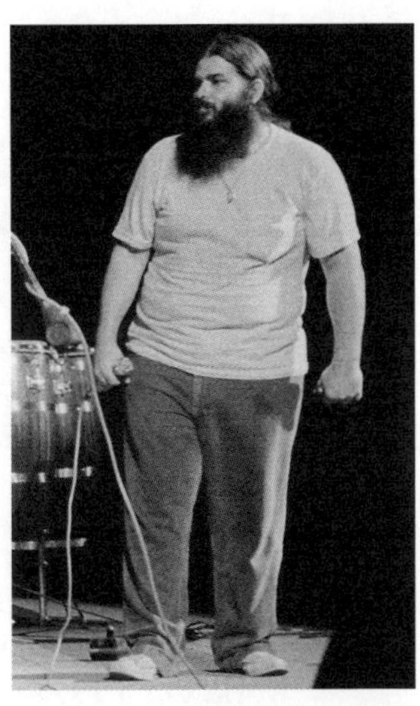

© Henry Diltz/CORBIS

Bob Hite (two years later at Woodstock)

2. Turtles

© Henry Diltz/CORBIS

3. Rolling Stones
4. Badfinger

Worst teeth:

1. Rick Derringer (McCoys)
2. Peter Noone

© Hulton-Deutsch Collection/CORBIS

3. Stephen Stills (He failed the Monkees audition because of "bad teeth." Three years later, at Woodstock, still no dental work. On a 1977 cover of *Rolling Stone*, a drawing of him accentuates the bad teeth.)

© Henry Diltz/CORBIS

4. Robbie Krieger

© Henry Diltz/CORBIS

5. Ray Davies (Had a gap between his front two teeth wide enough to place three guitar picks.)

© Debi Doss/Hulton Archive/Getty Images

6. Ginger Baker

These six were told by their publicists to keep their mouths closed when smiling☺.

Most distinctive noses:

1. Pete Townshend
2. Bob Dylan
3. Ray Davies
4. Ringo Starr
5. Gene Clark

Large or Protruding ears:

1. Keith Richards
2. George Harrison
3. Frank Zappa (extra large, but not protruding)
4. Eric Burdon (He looked like an elf.)

Old-timers: (Year born followed by age when person's group had first charting music release.)

1. Tiny Tim (1925; 43)
2. Skip Battin (1934; 34)
3. John Phillips (1935; 31)
4. Glen Campbell (1936; 31)
5. Garth Hudson (1937; 31)
6. James Griffin (1940; 30)
7. David Gates (1940; 30)
8. Sonny Bono (1935; 30)
9. Ike Turner (1931; 29)
10. Ginger Baker (1939; 29)
11. Bill Wyman (1936; 28)
12. Ray Manzarek (1939; 28)
13. Grace Slick (1939; 28)
14. Barry McGuire (1937; 28)

Youngsters:

1. Michael Jackson (1958; 11)
2. Stevie Wonder (1951; 12)

3. Carl Wilson (1946; 16)
4. Leslie Gore (1946; 17)
5. Dennis Wilson (1944; 18)
6. Michael Monarch (1950 [Steppenwolf]; 18)
7. Mel Schachner (1951 [Grand Funk]; 18)
8. Robin Gibb (1949; 18)
9. Maurice Gibb (1949; 18)
10. Peter Noone (1947; 18)
11. Dave Davies (1947; 18)
12. Howard Kaylan (1947; 18)
13. Mark Volman (1947; 18)
14. Michelle Phillips (1947; 19)
15. Donovan (1946; 19)
16. Barry Gibb (1947; 20)

- Biggest age gap between two members of a group: thirteen years, Mick Taylor and Bill Wyman of the Rolling Stones; eleven years, Sonny and Cher, John and Michelle Phillips of Mamas and Papas.

- Ginger Baker looked the oldest , followed by Mike Love

Style

In 1964, all individuals were clean shaven, wore ties (with the exception of Bob Dylan, Keith Richard and Mick Jagger), and did not wear glasses. There were also no tattoos (visible, at least) or earrings. These were added later, when the shock value of long hair wore off. Later added were moustaches (first were John Phillips and Sonny Bono [1966]), then beards (George Harrison and Mike Love [1967]). Later to come were longer beards (Mike Love), and untrimmed long hair. (John Lennon had this look on *The Beatles (White Album)*, but the first was probably Jack Casady of the Jefferson Airplane, or Bob Weir of the Grateful Dead. The longest pre-1967 hair was the Kinks' Dave Davies, the first to part it down the middle.)

- **First to wear sunglasses on stage:** Jim McGuinn, followed by Keith Relf and John Kay. Bob Dylan wore them only off stage.

- **First earring:** Keith Richards (1969, a bone earring in his right ear)

© Hulton Archive/Getty Images

Oddities and Obscurities

- **Best record scam:** There was a compilation album of different groups "by the original artists." Unfortunately, all the songs were done by one group, whose actual name was the "Original Artists."

- **Most original name:** Jorma Kaukonen (Jefferson Airplane), Devadip (Carlos) Santana, Joachim Krauledat (John Kay)

- **Least original names**: two Mike Smiths (Dave Clark Five and the Raiders) and John Paul Jones (Led Zeppelin)

- **Worst luck:** Roy Orbison: He divorced his wife on grounds of adultery in 1964. He planned to re-marry her in 1966, but she was killed on her motorcycle. His two eldest sons died when their family house burned down. In 1988, after a long musical absence, he teamed up with Bob Dylan, George Harrison, Jeff Lynne, and Tom Petty to form the Traveling Wilburys. He died later that year. ("If I didn't have bad luck, I wouldn't have no luck at all")

- **Fame vs. success:** The most famous musician in contrast to his success was Tiny Tim. In the running for second place were Arlo Guthrie and Country Joe McDonald.

- **Musicians who served in the military:** 1. Jimi Hendrix 2. Jerry Garcia (!) 3. Joe McDonald

- **Best movies for music:** 1. *Forrest Gump* 2. *Easy Rider* It had the rare music of Electric Prunes, Holy Modal Rounders, and Fraternity of Man, along with Roger McGuinn singing "It's Alright Ma (I'm Only Bleeding)." According to actor Dennis Hopper, the locals in the Louisiana café were *not* actors, but townspeople. That makes sense to me, because when I first saw the movie, I thought, "Where in the world did they find these actors?"

Rock and Roll Hall of Fame

Groups become eligible twenty-five years after the release of their first recording. The groups are listed by the number of years it took to be inducted after the twenty-five year waiting period. The year listed is the year inducted.

Inductees who were significantly active during 1964-71

No Waiting Period

James Brown (1986)
Ray Charles (1986)
Marvin Gaye (1987)
Smokey Robinson (1987)
Elvis Presley (1986)
Beatles (1988)
Aretha Franklin (1987)
Beach Boys (1988)
Bob Dylan (1988)
Supremes (1988)
Otis Redding (1989)

Rolling Stones (1989)
Temptations (1989)
Four Tops (1990)
Who (1990)
Jimi Hendrix Experience (1992)
John Lennon (1993)
Rod Stewart (1993)
Band (1993)
Elton John (1993)

One Year

Simon and Garfunkel (1990)
Kinks (1990)
Byrds (1991)
Ike and Tina Turner (1991)
Creedence Clearwater Revival (1994)
Grateful Dead (1993)
Sly and the Family Stone (1994)
Neil Young (1995)
Led Zeppelin (1995)

Two Years

Four Seasons (1990)
Yardbirds (1992)
Doors (1994)
Cream (1994)
Jackson Five (1997)

Three Years

Frank Zappa (1995)
Janis Joplin (1995)
Crosby, Stills and Nash (1997)

Four Years

Animals (1993)
Van Morrison (1994)
Velvet Underground (1996)
Pink Floyd (1996)
Joni Mitchell (1997)
Santana (1998)
Paul McCartney (1999)

Five Years

Booker T. And The M.G.s (1992)
Jefferson Airplane (1996)
Bee Gees (1997)
James Taylor (2000)
Eric Clapton (2000)

Six Years

Buffalo Springfield (1997)
The (Young) Rascals (1997)

Seven Years

Martha and the Vandellas (1995)

Eight Years

The Mamas and the Papas (1998)

Nine Years

George Harrison (2004)

Ten Years

Dusty Springfield (1999)
Lovin' Spoonful (2000)

Thirteen Years

Righteous Brothers (2003)

- The individuals that are in the Hall of Fame with two or more groups (including solo careers):

Eric Clapton: Yardbirds, Cream, Clapton
David Crosby: Byrds, Crosby Stills and Nash
George Harrison: Beatles, Harrison
John Lennon: Beatles, Lennon
Paul McCartney: Beatles, McCartney
Jimmy Page: Yardbirds, Led Zeppelin
Stephen Stills: Buffalo Springfield, Crosby Stills and Nash
Neil Young: Buffalo Springfield, Crosby Stills and Nash
Paul Simon: Simon and Garfunkel, Simon

- The most commercially successful groups *not* in the Hall:

Dave Clark Five, Herman's Hermits, Chicago, the Monkees, Three Dog Night, and the Moody Blues

Non-songwriters have a much tougher time getting into the Hall unless they can be seen as excellently "interpreting" someone else's music.

If an individual dominates a group, should he get in with or without the rest of his group? Buddy Holly is in, but not the Crickets. He had four charting singles with the Crickets and four without. Jimi Hendrix is in, but with the Experience. What about his work from 1969 and forward without the Experience? John Sebastian and John Fogerty are both in with their groups, even though they were the dominant players. Why does Tom Fogerty get in, but not Joe Mauldin (Crickets)? Paul McCartney is in, but not Wings or Paul McCartney and Wings. Why isn't Yoko Ono in, as she was part of John Lennon's band on many releases, or how about the Plastic Ono Band? Why is CSN in, but not CSNY? Michael Jackson is in, along with the other four. Neil Young is in, but not Crazy Horse or the Stray Gators. Eric Clapton is in, but how about Derek and the Dominoes? The Animals are in, but which ones of the nine? (Eric Burdon was the only original member by the time the group played at Monterey.) The Byrds had ten members, with only McGuinn remaining from the originals in 1968. Which ones, of the living, were invited to the 1991 induction? Was Kevin Kelly invited? If they were all invited, how do they all play together on stage? Did the Band get in on Bob Dylan's coattails, or on their own? Why aren't Scotty Moore and Bill Black, Elvis Presley's musicians, in? Frank Zappa is in, but not the Mothers of Invention. The Bee Gees had five or four members at different times. Janis Joplin is in, but not Big Brother and The Holding Company, Cosmic Blues Band, or Full Tilt Boogie Band.

An alternative method for choosing who gets into the Hall is by inducting individuals, rather than groups, as is done in all team sports.

If one is adamant that individuals in a group should not be inducted, then Yoko Ono, Linda McCartney, and Elephant's Memory should have been inducted along with Lennon and McCartney.

It appears that if one of the band members is part of the group name, it improves his chance of getting in as an individual. If Buddy Holly's group were always called the Crickets, the group would have probably gotten in. If Creedence Clearwater Revival would have been called John Fogerty and the Malcontents, Fogerty would have probably been inducted as an individual. Thus, the name of the group seems to have an effect on who gets inducted.

What about the musicians used for The Mamas and the Papas, Simon and Garfunkel, Beach Boys, and others? The answer could be, "Well, they were just session musicians." All right, what if the same session musicians were used each time? How is that any different than being a band member who does not sing or write?

Groups that used session musicians in the studio obviously needed other musicians to play during the live shows. One could always tell who was not officially in the group because they would never have a spotlight shown on them. Thus, being in a group got your picture on the album cover and a spotlight on you during a live performance.

An interesting example of this is with the Rolling Stones. When Mick Taylor replaced Brian Jones and Ron Wood replaced Mick Taylor, both replacements were official band members, with their pictures on the album covers and the spotlight on them at the shows. However, when Daryl Jones replaced Bill Wyman, he got neither recognition.

It probably boils down to finances. Money is divided up fewer ways with Jones as a hired hand, rather than an official member of the band. Ron Wood started as a hired hand, but evolved into an official group member.

Favorites of the Elite

A good portion of the bands inducted into the Hall of Fame also dominated the sales chart. They obviously appealed to both the elite and the proletariat. The ones that did not were favorites of the elite, including Buffalo Springfield, Velvet Underground, Frank Zappa, and Yardbirds. The least successful commercial group was the Velvet Underground, and next Frank Zappa. Any elite who lists these last two as his favorite bands will be instantly admired by other elites.

Frank Zappa

Frank Zappa disbanded the Mothers of Invention in 1969, saying he was "tired of playing for people who clap for all the wrong reasons." Zappa had no intention of becoming commercially successful. He refused to adapt his lyrics to a non-offensive level. He released fifty albums, with two of them reaching gold status. What made him popular were his entertaining, satirical lyrics, and the fact that he hated censorship. He also had a distinctive guitar-playing style, and many liked his orchestral/jazz rock style music.

"Most reviews of my albums bypass the musical content, because writers that have sufficient knowledge of music hardly ever write about rock 'n roll. Whatever image I have in the pop music business, it's mostly based upon opinions by people who aren't qualified to give such opinions at all."

"My job," he once said, "is extrapolating everything to its most absurd extreme."

Zappa described rock journalism as "people who can't write interviewing people who can't talk for people who can't read."

Velvet Underground

While most people have heard of Frank Zappa (though probably not his music), most have not heard of the Velvet Underground, even people who were music fans during that era. They released four albums, the top two peaking at number 171 and number 199. A famous remark, usually attributed to Brian Eno, is that while only a few thousand people bought a Velvet Underground record, every single one of them was inspired to start a band. This group had a small, but very enthusiastic, cult following, and claim they had a huge influence on 1970s music, especially punk.

In the Andy Warhol Museum (Warhol designed their first album cover) in Pittsburgh, Pennsylvania, lies an unpublished essay on popular music written in 1966 by Lou Reed, lead singer, guitarist, and songwriter of the group. Reed sees California as characterized by bands like the Grateful Dead and the Jefferson Airplane, composed of a bunch of drugged-up suburban kids looking for a false salvation in hallucinogenics and psychedelics. Reed seethes with disdain at such misguided and pretentious audacity. Referring to the Beatles' then recent experimentations with pot and LSD, he summarily dismisses such exploits with a blunt, searing vengeance, declaring "What a bore."

Salute to Songwriters

Following is a list of songwriters who wrote various popular songs during the era for other people. These people should get more recognition than they do:

Writer	Song	Performer
Jimmy Webb	"Wichita Lineman"	Glen Campbell
	"Galveston"	Glen Campbell
	"Up, Up, and Away"	Fifth Dimension
	"MacArthur Park"	Richard Harris
Joni Mitchell	"Both Sides Now"	Judy Collins
	"Woodstock"	CSNY
Laura Nyro	"Stoned Soul Picnic"	Fifth Dimension
	"Wedding Bell Blues"	Fifth Dimension
	"Eli's Coming"	Three Dog Night
Otis Redding	"I Never Loved a Man"	Aretha Franklin
	"Respect"	Aretha Franklin
	"Baby I Love You"	Aretha Franklin
Jerry Goffin and	"A Natural Woman"	Aretha Franklin
Carol King	"Pleasant Valley Sunday"	Monkees
	"Just Once in My Life"	Righteous Brothers
	"You've Got a Friend" (King only)	James Taylor
P.J. Sloan and	"Where Were You When I Needed You?"	Grass Roots
Steve Barri	"Things I Should Have Said"	Grass Roots
	"A Must to Avoid"	Herman's Hermits
	"Secret Agent Man"	Johnny Rivers
Graham Gouldman	"Listen People"	Herman's Hermits
	"Bus Stop"	Hollies
	"Heart Full Of Soul"	Yardbirds
	"For Your Love"	Yardbirds
Hal David and	"What's New Pussycat"	Tom Jones
Bert Bacharach	"Raindrops Keep Falling on My Head"	B.J. Thomas
	"Anyone Who Had a Heart"	Dionne Warwick
	"Walk on By"	Dionne Warwick
	"Message to Michael"	Dionne Warwick

Songwriter	Song	Performer
	"I Say a Little Prayer"	Dionne Warwick
	"Do You Know the Way to San Jose?"	Dionne Warwick
	"This Girl's In Love with You"	Dionne Warwick
	"I'll Never Fall in Love Again"	Dionne Warwick
Neil Diamond	"I'm a Believer"	Monkees
	"A Little Bit Me, a Little Bit You"	Monkees
Tommy Boyce and	"Last Train to Clarksville"	Monkees
Bobby Hart	"Valleri"	Monkees
Scott Davis	"In the Ghetto"	Elvis Presley
	"Don't Cry Daddy"	Elvis Presley
Barry Mann and	"Kicks"	Paul Revere and the Raiders
Cynthia Weil	"Hungry"	Paul Revere and the Raiders
	"You've Lost That Loving Feeling"	Righteous Brothers
	"Soul and Inspiration"	Righteous Brothers
	"I Just Can't Help Believing"	B.J. Thomas
Lee Hazlewood	"These Boots Are Made for Walking"	Nancy Sinatra
	"How Does That Grab You Darlin'"	Nancy Sinatra
Barry Bonner and	"Happy Together"	Turtles
Alan Gordon	"She'd Rather Be with Me"	Turtles
Jerry Fuller	"Young Girl"	Union Gap
	"Over You"	Union Gap
	"Lady Willpower"	Union Gap
Shel Silverstein	"A Boy Named Sue"	Johnny Cash
	"The Unicorn"	Irish Rovers
	"Cover of The Rolling Stone"	Dr. Hook and The Medicine Show
Bert Berns	"Twist and Shout"	Beatles, Isley Brothers
	"Hang on Sloopy"	McCoys
	"Piece of my Heart"	Janis Joplin
Jeff Barry and	"Chapel of Love"	Dixie Cups
Ellie Greenwich	"Do Wah Diddy Diddy"	Manfred Mann
	"Leader of the Pack"	Shangri-Las
Paul McCartney	"World Without Love"	Peter and Gordon
	"Come and Get It"	Badfinger
	"Goodbye"	Mary Hopkin
	"Woman"	Peter and Gordon

Underrated Songwriters that Wrote for Their Own Groups

Doug Ingle, Iron Butterfly
Felix Cavaliere, Rascals
Sonny Bono, Sonny and Cher
Ron Artest, Zombies
Sylvester Stewart, Sly and the Family Stone
Pete Ham, Badfinger
Robbie Robertson, the Band
Robert Lamm, Chicago
Jack Bruce, Cream
Robby Krieger, Doors
Bob Gaudio, Four Seasons
Justin Hayward, Moody Blues

Still Touring After All These Years:

(Or at least the group name is on tour)

It seems that most groups just fade away as their record sales decline. Other groups end because of a death. The Doors did put out two more albums after Jim Morrison's death, but were not the same. The Grateful Dead announced they were done after Jerry Garcia's death, but changed their minds (missed the good life?).

The Rolling Stones are still active, though they have lost two of their original members. The Beach Boys are also active, but only as a stage show, and it is just Mike Love and Associates.

Then there are all the groups that reappear (probably after running out of money). Two of the more amusing ones are Creedence Clearwater Revisited (Cook and Clifford) and Herman's Hermits (without Noone). McGuinn, Crosby, and Hillman played in the late 1980s to try to keep the name Byrds, but were unsuccessful, as Michael Clarke kept the name.

These re-formed groups are never successful with "new" albums. I remember both the Mamas and the Papas and the Association playing live songs off their "new" albums. They were awful and I doubt if those albums were even released.

America: Gerry Buckley and Dewey Bunnell

Animals: Eric Burdon with the New Animals

Association: Russ Giguere and Larry Ramos

Beach Boys: Mike Love and Bruce Johnston

Bee Gees: Until 2003, when Maurice died

Byrds: McGuinn, Crosby and Hillman in 1989; Byrds with Michael Clarke (drummer) until he died in 1993

Canned Heat: Fito de la Perra (drummer; not in the original lineup, but joined in 1968; he does a remarkable job imitating Al Wilson's falsetto)

Creedence Clearwater Revival: Creedence Clearwater Revisited with Stu Cook (bass) and Doug Clifford (drums); John Fogerty in a separate group

Crosby, Stills, Nash, and Young*

Doors: Robbie Krieger (guitar) and Ray Manzarek (keyboards)

Grass Roots: Rob Grill

Guess Who: Randy Bachman (guitar) and Burton Cummings (lead singer)

Jan and Dean: quit touring just recently

Jethro Tull: Ian Anderson (lead vocals, flute)

Kinks: Ray Davies (lead singer) and Dave Davies (lead guitar)

The Mamas and the Papas: in the 1980s with John Phillips and Denny Doherty; until 2001 with John Phillips

Moody Blues: Justin Hayward, John Lodge, Ray Thomas, and Graeme Edge

Monkees: Peter Tork, Davy Jones, and Mickey Dolenz touring separately; Mike Nesmith in the 1990s; he was too hip in the 1980s.

Peter, Paul and Mary*

Paul Revere and the Raiders: Paul Revere; Mark Lindsay separately

(Young) Rascals: touring as the "Old Rascals" ☺

Rolling Stones: Mick Jagger, Keith Richards, Charlie Watts

Simon and Garfunkel*

Three Dog Night: Danny Hutton and Cory Wells

Turtles: Mark Volman and Howard Kaylan ("Flo and Eddie")

Yardbirds: Chris Dreja (bass) and Jim McCarty (drums)

* original group

Major groups that have disappeared since 1972:

Donovan
Dave Clark Five
Sly and the Family Stone
Buffalo Springfield
Cream (until 2005)
Lovin' Spoonful
Hollies

Rhythm and Blues

Little Richard said, "It used to be called boogie-woogie, then blues, then rhythm and blues. It's called rock, now."

Blues originated from African American spiritual music in the first half of the 1900s. The music emphasized rhythm over harmony. Blues became "rhythm and blues" with Muddy Waters in 1944, when he electrified the music and changed lyrics from sad to upbeat. Rock-and-roll is often described as rhythm and blues performed by white bands.

In blues music, the second line of lyrics is usually repeating the first. The lyrics are sung without instrumental backing. The instruments, almost always including a harmonica, are played between the lines. (The playing of harmonica only during instrumental breaks, and only by the vocalist, carried over into rock-and-roll. More current blues guitarists will always close their eyes and look upwards, or grimace, while playing). An example would be:

> "I woke up this morning (or "my house burned to the ground" or some other disaster) (instrumental break) and I saw my woman with another man (instrumental break). Yes, I woke up this morning, (instrumental break) and I saw my woman with another man."

By 1956, with the help of Chuck Berry and Little Richard (the "half-moustache" men; Berry's was thin vertically, and Richard's was thin horizontally), rhythm and blues evolved into rock-and-roll, a euphemism for sexual intercourse. However, rhythm and blues still remained with black groups.

The closest two songs to real blues during this era were "Rollin and Tumblin" (Canned Heat) and "Around and Around" (Rolling Stones and Animals).

Motown: "Can't forget the motor city".

Barry Gordy was both the founder of Motown records and an occasional songwriter (a rare combination; see below). He hired Maxine Powell, who had experience running a finishing and modeling school, to refine his performers. Powell has said, "The singers were raw. They were from the streets, and like most of us who came out of the projects, they were a little crude; some were backward, some were arrogant. They had potential, but they were not unlike their friends in the ghetto. I always thought of our artists as diamonds in the rough who needed polishing. We were training them for Buckingham Palace and the White House, so I had my work cut out for me. Many of them had abusive tones of voice, so I had to teach them how to speak in a non-threatening manner.

Many of them slouched, so I had to show them what posture meant. Some were temperamental and moody; I would lecture them about their attitude. I chose which clothes were best for them as well. We used to call them 'uniforms,' and before we had them specially made, I would have to choose outfits that would complement all the people as a group, which wasn't easy. As far as makeup, I worked with all of the girls on wigs, nails, and that sort of thing. And on stage technique, I taught them little things like never turning their back to an audience, never protruding their buttock onstage [no matter what Mick Jagger says!], never opening their mouths too wide to sing, how to be well-rounded professionals." Powell also helped with interview technique.

Gordy also tried to appeal to as many people as possible. He wanted to disassociate the apparent connection many had between liquor and other drugs, and rhythm and blues music. He also rejected anything that had a strong blues sound to it.

He limited each of the Supremes to a $100/week allowance, and put the rest of the $300,000 earned in 1965 into a joint bank account. He did not allow them to date, and gave each a diamond ring to discourage possible paramours.

The Supremes, Four Tops, and the Temptations were the most successful benefactors from Motown. From 1964 to 1967, the label realized fourteen number-one pop singles and twenty number-one R&B singles. Seventy percent of its sales went to whites. Motown did a lot to bring the two races together, beginning with concert attendance.

Songwriting

The Motown groups usually consisted of one lead singer and several backup singers, none of whom played any instruments. (The backup singers became very good at snapping their fingers and dancing☺; the instruments were played by others in the background.) Many of them could not afford to buy their own instruments earlier in life. With the huge exception of William "Smokey" Robinson, and others listed below, they did not write their own music (Gordy, Holland-Dozier-Holland, and Stevenson and Whitfield were not performers). There was also a regular large group of session musicians, including vibes, trumpet, trombone, saxophone, flute and strings.

Smokey Robinson:

The Miracles: "Shop Around," "You've Really Got a Hold on Me," "Track of My Tears," "Tears of a Clown"

Mary Wells: "The One Who Really Loves You," "You Beat Me to the Punch," "Two Lovers, My Guy"

The Temptations: "The Way You Do the Things You Do," "My Girl," "Ooo, Baby, Baby," "I Second That Emotion"

Carolyn Crawford: "My Smile Is Just a Frown (Turned Upside Down)"

The Marvelettes: "Don't Mess with Bill"

Rare Earth: "Get Ready"

Four Tops: "Still Water"

Berry Gordy:

The Miracles: "Shop Around"

The Contours: "Do You Love Me, First I Look at the Purse" (some of the best lyrics ever)

The Marvelettes: "Beechwood 4-5789"

Jackson Five: "I'll Be There"

Marvin Gaye:

The Marvelettes: "Beechwood 4-5789"

Martha and the Vandellas: "Dancing in the Streets"

William "Mickey" Stevenson:

The Marvelettes: "Beechwood 4-5789"

Marvin Gaye: "Pride and Joy," "It Takes Two"

Shorty Long: "Devil with the Blue Dress"

Martha and the Vandellas: "Dancing in the Streets"

Carolyn Crawford: "My Smile Is Just a Frown (Turned Upside Down)"

Brian Holland-Lamont Dozier-Eddie Holland:

Martha and the Vandellas: Heat Wave, Nowhere to Run, Jimmy Mack

Four Tops: "Baby, I Need Your Loving," "I Can't Help Myself, It's the Same Old Song," "Reach Out, I'll Be There," "Standing in the Shadows of Love," "Bernadette"

The Supremes: "Baby Love," "Come See about Me," "You Can't Hurry Love"

Marvin Gaye: "How Sweet It Is to Be Loved by You"

Junior Walker and the All Stars: "How Sweet It Is to Be Loved by You"

Honey Cones: "Want Ads"

Norman Whitfield:

Marvin Gaye: "Pride and Joy"

The Temptations: "Ain't Too Proud to Beg," "Beauty Is Only Skin Deep," "I Know I'm Losing You," "Cloud Nine,"

"I Can't Get Next to You," "Just My Imagination (Running Away with Me)"

Gladys Night and the Pips: "I Heard It through the Grapevine"

Edwin Starr: "War"

The Undisputed Truth: "Smiling Faces Sometimes"

Barrett Strong:

Gladys Night and the Pips: "I Heard It through the Grapevine"

The Temptations: "Cloud Nine," "I Can't Get Next To You," "Just My Imagination (Running Away With Me)"

Edwin Starr: "War"

The Undisputed Truth: "Smiling Faces Sometimes"

Rhythm and Blues Chart

Billboard started its first R&B singles sales chart, called the *Harlem Hit Parade*, in 1942. By 1958, there was the Hot R&B chart, replacing three separate charts that existed before that. From 1955 (when the white groups started) until 1963, the R&B charts included most of the white groups, such as Elvis Presley, Buddy Holly, Pat Boone, and even the Beach Boys. Presley disappeared from the R&B charts in 1963.

- Groups that were bigger on the R&B Billboard charts than the pop charts during 1964-1971:

  ( ) = all-time R&B ranking

  Bobby Bland (15): twenty-six charting songs
  James Brown (see next section)
  Jerry Butler (21): twenty-nine charting songs
  Gene Chandler (69): twenty-two charting songs
  Ray Charles (6): twenty-seven charting songs
  Dells (49): eighteen charting songs
  Four Tops (25): twenty-six charting songs
  Aretha Franklin (2): thirty-six charting songs

Marvin Gaye (7): thirty-six charting songs
Impressions (28): thirty-three charting songs
Isley Brothers (9): eighteen charting songs
B.B. King (11): twenty-nine charting songs
Martha and the Vandellas (110): twenty charting songs
Miracles (24): twenty-six charting songs
Wilson Pickett (32): thirty-one charting songs
Otis Redding (73): twenty-nine charting songs
Joe Simon (35): twenty-four charting songs
Johnnie Taylor (45): sixteen charting songs
Temptations (3): thirty-five charting songs
Joe Tex (67): twenty-four charting songs
Ike and Tina Turner (154): fifteen charting songs
Junior Walker and the All Stars (106): twenty-one charting songs
Jackie Wilson (36): twenty charting songs
Stevie Wonder (4): twenty-three charting songs

Number-one Songs on Both Billboard Charts

1964

"My Guy," Mary Wells
"Where Did Our Love Go," Supremes
"Baby Love," Supremes

1965

"My Girl," Temptations
"Back in My Arms Again," Supremes
"I Can't Help Myself," Supremes

1966

"When a Man Loves a Woman," Percy Sledge
"You Can't Hurry Love," Supremes
"You Keep Me Hanging On," Supremes

1967

"Love Is Here and Now You're Gone," Supremes
"Respect," Aretha Franklin

1968

"Sitting on the Dock of the Bay," Otis Redding
"Tighten Up," Archie Bell and the Drells
"Grazing in the Grass," Hugh Makakela
"I Heard It through the Grapevine," Marvin Gaye

1969

"Everyday People," Sly and the Family Stone
"I Can't Get Next to You," Temptations
"Someday, We'll Be Together," Diana Ross and the Supremes

1970

"I Want You Back," Jackson 5
"Thank You (Falettinme Be Mice Elf Agin)," Sly and the Family Stone
"ABC," Jackson 5
"The Love You Save," Jackson 5
"Ain't No Mountain High Enough," Diana Ross
"I'll Be There," Jackson 5
"The Tears of a Clown," Smokey Robinson and the Miracles

1971

"Just My Imagination (Running Away with Me)," Temptations
"Want Ads," Honey Cone
"Family Affair," Sly and the Family Stone

1972

(None)

Whites bands on the R&B chart from 1964-1972:

Bobby Gentry ("Ode to Billie Joe," number eight [reached number one on the pop charts])

Rare Earth (four songs)

If a song reaches number one on the R&B chart, it does not necessarily reach the same on the pop chart, because the pop chart includes all songs. For example, "Hey Jude" was not an R&B song. Whatever was number one on the R&B chart when "Hey Jude" was number one on the pop chart obviously would not have also been number one on the pop chart. If a song reaches number one on the pop chart, and is considered an R&B song, one would think it would also reach number one on the R&B chart, but that did not always happen. The answer has to be that only select radio stations are used for the radio-playing portion of the ranking for each chart. The sales volume obviously has to be the same for each ranking. For example, "Ode to Billy Joe" did not get nearly the amount of airplay on R&B stations as on pop stations.

- James Brown was the number-one all-time seller, with 118 charting songs, including sixteen number ones. Brown's number ones between 1964-1972 were:

Song	Pop Chart Peak
"Papa's Got a Brand New Bag"	8
"I Got You (I Feel Good)"	3
"It's a Man's Man's Man's World"	8
"Cold Sweat"	7
"I Got the Feeling"	6
"Say It Loud, I'm Black and I'm Proud"	10
"Give It Up or Turn It Loose"	18
"Mother Popcorn"	11
"Super Bad"	13
"Hot Pants"	15
"Make It Funky"	22
"Talking Loud and Saying Nothing"	27

Chapter Thirteen

Other Music Comments and Facts

Group Names:

Group names were one of three types: an individual name (or last names of two or more individuals), a band name, or a combination of both. Many groups were a combination throughout, but many group names added the lead singer's name when he wanted more attention, i.e., Diana Ross and the Supremes, Eric Burdon and the Animals, Smokey Robinson and the Miracles, Kenny Rogers and the First Edition, Paul McCartney and Wings, Frankie Valli and the Four Seasons, or Tony Orlando and Dawn. Only one band name actually *dropped* the individual's name: Paul Revere and the Raiders became the Raiders in 1970, when Paul Revere was still in the group.

- Paul McCartney's band has been named Paul McCartney, Paul and Linda McCartney, Paul McCartney and Wings, Wings, back to Paul McCartney and Wings, and then Paul McCartney again.

- The Union Gap, The Union Gap Featuring Gary Puckett, Gary Puckett and the Union Gap, Gary Puckett

Band Formations:

A band could be formed by friends attending the same high school, members chosen for musical ability rather than friendship or geography, or any combination. Bands formed by friendships were more likely to have members less musically talented than the other band formation, and have one band member with most of the musical talent.

- Creedence Clearwater Revival were all friends before the group began, and included two brothers. They were all from El Cerrito, California.

- The Beach Boys were three brothers, one cousin, and one friend. They were all from Hawthorne, California, but Jardine was born in Ohio.

  In these two "friend" bands, one of the members had almost all of the talent and the others went along for the ride.

- Cream and Crosby, Stills, and Nash were at the other end of the spectrum, as the members knew each other strictly through music. They were born an average of about five thousand miles apart from each other. I do not think they went to the same high school.

- The Grateful Dead members were all born in the San Francisco area, three of the five actually born in the city.

- Another San Francisco band, the Jefferson Airplane, had only one member, Paul Kantner, born in California (San Francisco).

- The Beatles were the only band where all were *born* in the same city, but only George and Paul knew each other before joining the band, and not well. John asked Paul to join the Quarrymen because of his musical ability, but they were not previous friends. George was recommended by Paul because of his musical ability, and Ringo was picked for his drumming in other bands.

- The Byrds, as with many "Southern California" groups, were mostly not made up of Southern Californians. McGuinn grew up in Chicago and then moved to Greenwich Village. Gene Clark was from Missouri. These two met in Los Angeles in 1964. Crosby *was* born in Los Angeles, and was the third to join the group. Chris Hillman was from San Diego, and Clarke was from New York City.

- The Buffalo Springfield formed in Los Angeles. Neil Young had just arrived from Canada. Steve Stills was born in Dallas, then he moved to New York City. Furay was from Ohio. Palmer and Martin were also from Canada.

- The Doors also formed in Los Angeles. Morrison was attending UCLA, but was from Florida. Manzarek was from Chicago. Krieger was born in Los Angeles and Densmore, in Santa Monica.

- The Turtles formed in Westchester, California. Kaylan was born in the Bronx, but moved to Westchester at age nine. Volman was born in Redondo Beach, and soon moved to Westchester. Those two, along with Nichol and Portz, attended Westchester High School. Tucker and Murray were also from the same area.

- In The Mamas and the Papas, only Michelle Phillips was from Southern California. Cass and John both went to high school in Alexandria, Virginia. Denny was from Nova Scotia, Canada.

- The Rolling Stones formed in London. Mick Jagger and Keith Richards were the only two that knew each other from earlier years. They were both born in Dartford, Kent, England, but went to different schools after primary school. Jones was born in Cheltenham, England. Wyman was born in Penge, Kent, England. Watts was born in London.

Hard to Discern Lyrics:

- "Woodstock" (Crosby Stills Nash and Young): "We are stardust. We are golden. *We are billion-year-old carbon.* And we've got to get ourselves back to the garden" for the first three choruses, and "*We are caught in the devil's bargain*" for the fourth.

- "Help Me Rhonda" (Beach Boys): First line: "*Since she put me down, I've been out doing in my head.*"

- "Chimes of Freedom" (Byrds): First line: "*For between sundown's finish, and midnight's broken toll.*"

- "Hard Day's Night" (Beatles): "You're gonna give me everything. *So why on earth should I moan?* 'Cause when I get you alone...."

- "Slow Down" (Beatles): "Carry her books home, too. *But now you've got a boyfriend down the street.* Baby, what you trying to do?"

- "I Get Around" (Beach Boys): "Get around round round. I get around. *From town to town.* Get around round round I get around. *I'm a real cool head.* Get around round round I get around. *I'm makin' real good bread*" (Brian had recently purchased a bakery☺).

- The most difficult of all is "Get Off of My Cloud" (Rolling Stones). "Then in files a guy who's all dressed up like a Union Jack and says, '*I've won five pounds if I have his kind of detergent pack.*' Next is, "I laid myself out, I was so tired and I started to dream. *In the morning, the parking tickets were just like flags stuck on my window screen.*" Also from the Rolling Stones is the first line of "Brown Sugar," "Gold Coast slave ship bound for cotton fields."

English Accents:

The age-old question of why English singers do not have an English accent while singing has various answers. The best answer is that part of singing has always been mimicking. The earliest rock-and-roll records heard in England were from the United States. In the same line, country music singers have the same twang, whether they are from the South or not. There are also no real regional singing dialects in the United States, though LeVon Helm of the Band comes the closest. Musicians have their own singing "language."

The Irish Rovers had a distinct Irish accent, however. Petula Clark also let a few British sounds come through like "grahs" for grass, "cahn't" for "can't," and "ahsk" for "ask."

Two words that do survive as British sounds are been ("bean") and again (a gain).

When one hears Mick Jagger being interviewed, he will pronounce "cahn't," but in the song "(I Can't Get No) Satisfaction," it becomes "can't"; it's the same when "bond" becomes "band" in "Sgt. Pepper's Lonely Hearts Club Band," and "hahd" becomes "hard" in "Hard Days Night."

Another theory is that vowels, when sung, sound the same. However, this does not explain the "r's" that are dropped in British speech, if it does not start a syllable. For example, the "r" is dropped in "word," but not in the Beatles song "The Word"; same for "work" in the Beatles' "We Can Work It Out"; and "better," pronounced "bettah" in British speech, but not in "It's Getting Better All the Time."

The same phenomenon is true for many lyrics. For example the U.S. word "pennies" is used, rather than the UK word "pence," in the Beatles' "Taxman"; in The Rolling Stones' "19th Nervous Breakdown," "dollars" is used instead of "pounds."

Entertainers or Musicians?

Songwriting is a much rarer, and more valuable, talent than singing. For every singer that makes it big, there are probably thousands with a fraction less talent, connections, or luck, that were very close to doing the same. An excellent songwriter should be able to find numerous singers to perform his work.

"You can be a great singer from here to hell and back, but unless you have the material, you're just standing there," said Cass Elliott of the Mamas and the Papas. "John (Phillips) is a great, great songwriter."

Are singers who play no instruments and write no songs more accurately entertainers than musicians? Obviously, anyone who sings *is* a musician. However, singers-only often rely significantly on visual effects, like stage antics and charisma. No matter how much talent they had as singers, Frank Sinatra and Elvis Presley are not in the same musical class as the top songwriters; same with Barbra Streisand, Cher, and Michelle Phillips. They relied at least as much on charisma as musical talent. The latter two became famous singers without having any musical background, as did Jones and Dolenz of the Monkees. Songwriters do not start from scratch, without some type of a musical background. Lennon and McCartney had no academic music training, but were instrumentalists before they became songwriters. While singers-only often also go into acting, it is rare that a songwriter will do the same.

Who would you rather listen to, Elvis Presley singing songs that he had written, or Jimmy Webb singing songs that he had written?

It seems as if the concerts during the era were primarily for music, while in later years, there were a lot of extras, such as pyrotechnics, added, and much more activity onstage, such as costume and gimmicks. Mick Jagger, prancing around onstage and moving his arms, does nothing for a lot of people. The Doors' music was certainly good enough without Jim Morrison's drunken stage performances. The audience dancing and clapping their hands over their heads, thankfully, seems to have started after this era.

Go-go dancers were the one exception to this. These were woman dancers with mini-skirts and go-go boots who danced on stage behind, or to the side of, the musicians on television shows. These, along with the screaming female fans, completely died out by 1967, when the music became more serious.

The lead singer is the most recognizable sound from a group, and later "patch-up" versions of original groups can be poor, if they do not contain the lead singer. For example, when two of the Lovin' Spoonful's members, drummer Joe Butler and bass player Steve Boone, performed Lovin' Spoonful songs, the result could only be described as "awful." Any four people out of an audience with reasonable musical talent could have done as well. There was a "Byrds" band touring in the late 1980s whose only original member was drummer Mike Clarke. (That is the topic of another book: who ends up with the legal ownership of a group's name? Clarke actually owned the name "Byrds." Also, how do members of a group split up revenues? How much did John Fogerty earn, compared with the other three?)

A group could replace anyone but a singer and a lead guitarist and most people could not tell the difference. How many listeners, at the time, could tell that Bill Wyman did not play bass on ten of the eighteen songs on *Exile on Main Street*.

Lip Synching:

Lip synching, unfortunately, was commonplace during this era. There were two reasons for this:

- Poor acoustics where the group was playing, and
- Poor musicianship, which made it impossible to recreate the studio sound on the stage.

The Beatles rarely lip synched (they did on "Hello Goodbye" and "I Am The Walrus"), and the Doors never did. I cannot picture Jim Morrison lip synching. The Dave Clark Five and the Mamas and the Papas almost always did. The latter did because only John Phillips played an instrument and they did not have stage musicians. The worst example of the lip synch was the Yardbirds' "Heart Full of Soul" on the *Shindig* show, two years after it was released, in which Jimmy Page played guitar, when Jeff Beck had been the studio guitarist. Also, on many lip synchs, there are instruments heard that are not on stage

Musicians as Athletes:

Musicians are not known for being well coordinated and rarely are they good athletes. Think back. How many band members also played a sport? Exceptions include the following: Brian Wilson played football and baseball and knew Al Jardine from the football team. James Brown was a professional bantamweight fighter. Dave Clark was a soccer player. Bobby Hatfield earned a baseball tryout with the Dodgers. Kris Kristofferson played football in high school. Rod Stewart played soccer. Jackie Wilson was a Golden Gloves boxer. Mark Farner was a football player until an injury at age fifteen. Ginger Baker was a racing cyclist. Going in the reverse direction, two major league athletes who were professional musicians were Mike Reid and Denny McLain, both pianists.

Diversity:

To use a current-day buzzword, there was little “diversity” in music of this era. There were no white, all-girl groups. In fact, there were very few women in any groups. Joni Mitchell and Grace Slick were the only singer/songwriters, and only Mitchell played an instrument In fact, she is the only female on the current *Rolling Stone* list of top 100 guitarists of any era.

Some multi-racial groups were Love, Sly and the Family Stone, CSNY, who used Greg Reeves briefly as a bass player, Jimi Hendrix Experience, and Booker T. and the MG’s. Hendrix played almost exclusively to white audiences.

The attendance at all the music festivals was hardly diversified, either. The audiences were almost entirely made up of middle- to upper-class whites who had attended, or were attending, college.

Record Turntable Speeds:

Records players usually had four turntable speeds in the mid-1960s. For the spoken word, where sound quality is not as important, 16 2/3 RPM was used. Formal standardization at 78.26 RPM (shown as 78 on the turntable and applied to a ten-inch diameter record) didn't come until 1925. In 1931, RCA Victor badly bungled an attempt to put a cheap, imperfect 33-1/3 system on the mass market, and no one tried it again until 1948. Columbia called these records "long playing" or "LPs." To compete with Columbia, RCA put out the first 45 RPM, also in 1948. The 78 was defunct by 1950, while the 45 (with a seven-inch diameter) was used for singles, and the 33-1/3 (with a twelve-inch diameter) for albums. These two formats remained until the late 1980s, when compact discs arrived.

The Eight-track Tape:

There was also a music format called an eight-track tape player, which appeared about 1968. This played an endless magnetic tape, enclosed inside of a rectangular container. There were four separate music programs, each having a two-part stereo. There was a button to push to move from one track to another. Pushing the button four times would get you back to where you started. It was impossible to skip over just one song or start the tape on a certain song. After some wear or misalignment, it would play two songs at once. Fortunately, this format mostly died out a few years later.

Some Surprising Comments From Fan Magazines

Dino, Desi & Billy

16 Magazine, July 1965

~~group?~~ . . . The groups to watch on the rise in England are WAYNE FONTANA AND THE MINDBENDERS and the GONKS . . . My special fave is attractive (and what a voice!) GEORGIE FAME. He is going to be IT, chickies!

16 Magazine, May 1965

To squelch another rumor — The Monkees DO sing & play on their own records — I know, I've been to their sessions. PHIL OCHS' first single record, Cross My Heart, is gonna be the living end — as is TERRY MELCHER's recording of Phil's tune, Miranda. If either of them ever get released by these two perfectionists!

16 Magazine, February 1967

CAN YOU DIG IT??? Mick's and John's clothes are the freakiest and grooviest gear on the scene. They have been recording together recently, which should produce some wild sounds.

(Jagger and Lennon) *Tiger Beat*, October 1967

Keith Allison

Ian Whitcomb

From *16 Magazine* (various)

Some Fan Clubs You Might Have Missed

From *16 Magazine*

MIKE CLIFFORD FAN CLUB
Kathie Rantz
2010 Elkins Place
Arcadia, Calif. 91006

WAYNE FONTANA FAN CLUB
c/o Stuart Martin
8 Capel Road
Lawrence Weston,
Bristol, England

THE BARBARIANS FAN CLUB
c/o Verne Drew
Box 152
Fort Montgomery,
New York 10922

THE LEWIS & CLARKE
EXPEDITION FAN CLUB
Box 928, Radio City Station
New York, N. Y. 10019

JOHNNY MAESTRO FAN CLUB
c/o Glenda Kaufman
1171 Leland Ave.
Bronx, New York 10472

THE WILD ONES FAN CLUB
c/o Tina Parascondola
1342 West 7th St.
Brooklyn, New York

THE GREAT NEW
PETER & GORDON FAN CLUB
NATIONAL HEADQUARTERS
Suite 236, 2770 Belknap N.E.
Grand Rapids, Mich. 49505

PHILLIP ALFORD FAN CLUB
c/o Universal-International
Studios
University City, Calif.

Replacing the "Old Insignificant" Peter & Gordon Fan Club

CRYAN' SHAMES FAN CLUB
c/o Nikki
P.O. Box 136
Hinsdale, Ill.

ROGER EWING FAN CLUB
CBS-Studio Cntr.
4024 Radford
Studio City, Calif.

TONY & THE TIGERS FAN CLUB
Carolyn McCombs
146-16 123rd Ave.
South Ozone Park, N.Y.

Chapter Fourteen

Music Festivals

Monterey International Pop Music Festival

June 16-18, 1967; Monterey County Fairgrounds, Monterey, California

The music here was the best and some previously unknown groups that were "introduced" here went on to great success including: the Who, Jimi Hendrix Experience, and Big Brother and the Holding Company (mainly Janis Joplin). Otis Redding would have gone on to the same type of success, but unfortunately was killed in a plane crash in December 1967. Plus, the festival was centered more on music than on being a gathering of people watching each other. It was civilized, and people actually sat on folding chairs.

The Who had begun releasing music two years earlier in the UK. "I Can't Explain" (peaking at number eight), "Anyway Anyhow" (number ten), "My Generation" (number two), "Substitute" (number five), "I'm a Boy" (number two), "Happy Jack" (number three), and "Pictures of Lily" (number four) were all hits in the UK prior to Monterey. After that, they had sixteen top-forty songs in the U.S., the most successful being "I Can See for Miles," which reached number nine. They were a more successful album group, selling twenty million, which is number 105 all time.

Jimi Hendrix had been performing in the UK since September 1966, and Monterey was his first journey back home. Janis Joplin, who many considered the best of the Monterey performers, had signed with Big Brother a year earlier, but the group had not released anything.

What was the point of Hendrix and Townshend smashing instruments? I guess, at that point, the shock value of long hair was wearing off, and some musicians felt the need to draw attention to themselves with stage theatrics, which would imply that their music was not good enough. The music was good enough, however. Townshend took a long time to outgrow that nonsense. Each time it happens, it loses some of its effect, and then something else must be dreamt up. Some of the audience is there, though, just to see the theatrics, like hockey fans attending just to see a fight.

The festival was the first of its kind, a true original. There were only seven thousand seats (at the Monterey County Fairgrounds), but there were a total of two hundred thousand people in and out of the fairgrounds. The groups performed for free. For Hendrix, Joplin, Redding, and the Who, it was still a huge bargain, as no amount of money could have produced the exposure that they received.

David Crosby was a loudmouth at Monterey, strutting around on stage like a peacock.

Crosby said, "They are shooting this for television. I'm sure they will edit it out. I want to say this anyway, even though they will edit it out. When President Kennedy was killed, he was not killed by one man. He was shot from a number of different directions, by different guns. The story has been suppressed. Witnesses have been killed, and this is your country, ladies and gentlemen."

Lou Adler responded, "Vintage Crosby regarding Kennedy and the assassination. People hadn't had the forum yet to speak out in that manner and have it heard by that many people." Sure they had. However, in the past, musicians did not feel compelled to tell the audience what their political opinions were.

> Roger McGuinn gave a more realistic response, "I think David was just trying to be hip. Come on. Give me a break. We all knew that. He didn't know anything more than anyone else. He was just being Mr. Cool up there. I resented it, frankly."

Crosby again put his foot into his mouth two years later. On the Dick Cavett Show, right after Woodstock, he wished that seven major automobile and oil companies would go out of business because of the air pollution they caused. Four of them were show sponsors. He also got into an argument with the Ed Sullivan producer (Ed's son-in-law), which meant they were never invited back. Chris Hillman commented, "David was the cause of ninety-nine percent of the bad business moves in the Byrds."

Ravi Shankar played his sitar for three hours on Sunday afternoon and was the only musician who was paid. No question that Shankar was an influence on George Harrison, and it was very chic to say that his performance was the highlight of the festival, but how many people *really* preferred his music to the other performers, especially three-hours worth? How popular was his "no drugs" position?

The recording of his three-hour performance was released as a triple "concept" album, and a shortened two-and-one-half-minute version was released as a single. These two only charted in India☺.

> Pete Townshend said, "Our anger was not all our own anger; our anger was a reflection of the anger in the audience." How does he know what the anger level is in an audience of seven thousand? How many people did he interview?

> Jerry Garcia explained, "There is a community. We are all the people who are the weird ones, all of a sudden you discover people who are like you; like the beatniks."

That was a huge drawing card for most music, and any counterculture-type events. They had never been together with as many people with their looks and ideals.

Michael Bloomfield said, "Monterey is very groovy, man. This is something, man. This is our generation, man. All you people, we are all together, man. It is groovy. Dig yourselves, it is groovy."

Dionne Warwick, the Impressions (featuring Curtis Mayfield), and the Beach Boys were all scheduled to appear at the festival but dropped out at the last minute. (Brian Wilson decided that the Beach Boys were not hip enough.) Chuck Berry was also invited to perform, but refused to come because he would not be paid.

During Ravi Shankar's performance, was she in deep meditation or sleeping?

Performers (In order)

Friday Night

© Elaine Mayes and Britannia Press

The Association

(the last time any group was seen in coats and ties?)

Since they were one of the most anonymous groups, it was difficult for me to research who was who, as none of their albums that I know of provided names with faces. Left to right: Larry Ramos, Jim Yester, Russ Giguere, Terry Kirkman, Brian Cole. Ted Bluechel (not pictured) was the drummer. Jules Alexander had temporarily left the group to "find himself" in India.

The Paupers

Lou Rawls

Johnny Rivers

The Animals

Simon and Garfunkel

Saturday Afternoon

Canned Heat (had not released an album yet)

Big Brother and the Holding Company (hard to believe, but guitarist Sam Andrews sang lead on "Combination of the Two")

Country Joe and the Fish

Al Kooper

Butterfield Blues Band

Quicksilver Messenger Service

Steve Miller Blues Band

Electric Flag

Saturday Night

Moby Grape

Hugh Masekela

The Byrds

Laura Nyro

Jefferson Airplane

Booker T and the MGs

Otis Redding

Sunday Afternoon

Ravi Shankar

Sunday Night

Blues Project

Big Brother and the Holding Company (brought back for an encore)

The Group with No Name (self contradictory)

Buffalo Springfield

The Who

Jerry Garcia

Jimi Hendrix photographed as just another spectator prior to his act

These pictures are from an excellent photo book on Monterey, *It Happened in Monterey*.

Scott McKenzie

The Mamas and the Papas (second-to-last live performance)

Woodstock

Friday, August 15-17, 1969; Bethel, New York

A three-day ticket was $24. With four hundred thousand people, this should have raised $9.6 million. However, it became impractical to collect money, as fans were climbing over the fences, and it became a "free concert." The only revenues were from tickets purchased before the event, which amounted to $1.1 million. (These three amounts in 2004 dollars are $120, $48 million and $5.5 million, respectively.) Abbie Hoffman and Paul Krassner handed out thousands of fliers urging guests not to pay the admission fees.

When Hoffman, Yippie (member of the Youth International Party, an informal counterculture political organization) and political activist, took the stage and grabbed a microphone, Pete Townshend literally kicked his ass and Hoffman fell off the stage. Hoffman screamed at the Who, but no one could hear him because of the loud music.

To the attendees' credit, there was no violence. The drugs of choice were LSD and marijuana, neither of which induces violence. If the chic drug were alcohol, it would have been an entirely different story.

> Michael Lang, an organizer: "You see how they function on their own, without cops, without guns, without clubs, without hassles, everybody pulls together, and everybody helps each other. It has been working since we got here, and will continue working when we go back. This thing is happening."

The festival got off to rough start. The scheduled starting time was four in the afternoon. However, the performers were spread around in hotels miles from the site. Because of the traffic jam, the promoters were frantically contracting for helicopters to shuttle in the performers and supplies. But the helicopters were late. A four-seater finally arrived after four o'clock; it could handle only single acts. Lang had two choices: Hardin, who was drifting around backstage stoned, or Richie Havens, who looked ready. Three days of music started at 5:07 p.m. Eastern Daylight Time on August 15, 1969, with Richie Havens. Every time Havens tried to quit playing, he was coaxed into continuing. The other acts hadn't arrived. Finally, Havens had played for nearly three hours (!) — improvising his last song, "Freedom."

> The most profound response during the Woodstock movie was to the following question, "What is it that the musicians have that they can communicate so well to the kids?"
> Michael Lang answered, "Music."
>
> John Sebastian said, "This is really a mind-f_____ of all times, man. I have never seen anything like this, man. Wow, just love everybody around you, and clean up a little garbage on your way out. There is a cat whose old lady had a baby, and it made me think that this really is a city. This is for you and your old lady, and whew, the kid is going to be far out."
>
> (A more mature Sebastian had this to say about the Lovin' Spoonful many years later: "We were accused of optimism. We did not want to have any part of 'I kind of have my toe in pop music, but I really have a concern for international affairs.' We are entertainers. What kind of insight are you going to get from us? The protest movement was done well by Bob Dylan, but not necessarily by the second tier after him.")

Woodstock did not launch any new music stars, but the festival, and especially the movie, did wonders for the fame of many of the groups (much more than Monterey Pop). This book's survey showed that if there were no Woodstock movie, the portion of people who would have heard of Joe Cocker was sixty-six percent, Country Joe and the Fish, forty-eight percent; Ten Years After, forty-five percent; and Richie Havens, forty-one percent. There were quite a few other groups that remained obscure because they were not featured in the movie.

Arlo Guthrie got a boost from the movie, but was better known than those above, largely from having a famous father.

> Guthrie: "I don't know like how many of you can dig how many people there are, man. Like, I was rapping with the fuzz. Can you dig it? There are supposed to be a million and a half people here by tonight. Yeah, it's far out, man."

> Country Joe McDonald believed that his fate was sealed right after he shouted: "Gimme an F." McDonald said, "After the movie came out, that's all I was known for. ... It's pretty hard to top the 'Fish Cheer.' I don't know if I can do that."

What did he expect? That act ranked in the same juvenile category as the destruction of instruments at Monterey. However, McDonald did not have near the commercial success that Hendrix and the Who had.

By the 1980s, McDonald said he was done with the music business. "I won't make another record again unless it seems commercially viable," he said in 1989.

> McDonald continued, "I just don't have the burning desire to make a record that nobody wants to hear. You spend a year to do it, and it doesn't sell more than one thousand copies. That's not cost-effective. Music is something that needs to be heard."

> McDonald said the problem was that he was still writing "sociopolitical and anti-war" songs.

> McDonald also said, "Today, politics and war isn't good box office. I don't like doing these nostalgia things, but when people offer me the right amount of money, I'll do it. I wouldn't even write a story about myself. I wouldn't waste my time."

By 1991, the year he recorded an acoustic album, *Superstitious Blues*, McDonald had changed his tune. In 1994, he appeared in a Pepsi commercial featuring a Woodstock reunion for yuppies. Sounds like someone who got in touch with reality at an advanced age.

> Artie Kornfeld, another organizer admitted, "Financially, this is a disaster."
>
> An interviewer asked, "Then why do you look so happy?"
>
> Kornfeld explained, "It has nothing to do with money, nothing to do with tangible things."
>
> Michael Lang also said, "Financially, this is a disaster."
>
> The interviewer commented, "You look so happy."
>
> Lang replied, "I am very happy. You could not buy that for anything. It has nothing to do with money. These people are communicating with each other."
>
> The interviewer reminded him, "You have to make $2 million to break even?"
>
> Lang insisted, "The point is that it is happening, and that is enough for now."

Yeah, right. Of course it has nothing to do with money for them, because they were not paying the $2 million costs to run the festival. If it had nothing to do with tangible things, there would be no sound system, land lease, food, water, restrooms, stage, paid musicians (all of them), security, etc. Jimi Hendrix was the top-paid performer at $18,000, and the land lease cost $50,000, plus a $75,000 deposit to cover damages.

> The announcer told the crowd, "It is a free concert from now on. We are going to put the music up here for free. The people who put up the money for it are going to take

> a bit of a bath, a big bath. They are going to get hurt. These people have it in their heads that your welfare is hell of a lot more important, and so is the music, than a dollar." The financial backers had no choice.

When Woodstock became a "free" festival, this, of course, did not apply to the performers. When groups refused to go onstage without being paid their full fee (the groups had received a small amount up-front, but much less than the standard fifty percent), they were threatened by the promoters that an announcement would be made about the situation. The groups certainly did not want to be seen as greedy. However, the promoters also had reasons not to upset the crowd, including destruction of all the equipment ("peace and love" had its limits). The management of the Who held firm, and was paid the remaining $11,200 fee ($1,300 was paid in advance) with a certified check at 3:30 a.m., from financial backer Joel Rosenman. Michael Lang was nowhere to be seen, as he did not want to be bothered with paying the performers.

John Roberts was the other brave individual who risked his own money to finance Woodstock Ventures, the business that funded the festival. Without him, there would have been no festival. Woodstock Ventures got into financial difficulty because there were two people spending money who had no incentive to control costs. Kornfeld's promotional expenses were more than $150,000, seventy percent over budget. Lang's production expenses had soared to $2 million, more than three hundred percent over budget.

> Lang recalled, "My idea was just to get it done, whatever it took. We had a vision, and it all came true. I made a decision that we needed three major acts, and I told them I didn't care what it cost. If they had been asking $5,000, I'd say, 'Pay 'em $10,000.' So we paid the deposits, signed the contracts, and that was it, instant credibility."

> To convert the above dollar amounts to 2004 dollars, multiply by five.

Woodstock Ventures paid bands money unheard of in 1969. Bands were reluctant to sign up with an unknown entity, but the big breakthrough came with the signing of the top psychedelic band of the day, the Jefferson Airplane, for the incredible sum of $12,000. The Airplane usually took gigs for $5,000 to $6,000. Creedence Clearwater Revival signed for $11,500.

Woodstock Ventures spent $100,000 to clean the trashed festival site. Not many people heeded John Sebastian's advice about picking up trash. A huge hole was dug and filled with tons of shoes, bottles, papers, clothes, tents, and plastic sheets, which were burned. The smoke that lasted for days brought Ventures a charge of illegal burning from Bethel officials.

A local banker, Charlie Prince, went way out on a limb and extended $250,000 of credit to Woodstock Ventures at a crucial time. Because additional ticket revenues were not coming in, and some acts (Janis Joplin, the Who, and the Grateful Dead) refused to perform until they were paid, the festival could not continue without more money.

Organizers Roberts, Lang, Kornfeld, and Rosenman had made personal guarantees to pay the bills. But only Roberts' family had enough assets to pay off Woodstock's debt, and did. Roberts' father and brother told the Wall Street bankers that they never had run out on debts and they weren't going to start now.

The following were at both Monterey and Woodstock:

- Stephen Stills
- David Crosby
- Country Joe and the Fish
- Ravi Shankar
- Janis Joplin
- Jefferson Airplane
- Jimi Hendrix
- Canned Heat
- Grateful Dead
- The Who

Performers: (In order)

Friday

Richie Havens

Sweetwater (the movie advertisement says that they were the first "band" to appear)

Bert Sommer

Swami Satchadinanda

Tim Hardin

Ravi Shankar (a bearable fifty-five minutes because he was stopped by the rain)

Melanie

Arlo Guthrie

Joan Baez

Saturday

Quill

Country Joe McDonald

John Sebastian

Keef Hartley Band

Santana

Incredible String Band

Canned Heat (rare obscure group with two lead singers,

Bob Hite and Al Wilson; Wilson has the falsetto voice, and Hite the raspy one)

Creedence Clearwater Revival (eleven songs)

Janis Joplin

Sly and the Family Stone

The Who

Jefferson Airplane

Sunday

Joe Cocker

Country Joe and the Fish

Mountain

Ten Years After

The Band

Johnny Winter

Crosby Stills Nash and Young (sixteen songs)

Early Monday Morning

Paul Butterfield Blues Band

Sha-Na-Na

Jimi Hendrix (there were only about thirty thousand people left for his performance)

- Iron Butterfly was scheduled, but got stuck at the airport

Isle of Wight (1970)

Wednesday, August 26-30, 1970; UK

This was the largest of them all, with six hundred thousand in attendance. The island, of course, could only be accessed by boat. The crowd was a much angrier one than at Woodstock. At Woodstock, there were no ticket booths set up; it was impractical to sell tickets and it quickly became a free concert. At Isle of Wight, there were barricades set up, police dogs, and more visible security.

There were many there who wished to attend, but did not want to pay the fee. There was a class warfare-type anger from those outside the fences. They had shown up expecting to get something for nothing (three pounds was the entrance fee). They were not in the least bit interested that these festivals cost a huge amount of money to put on, that the musicians were paid a big part of that, and they would have to be paid before they would perform.

Tiny Tim wanted the event to be free, but, of course, insisted on being paid.

> Here is a comment from someone on the outside: "Power to the people, mother-f______. I have been to Woodstock, and I dug it very much. I have been to about ten f______ _ festivals and I love music. I just think one thing — this festival business is becoming a psychedelic concentration camp where people are being exploited, and there is enough of that. What is all this peace and love s___, when you have police dogs out there? What about that? That reminds me of a lot of bad things, you know. I do not like police dogs."

Performers: (In order)

Wednesday, August 26

Judas Jump

Kathy Smith

Rosalie Sorrels

David Bromberg

Redbone

Kris Kristofferson

Mighty Baby

Thursday, August 27

Gary Farr

Supertramp

Andy Roberts Everyone

Howl

Black Widow

Groundhogs

Terry Reid

Gilberto Gil (or was it Gil Gilberto? ☺)

Friday, August 28

Fairfield Parlour

Arrival

Lighthouse

Taste

Tony Joe White

Chicago

Family

Procol Harum

The Voices of East Harlem

Cactus

So far not an impressive lineup, but wait …

Saturday, August 29

John Sebastian

Shawn Phillips

Lighthouse

Joni Mitchell

Tiny Tim

Miles Davis

Ten Years After

Emerson Lake and Palmer

The Doors (last live appearance)

The Who

Melanie

Sly and the Family Stone

Sunday, August 30

Good News

Kris Kristofferson

Ralph McTell

Heaven

Free

Donovan

Pentangle

Moody Blues

Jethro Tull

Jimi Hendrix (died eighteen days later)

Joan Baez

Leonard Cohen

Richie Havens

Hawkwind

The Social Movement

Chapter Fifteen

Relationship between the Music and the Social Movement

Background

During the twentieth century, the original word for those who rebelled against society's norms was "bohemian," which originated in the 1920s. The word came from the Bohemia area of Czechoslovakia, where Gypsies came from. The word "beat" originally meant "robbed" or "cheated" (as in a "beat" deal), and had nothing to do with music. Herbert Huncke picked up the word from his show business friends on the Near North Side of Chicago, and in fall 1945, he introduced the word to William Burroughs, Allen Ginsberg and Jack Kerouac. From this came the "beat generation." This was first used in the late 1940s as slang for young people who were exhausted or "beat down." The movement was also said to originate from Eastern religion, where "beat" came from beatitude that could be discovered through Zen Buddhism. It was a relatively small group of struggling writers, artists, and drug addicts who felt out of the mainstream of society. The word "generation" was probably used to make the group seem larger than it actually was.

San Francisco columnist Herb Cain added the suffix "nik," supposedly related to a Russian or communist influence, in the late 1950s. They were known for unkempt appearance, bongo playing, and poetry reading. A popular hangout was the North Beach area of San Francisco.

Folk music, a dominant form of music prior to 1964, and left-wing politics have always had a strong connection in the twentieth century. The marriage began when Joe Hill ("I dreamed I saw Joe Hill last night") adjusted old folk songs and hymns into pro-labor music that was used to rally workers into joining unions in the 1910s. The term "folk music" had previously meant songs with no known origin or author, but that changed with Woody Guthrie. It has always been a left-wing movement from Guthrie to Pete ("If I Had a Hammer" [and sickle]) Seeger to Bob Dylan (at first). There is no question that the two kingpins of folk music, Woody Guthrie and Seeger, were Socialists. (John Sebastian correctly used the term "Commie Folk Singers.") Guthrie had applied for Communist Party membership in 1943, but was turned down because of personal unreliability and his rejection of any authority. Irwin Silber recalled that "the puritanical nearsighted left…didn't quite know what to make of this strange, bemused poet who drank and bummed and chased after women and spoke in syllables dreadful strange…they never really accepted the man himself."

On Guthrie's guitar were the words "This Machine Kills Fascists," and should have included that it was sympathetically favored toward another totalitarian regime, communism. Maybe there was not enough space.

Guthrie portrayed Jesus as a "Socialist outlaw" and tended to glamorize crime, gambling, and drinking. He enjoyed hating and tormenting his class enemies, the rich, and police and security guards.

> "The honest and hungry prophets raving and snorting and ripping into the bellies of the rich and powerful rulers and lying priests who beat their people into slavery and dope them with superstitions and false ceremonies and dictate to them what to do, where to go, what to read, who to love, what to eat, what do drink, what to wear, when to work, when to rest, and where to bring your money." Guthrie.

He was talking about the United States, but it sounds to me more like his beloved Soviet Union.

> Seeger did join the Communist Party in 1942. "I *like to say I'm more conservative than Goldwater. He just wanted to turn the clock back to when there was no income tax. I want to turn the clock back to when people lived in small villages and took care of each other.*"

Fine, in a free country one can move to a small village and take care of whomever he wants. However, his idea is to force everyone else to do the same.

Because the terms "left wing" and "right wing" mean so many things to so many different people, for the purposes of this book they are defined below. I have avoided the terms "liberal" and "conservative" because the current usage is so very different from the dictionary definition.

> Left-wing: People who favor civil liberties (freedom to use any drugs, engage in activities that others might deem to be immoral, and be uncensored. This does not include theft, or anything else that infringes on others' freedoms), but despise certain economic liberties (some voluntary exchanges, disparity in wealth, free trade among nations, people keeping what they earn). [Examples: most Democrats, but most in public office are moderate on social issues — drug legalization is almost never mentioned; most university professors and economic textbook authors; Paul Krugman.] The Far Left are also called "radicals" or "Socialists," and are labeled that way because of their views on economic liberties.

> Right-wing: People who want to restrict civil liberties, but favor economic liberty. (Examples: most Republicans, but almost all in office are moderate on economic issues — including George W. Bush; many Christian groups, who usually focus on restriction of personal liberties.) Most people identified as Far Right are labeled that way because of their views on civil liberties, not economic ones.

Both groups claim to favor "freedom" and accentuate the other's opposition to the same. The left wing included social activists that hated the oppression of any minority group and war, and despised "social injustice," which also included an unequal distribution of wealth, which, in theory, could be dismissed through socialism. (In practice, the ones who do the distributing end up with all the money.)

Both groups claim that the other tries to force its morality on everyone else. The right wing tries to impose its religious beliefs on others through laws. The left wing's belief that disparity of wealth and income (CEO pay, etc.) is immoral and tries to impose those beliefs through forced income re-distribution.

One who believes in both civil and economic liberties is a libertarian. (Examples: Ron Paul is one of the few in the current political arena, but Jefferson, Madison, Adams, and other Founding Fathers definitely were; Milton Friedman, Walter Williams, and a few other economists.) One who believes in neither freedom is an authoritarian. (Examples: Adolph Hitler, Josef Stalin, and most other dictators, especially with theocracies. To a much lesser degree, Richard Nixon).

Prior to 1960, the main left wing activism was through the folk singers railing on disparity of wealth. However, during the next decade, it concentrated on civil liberties and ending the Viet Nam War.

Free Speech Movement

This left-wing idea started at University of California in October 1964, and had *nothing* to do with the First Amendment. This amendment states that no one can be arrested for what he says in speech. It does *not* give the right for anyone to speak wherever he wants, especially on private property. The protesters believed that they were being suppressed from expressing their political freedoms. It started with trapping a police car and giving speeches on top of the car for three days. They were again upset when the political information tables on the corner of Bancroft and

Telegraph were banned. Even though UC Berkeley was a publicly funded university, the property was owned by the university, and was not owned by "the people." The students had a collectivist view that everything was owned by everybody. These young, privileged children actually began to see *themselves* as being oppressed.

They also occupied Sproul Hall before they had to be forcibly evicted. Their self-appointed leader, Mario Savio, tried to speak at a Regents meeting, but was not allowed to because it was not an open meeting. He thought that his free speech rights were being violated. Wrong. How would he have liked it if the University president, Clark Kerr, kept interrupting his private meetings, claiming "free speech" as the reason?

"Anybody who wants to say anything on this campus, just like anybody on the city street, should have the right to do so," Savio declared, "And no concessions by the bureaucracy shall be . . . considered by us, until they include complete freedom of speech!"

Certainly universities, and even state universities, then and now, have a right to regulate the time and place of speech so that "free" speech does not disrupt the university's teaching and research mission. Of course, there is no constitutional right for a mob or even a peaceful student group to take over a piece of property. Like speech, universities can regulate the use of property so that it does not interfere with teaching and research.

Later, in 1969, again at Berkeley, a large group tried to expropriate a piece of land that was purchased the year earlier by the university. It was an eight-block section on Telegraph Avenue, just to the south of the campus. It was previously home to old wooden houses that were rented by hippies and students. These were torn down to make room for student dorms (which were never built). The group wanted the land for concerts and a playground for children, and named it "Peoples' Park." After four weeks, the police bulldozed the improvements, and put up a fence. This led to a violent confrontation between police and students, including burning a police car and a building, and the police using shotguns. At a corresponding student rally, tear gas was dropped by helicopters. In the end, the university took back what was theirs.

Vietnam War and Forward

The escalation of the Vietnam War in 1965 turned the main focus of protest from other social issues to the war. This immediately increased the popularity of the protests by enrolling a huge number of young men who were eligible for the draft, but did not want to fight in a war.

Following are two comments made on the war in 1964, one a correct prognostication, the other a blatant lie. Wayne Morse, after casting one of only two Senate votes against the war resolution, said, "I believe that history will record that we have made a great mistake." Lyndon Johnson, "The role of the United States will remain limited, and I have no intention to have American boys do the fighting of Asian boys."

Beatniks became "hippies" during the middle 1960s, and many moved to the Haight-Ashbury district of San Francisco by 1967, adding long hair to their uniform. The word "hip" meant "characterized by a keen informed awareness of or involvement in the newest developments or styles." (Miriam-Webster Dictionary) The word might have come from describing opium smokers resting on their hips, or as a variant on the word "hep" which means "informed." These "hip" people started calling younger university students who were trying to emulate them "hippies." The word grew to mean everyone in the counterculture. While these people were non-conformists relative to the rest of society, there was a huge conformity within their group, including politics, drugs of choice, and appearance. Communal living, where everyone would share, was in vogue for the hippies.

"Music was the pied piper that led kids off the asphalt and out of the suburbs into some other kind of reality. So we began creating free stores, where the goods were free, and the roles were free. There were free crash pads, free food, and free medical clinics," said activist Peter Coyote. Sounds good, but when the reality set in that in actuality someone had to pay the costs, and it was not free, they were shut down.

This group consisted of many who just wanted to have a good time and get high, and other more serious ones that had a left-wing political agenda. They were much more interested (at least on the surface) in civil liberties than the redistribution of wealth. Occasionally, a redistribution idea, such as "jobs for everyone" or "production for use rather production for profit," would slip through, but this was rare.

There was always a fine line for musicians, especially folk singers, of playing music suited for their esoteric niche, or music that was commercially successful. Many "cult" groups (groups with a small, but very enthusiastic following), or individuals, would look down at commercially successful groups, as if they had "sold out" or that the music could not be that good if it were liked by the masses. Electra Records was one of the few companies that sought out the cult groups. The Doors were with Electra, but with their different sound, were probably initially not thought of as being commercially successful. Electra had folk-cult singers Phil Ochs, Tim Buckley, Tom Paxton, and Tom Rush. Bob Dylan was despised by many folkies when he started playing more commercial music.

The Grateful Dead and the Jefferson Airplane actually did perform free concerts in 1967. However, this type of thing ended about as quickly as the free health clinics and the communes.

Phil Ochs (probably the third most prominent folk singer in the mid-1960s, behind Joan Baez and Bob Dylan, but never commercially successful) complained that Electra was catering to the commercial market, specifically mentioning the Doors. Jac Holtzman, an Electra executive, countered that "Phil should remember that it was the open-mindedness of both Vanguard and Electra that caused him to be heard on records at all, and without censorship of any kind." What business of Ochs was it, anyway, what artists Electra was signing? They were a business, after all, and if all the musicians of theirs had the lack of commercial success of Ochs, they would be out of business.

Ochs had an excellent song, "I Ain't Marchin' Anymore," but it was only released as a single in the UK. His song "Outside of a Small Circle of Friends" would certainly have been a hit, but he included the lyrics "smoking marijuana is more fun than drinking beer," which, of course, blacklisted it on AM radio. It did not help that Bob Dylan criticized Ochs as a "singing journalist."

Frank Zappa was one of the few musicians who did not wish to become commercially popular. Eric Clapton quit the Yardbirds because they were shifting into popular music from the blues he wanted to play, even though he later became commercial.

What started out as peaceful protests turned more violent later in the decade. Groups such as The Weathermen and Students for a Democratic Society favored a violent overthrow of the government.

The 1968 Democratic Convention in Chicago was marred by violence between left-wing protestors and the police. Many musical groups were supposed to have been there, but only Phil Ochs, the Fugs, and the MC5 actually showed up.

Left-wing activists (it seems like activists are always left-wing) were also willing to confront the Democratic Party, as they did in Chicago at the 1968 convention. This would never happen today. Their hatred for Lyndon Johnson and the war offset any favor they showed for increased social programs. Also, they viewed the government as the enemy. Most in the Left today view government as the friend to enact more regulations on capitalism, and redistribute income through the income tax.

These groups continued their violence through the next few years. The Weathermen actually started meetings with all participants taking LSD, based on the idea that no undercover policeman could keep his cover while tripping. LSD had various effects on different users, including violent behavior.

It is ironic that many who despised any type of repression favored a type of government that is the most repressive of all — communism. The "revolution" talked about later in the decade certainly involved overthrowing capitalism with socialism.

Ian McDonald, in *Revolution in the Head*, said, "Much countercultural rhetoric — notably in its airy notion of a money-free, share-all society ('post-scarcity anarchism') — was adolescent nonsense."

Similarities between the counterculture and the musicians

Both the counterculture and the musicians tended to be "outside" the mainstream of society. "Virtually all rock musicians came from the outside of society," Bruce Springsteen once noted. The first time people in the counterculture got together in a large group was the San Francisco "Be-In" in 1966. As Jerry Garcia said, "After the Be-In, there are all these people who were the weird ones like you." Previously feeling isolated, this was an entirely new experience. To this day, the left wing generally is more group-oriented than the right wing.

The Monterey Pop Festival was the first large gathering to hear music performed. Part of the counterculture lifestyle was the music, which certainly separated its members from older people. The music, however, had a much broader appeal than just to this group.

The counterculture wanted to be different, but faced a dilemma. Followers tended to be different in almost the exact same way. They dressed the same, used the same drugs, talked the same, had the same political opinions, favored the same hairstyles, etc. The musicians all had Beatle haircuts (then longer), were clean-shaven (until 1967), (mostly) had two guitars, bass and drums, wore coats and ties (until about 1966), took the same drugs, etc. This "groupthink" still is in existence today. The chances of a band member, today, not having a tattoo and an earring is about the same as a 1967 musician wearing a crew cut.

Protest songs

A linkage between the music of the times and current events was the "protest song." This type of song usually focused on social injustices, not economic ones. Earlier folk songs protested more against economic disparities. Bob Dylan had various songs protesting racial inequality and war prior to 1964. Some songs considered as protest songs after 1963 and what they protested include:

Overtly Protesting:

"Eve of Destruction" (Barry McGuire): War

"Fortunate Son" (Creedence Clearwater Revival): Inheritance. (John Fogerty was not one, but his sons certainly are)

"Ohio" (Crosby Stills Nash Young): Kent State killings

"Imagine" (John Lennon): Religion, wealth disparity, war

"War" (Edwin Starr): War (about as open as it gets)

"I'm Not Marching Anymore" (Phil Ochs): War

"Society's Child" (Janis Ian): Racial intolerance

"Universal Soldier" (Buffy St. Marie): Soldiers. The song did not criticize government, but the actual soldiers. To blame the soldiers, who have almost no choice in the matter, is absurd.

"Taxman" (Beatles): High taxes. The only song that actually protested big government.

Protest Discernable, but More Hidden in the Lyrics:

"Run Through the Jungle" (Creedence Clearwater Revival): Vietnam War (jungle), even though there is nothing explicitly negative said about war.

"My Back Pages" (Bob Dylan): Protest songs

"Who'll Stop the Rain" (Creedence Clearwater Revival): Socialism (five year plans and new deals). Some consider this as an anti-war song, but this is not clear from the lyrics.

"Won't Get Fooled Again" (The Who): Revolution. "Meet the new boss, same as the old boss" indicates the Animal Farm idea that the new leaders are as self-centered as the old leaders. The French and Russian Revolutions are prime examples of this.

More of a commentary on then-current issues and attitudes than a protest

"The Times They Are a-Changin'" (Bob Dylan): No protest here, times are always changing.

"For What It's Worth" (Buffalo Springfield): About youth gathering on Sunset Boulevard, Los Angeles. The idea of the United States becoming a police state was nonsense, though. Compare the action of the police (anywhere except Kent State) to the reaction of a real totalitarian state anywhere else in the world.

"Street Fighting Man" (Rolling Stones): About civil unrest and a suggestion to take up arms. Because of this, many radio stations would not play the song. As with movies and video games, the value of lyrics promoting violence is highly overrated.

"Revolution" (The Beatles): Hate-filled and violent revolution and other people who do not like the way things are, but have no solution. *The Beatles* album version is equivocal about the violent part.

There are many more songs that some would put on the list of protest songs. However, whether a song is truly a protest song is often subjective. The same can be said of lists of songs that promote drug use. For example, the Beatle songs "Lucy in the Sky with Diamonds," "Being for the Benefit of Mr. Kite," "A Day in the Life," "Fixing a Hole," and "With a Little Help from My Friends" were thought to be drug songs, but were not, according to the authors.

John always got a kick out of "pseudo-intellectuals" who over-analyzed his lyrics.

Eight Miles High: The Drug Culture

The establishment drug of choice was alcohol and the new hip drug was marijuana and, later, lysergic acid diethylamide (LSD). These drugs scared the establishment, even though marijuana is less harmful than alcohol in both leading to violence and health problems. (To this day, marijuana is not socially acceptable and is still seen as a counterculture drug, while alcohol is socially acceptable. The term "alcohol and drugs" is commonly used, even though alcohol *is* a drug.) Non-alcohol drug use was glorified. The youth were supposedly using drugs not to temporarily escape their problems, but to expand their minds and for spiritual purposes. Yeah, right. Mind-altering drugs are said to temporarily reduce the intelligence of the user; they make the ordinary seem extraordinary. This is hardly "mind expansion." Illegal drugs were not common among pop musicians in 1964. Bob Dylan was one of the few at that time to use marijuana. Usage was mainly in London, by poets and jazz musicians.

LSD is a powerful hallucinogen that alters the mind's perceptions by removing prior censors. The doses taken back then (100 to 200 micrograms) were up to ten times as strong as the common dose currently taken (20 to 80). Sensations and feelings change much more dramatically than the physical signs. A "trip" causes a person to experience two or more different emotions at once or to swing rapidly from one emotion to another. If taken in a large enough dose, the drug produces delusions and visual hallucinations. The user's sense of time and self changes. Sensations may seem to "cross over," giving the user the feeling of hearing colors and seeing sounds. Hallucinations and vivid colors can also be seen. The drug takes effect between thirty and ninety minutes after it's taken, and the effects last for about twelve hours. A "bad trip" involves anxiety, confusion, psychosis, and panic.

Marijuana is a green, brown, or gray mixture of dried, shredded leaves, stems, seeds, and flowers of the hemp plant. The main active chemical contained is THC (delta-9-tetrahydrocannabinol). The THC content of marijuana has been increasing since the 1970s. The marijuana high is a complex experience, involving a wide range of psychical, physical, and emotional responses, based on one's personality, mood, disposition, and experience with the drug. The intensity of the marijuana high depends primarily on the amount of THC present in the marijuana. "High" experiences can include relaxation, euphoria, uncontrolled laughter, feelings of heightened sensitivity, and a distorted sense of the passage of time. On the negative side, some users feel anxious or paranoid, lose coordination, and have impaired judgment and reasoning skills.

Alcohol was the "establishment drug," but was the favorite of Janis Joplin and Jim Morrison (with heroin being a close second for both).

"Acid is not for every brain. Only the healthy, happy, wholesome, handsome, hopeful, humorous, and high-velocity should seek these experiences. This elitism is totally self-determined. Unless you are self-confident, self-directed, self-selected, please abstain," said Timothy Leary, Harvard University lecturer turned drug guru.

This is the same person who, after breaking out of jail, told the remnants of his audience to get off their "pious, nonviolent asses" and free by force all other incarcerated people in the alternative society.

"All healthy Americans over the age of fourteen should take at least one trip in order to preserve the New Wilderness of machine America as it really was. If there be necessary revolution in America, it will come this way," Leary declared.

George Harrison, in regard to his visit of the Haight-Ashbury district in August, 1967, said, "I expected them to all own little shops. I expected them to be nice and clean and friendly and happy." But what he saw were "hideous, spotty little teenagers" begging him for money and imploring him to play the guitar for them. "I don't mind anybody dropping out of anything. It is the imposition on somebody else that I don't like. The moment you start begging off someone else to help you, then it's no good." The folkies must have been appalled when they heard this comment.

"You had a lot of people talking to posts. They were ripping one another off, because it costs a lot of money, once you get strung out on speed," said Travis Rivers, owner of a psychedelic poster store in the Haight.

Psychedelic music evolved after psychedelic drugs (mind-altering or hallucinogenic, rather than narcotic) became popular. It could either be music created while under the influence of these drugs, or music used to enhance the feeling of being on psychedelics. Jimi Hendrix, Iron Butterfly, and Jefferson Airplane were moguls in this type of music.

Whether "mind-expanding" drugs influenced the music in a positive way is highly questionable, but it sounded good at the time.

Superimposing two identical dubs of the same material played at slightly different tempos resulted in a "whoosh" sound of a jet airplane. This became a staple of psychedelic music. The Beatles' "Blue Jay Way," the Small Faces' "Itchycoo Park" ("I feel inclined to blow my mind" and "It's all too beautiful"), and the Count Five's "Psychotic Reaction" are good examples of this. Jimi Hendrix used this sound (called "phasing"), which he said resembled the underwater sounds that he heard in his dreams.

Also used was the wah-wah pedal to vary the tone of a guitar. Used by Hendrix, and Cream's Eric Clapton in "White Room" and "Tales of Brave Ulysses," it makes the guitar sound "like something is reaching out" (Hendrix).

It became chic in 1967 to call one's own music "psychedelic" and to laud the use of hallucinogenic drugs. However, not all musicians toed the line. Graham Nash said, "Those who use the (hallucinogenic) stuff should know better… It's doing a lot of harm to the entertainment industry." And George Harrison said, "If you are really hip, you don't get involved with LSD."

Glorifying marijuana and psychedelic drugs was commonplace in song lyrics starting in 1966, with the term "getting high" the most frequent reference. Barry Melton, of Country Joe and the Fish, takes credit for his group being the most direct in the drug lyrics. "Other bands alluded to drugs; we talked about them, straight up. The Grateful Dead didn't have any songs that actually directly talked about drugs. If you listen to what's on the first record, there's some stuff there that's fairly shocking for its time. We were talking about weed on the first record, getting high. By the second record, we were singing the LSD commercial. So we were overt. We were the guys who said what other people alluded to. It was right there in the lyric content. Everybody else had the message coded in there."

Also by 1967, there were almost no coats and ties, go-go dancers, uniforms, screaming girls (the Beatles stopped touring), or surf music. John Lennon stopped smiling for pictures. First with The Mamas and the Papas and then with the Beatles, facial hair became chic.

> Jerry Garcia said, "To get really high is to forget yourself. And to forget yourself is to see everything else. And to see everything else is to become an understanding molecule in evolution, a conscious tool in the universe. ... The Grateful Dead is not for cranking out rock-and-roll, it's not for going out and doing concerts or any of that stuff; I think it's to get high."

Prior morals kept sex between married couples only (or at least the non-marital sex was well hidden), while the new "free love" had no boundaries. Jefferson Airplane's Grace Slick said, "It doesn't matter what the lyrics say, or who sings them. They're all the same. They say, "Be free — free in love, free in sex."" Fellow band member Marty Balin said, "The stage is our broad. We are not entertainers, we're making love."

Musicians, along with the elite, tended to overrate the value of lyrics for influencing other people. About seventy-one percent of survey respondents said that lyrics had no influence on them regarding drug use, twenty-nine percent said they had some influence, and zero percent said a lot. To the elite, a memorable "day in their lives" was finding out that *Sgt. Pepper* actually had all the lyrics printed on the album. To many others, it was inconsequential. They were more interested in the music, and were not interested in what hidden, or overt, message the musicians were trying to send.

The matter of musicians giving opinions between songs seems to be more commonplace as time goes on. Musicians, as everyone else, have every right to voice their opinions. However, a music concert is not the right place to do it. A good portion of the audience is there to hear music, not opinions. (Would it be any different if a politician, at a rally, started singing to the crowd on an unrelated subject?) Musicians spout political opinions because they know that a certain portion of the captive audience will cheer whatever they say. There is faulty logic behind this, that if someone is a musical expert, it somehow automatically makes him an expert on other subjects. Unfortunately, the same people who are influenced by lyrics are the ones who turn to musicians for political guidance. As George Harrison once said, "Think for yourself."

Art Linkletter certainly held the belief that most listeners were drooling over each lyric. He claimed his daughter jumped out of a window while on LSD (which was highly questionable), and he blamed it on music lyrics, which included "secret messages to teenagers to drop out, turn on, and groove with chemicals." He might have been right about the lyrics, but it is most likely that many young people would have ingested drugs, lyrics or no lyrics. Also, how many other LSD users jumped out of windows? He also said, "It isn't suicide because she wasn't herself. It was murder. She was murdered by the people who manufacture and sell LSD." Even if she were on LSD, blaming the manufacturer is absurd. Maybe if she had experienced a better home life, she would have stayed away from LSD, despite any lyrics.

Music lyrics tend to follow, not lead, social movements. For example, Bob Dylan said that he just wrote "what is already out there." Marijuana and LSD usage preceded any lyrics referring to them. The anti-war movement came first, then the corresponding song words.

The idea that drug use was propitious seems silly forty years later. Living in communes lost its appeal; no matter how little work one did, he received the same output. This leads to no incentives for the harder workers. Many people who rejected the "establishment" ended up taking white-collar jobs.

- Some drug arrests that amounted to nothing:

May 1967, Mick Jagger and Keith Richards
This was the closest call. They came within a day of having to serve jail time. Jagger was nailed with legally prescribed prescription drugs, and Richard owned the house where marijuana was used. The police waited until George Harrison left the house earlier that day.

May 1967, Brian Jones

July 1967, Steve Boone and Zal Yanofsky

March 1968, Neil Young, Richie Furay, Jim Messina, and Eric Clapton "at a place where it is suspected marijuana is being used"

May 1968, Jimi Hendrix (in court admitted that he had smoked pot four times and hashish five times, taken LSD five times, and sniffed cocaine twice, but had now "outgrown" drugs; December 1969)

May 1968, Brian Jones

October 1968, John Lennon

May 1969, Jimi Hendrix

May 1970, Marty Balin

Life Spans

Did this era's musicians' supposed heavy use of drugs shorten their life span on average? Let's consider this. Thirty-five of the men from the major groups listed in this book have died as of January 2005. Their average life span was 46.7 years. Three of the women (Cass Elliott, Janis Joplin, and Flo Ballard) have died, living an average of 30.7 years. This leaves 216 (eighty-six percent) of the men still alive, with an average age in 2004 of 60.0 years. Using life-expectancy tables, a man sixty years old should live another nineteen years. Eleven (seventy-nine percent) of the women are still alive, with an average age in 2004 age of 62.3 years. Using life-expectancy tables, a woman sixty-two years old should live another twenty-one years. Assuming those now alive will live the expected amount longer, the average male musician lives 75.1 years, and the average female, 71.8 years. This includes both the living and those who have died. In 1965, the average man at age twenty was expected to live another forty-nine years and a woman, fifty-one years. The average male musician is expected to live 6.1 years longer than average, and the average female, 0.2 years shorter. Since 94.7 percent of the musicians are men, the life span of a 1965 musician is 5.8 years *longer* than average. The one assumption in this analysis that may not turn out to be true is that the musician alive today will live as long as others his age, on the average. He might not live as long, or he may live longer. Until everyone dies, there cannot be a final comparison.

Why would most people expect the opposite? As with airplane crashes, the spectacular makes the news, not all the flights that landed safely. Musicians' deaths are highly publicized, but people forget about the vast majority that are still living. (The fact that Brian Wilson, Keith Richards, and David Crosby are alive should be making headlines every day!) There are all kinds of lists of the hundreds of musicians that have died, but there are never lists of the thousands that are still living. Of the four musicians who died before 1972, only one (Janis Joplin) died from a drug overdose.

Censorship

Musicians *hate* censorship. That is just part of the genetic makeup of musicians, as they have an intense need to express themselves. (That same gene also contains an attraction to drug experimentation and addiction.) As with the word "freedom," the word "censorship" is often misused and was a very common word in this era. Censorship is when the *government* suppresses or deletes anything it deems objectionable. No question that real censorship was attempted with "Louie Louie." There were also attempts, but few successes, with other songs. Musicians also hate what is *not* censorship, which is when record stores decide not to carry certain records and record companies don't permit certain songs or lyrics. This is called freedom of choice. They have every right to decide on what to sell or not to sell. They are businesses, and if these types of sales offend prior customers and hurt business, then they have the right to say "no." For example, let's assume that my favorite anthem is the "Fish Cheer," and I think the lyrics send a wholesome message to today's youth. I also own a record company and need to make a decision on whether this song will sell, regardless of what I think of the song. If I decide not to record it, it is hardly censorship. It is the same thing with the Smothers Brothers on CBS. It is common to hear that they were "censored" off the show. Nonsense. CBS probably decided that they were too offensive to some, and it was not profitable to keep them on the show. Even if they were wildly popular, CBS has the right to make any decision it wants.

If real censorship were carried out with music, it would not have worked, anyway. The "Louie Louie" example showed how long and involved a censorship issue can be. What about the between-the-lines messages? Should every song that implies "getting high" be outlawed? Censorship is just an attempt by people to have the government do the job they should be doing as parents. Parents, not the government, should decide what their children can and cannot listen to. If kids have a decent home life, they are not going to be influenced by the "messages" of song lyrics. There is also the buyer's attitude that if there is an attempt to censor something, it will be an encouragement to buy the product.

> Mick Jagger said, "I'm rather pleased to hear they have banned "Street Fighting Man" [on the radio] as long as it's still available in the shops. The last time they banned one of our records in America, it sold a million."

MusicSpeak

Musicians and other musical elite, when interviewed, speak an abstract language that more objective people find difficult to understand. Subtitles should be used during many of these interviews. These musicians, who often use their hands to help explain themselves, usually speak along the same theme and end up sounding the same. The theme is that musicians had previously followed "rules" and anyone who "breaks these rules" is a hero. Here are some examples:

> Paul Kantner said, "Cream came up challenging the musical landscape, making anything possible. The new music is total abandonment, rejecting everything, and looking for something positive and new."
>
> Judy Collins: "One of the things that happened was the rules were being broken. To me, it was the signal that we had now come of age, when Dylan went electric, and now we could do anything and everything, and we did it."
>
> Al Kooper said, "Jimi Hendrix was an envelope pusher. He was kicking, with extreme force, all the boundaries of music."
>
> Pete Townshend said, "The Stones made it dangerous, revolutionary … taking drugs on stage. We were allowed to be angry, the Beatles and Stones had broken enough rules."
>
> Bruce Springsteen said, "All of a sudden, everything is up for grabs."
>
> Bill Flanagan, MTV Networks, said, "'Blue' (Joni Mitchell) turned forever on its head the notion of what a songwriter was expected to be."
>
> Are these people all reading from the same script?
>
> Donovan said, "And how can we convince the sleepers that we are stardust? We all must contemplate the passing of our thought waves, to view the true reality. Be heavenly and turn off your mind for a pause."

> Keith Richards offered a rare counter-argument. "We thought it was a lark; starting treating us as revolutionaries, smoking dope on stage."

There was always an "unwritten rule" that singles could not be more than 2:30 minutes, to facilitate radio airplay. The Animals' "House of the Rising Sun," a number-one single in 1964, lasted 4:28, which proved "the rule" to be a myth, but musicians still talked about playing by this rule until at least 1969. Other pre-1967 hits that were well over 2:30 were "19th Nervous Breakdown" (3:57), "Satisfaction" (3:43), "Turn! Turn! Turn!" (3:52), "Like A Rolling Stone" (5:57), and "Good Vibrations" (3:37). As previously mentioned, almost all groups started with coats and ties, and facial hair was unseen until 1966. In 1967, especially after all four Beatles grew moustaches, facial hair became commonplace (again, the herd mentality). *All* musicians had long hair (for that era). Once the Byrds started performing both folk-rock, and psychedelic rock ("Eight Miles High"), other groups quickly played follow-the-leader. Most groups had two guitars and a bass guitar. (Before the invention of the electric guitar, which certainly helped in the creation of rock-and-roll, the guitar was an obscure, classical instrument, or one played only by folk musicians like Guthrie and Seeger. The guitar is amenable to singing and is portable, which was certainly important to those two.) Singing about the virtues of marijuana and other mind-expanding drugs took the same course. One of the first mentions was "turn me on" in the Beatles' "She's a Woman." Usually, advertising the groovy effects of drugs was mentioned in cryptic form.

Another area where all musicians seem to follow the same script is in admiration of other musicians. They all like the same groups of this era. Probably the number one "musician's musician" is Jimi Hendrix. Three other favorites are the Beatles, Cream, and Bob Dylan. Elvis Presley is also universally admired because he "opened the doors for other musicians and was a true pioneer"; he is admired not so much for his music. Do these musicians all have the same musical taste, or is it more of a "follow-the-herd" mentality?

One group that did not subscribe to the herd mentality was the Band. "The psychedelic craze was in, and we wanted to go against the grain," said Levon Helm. Another who was truly his own person was Frank Zappa. He poked fun at hippies and the elite's favorite Beatle album, *Sgt. Pepper*, and had the nerve to call himself a "devout capitalist." Instead of civil disobedience and property destruction, he favored infiltrating the "establishment." The only drug he used was nicotine. "Americans take drugs as a special excuse to behave as an asshole. Whatever way they misconducted themselves the night before, they'll always have the immediate answer that they were "high" doing it, so they can't be blamed."

Musicians, as with any other group of talented people, will not criticize their own. When they judge another musician, they are usually judging the technical ability, not how much they actually like the music. You would never hear a musician say, "I think so and so is a great guitarist, but I really do not care for his music." When Jimi Hendrix got started in London, Pete Townshend and Eric Clapton were concerned that they would be made obsolete because they felt that Hendrix was such a good guitar player. Wrong. While Hendrix is usually considered the best guitar player (it is all a matter of opinion), the songs he produced were not necessarily the best. Townshend and Clapton might have been knocked down a notch by Hendrix, but they lost nothing from the general music-buying public.

The exceptions to this are musicians who are "breaking the rules." Elvis Presley and Bob Dylan are not considered technically great musicians (especially Presley). However, they were doing things that others were not doing before.

> Paul Robbins of the *Los Angeles Free Press* said, "What the Byrds signify is a concept deeply applied to unification and empathy and a rich joy of life — together with a positive recognition of the bulbous clusters of sickness around us. It represents a passing through negative apathy and an approach into involvement. Dancing with the Byrds

becomes a mystic loss of ego and tangibility; you become pure energy some place between sound and motion and the involvement is total."

David Fricke, *Rolling Stone* magazine senior editor, said, "*Fifth Dimension* (Byrds) is actually a record of considerable beauty and great courage (?), an impressive display of shotgun enthusiasm ... "Eight Miles High's" open-ended, mantra-like lyricism, charged by the jagged modality of McGuinn's solos, shattered the verse-chorus-verse tyranny of top-forty tunecraft and defined the sound and ideal of psychedelia at a time when the Beatles had only just digested the lesson of folk-rock on *Rubber Soul*. That cliffhanging quality of unresolved melodic drama. ..."

Ian McDonald said, "*Tomorrow Never Knows* introduced LSD and Leary's psychedelic revolution to the young of the Western world, becoming one of the most socially influential records the Beatles ever made."

Donovan said, "[*Hurdy Gurdy Man*] is about the loss of the world's wisdom and the "call to awakening." My chord's like a mantra, and in my head I heard power guitar first and wild drums, like Keith Moon of the Who. Ecstatic trance vibes."

Kim Fowley, producer, songwriter, and performer said, "But the critical question remains: What's so important about the Doors? The answer is easy: They were the first band to scare the hell out of us. They mapped out a previously uncharted psychic landscape in rock-and-roll and they discovered that the music could convey the sounds of fear and beauty, passion, liberation, triumph, dementia and dread all at once."

Chuck Crisafulli, *Moonlight Drive* author, said "The Beatles had brought wit and intelligence to pop music, and the

Rolling Stones demonstrated a brash frankness about life in the modern world, but Morrison and the Doors asked rock-and-roll to do some heavy thinking."

David Anderle, an associate of Brian Wilson, said, "The beginning of the moment was a period of creativity that burned and died with supernova brilliance. It was a time when Brian ignored all the limits and boundaries as an artist and was operating in another area of consciousness."

Pete Townshend said, "Jimi Hendrix turned a guitar into an instrument." (What was a guitar before that?)

Bruce Springsteen said, "Hendrix came in and knocked all the doors down."

Paul Stanley said, "Rock-and-roll is as physical as it is anything else. The idea of jumping around, rolling around, setting your guitar on fire. Those are all avenues to be explored."

Al Kooper said, "Jimi Hendrix was an envelope pusher. He was pushing at all the boundaries of music."

Paul Kantner said, "Before that (the Monterey Pop Festival), there were rules that only certain songs were deemed capable of succeeding on the radio or pop landscape. But the Beatles broke all the rules, and got away with it."

Changing the World

Then there was the naive theme that music was somehow going to "change the world."

Ray Manzarek, of the Doors, declared, "A psychedelic revolution was happening. That was the point of rock-and-roll at the time, to become a new tribe, to bring America into a cleaner, purer form of existence."

Wavy Gravy, commenting on Woodstock, said, "We had a chance to show the world how it would be if we ran the show." (Good for Woodstock, not so good for Altamont.)

Peter Yarrow, of Peter Paul and Mary, said, "I remember Bobby Dylan was living with me in Woodstock for the summer when 'Blowing in the Wind' came out, and there was a sense of the enormous moment of the linkage of the movement to the political movements of the time."

Kantner warned, "Basic institutions are crumbling about you, and it is chaos."

Allen Ginsberg said, "The Beatles changed American consciousness and introduced a new note of complete masculinity allied with complete tenderness and vulnerability."

David Crosby mused, "Somehow *Sgt. Pepper* did not stop the Vietnam War. Somebody just wasn't listening. I would have thought *Sgt. Pepper* could have stopped the war just by putting too many good vibes in the air for anybody to have a war around."

Abbie Hoffman said, "Hearing *Sgt. Pepp*er, smoking reefers, and planning the revolution in my friend's loft, we were just overwhelmed by their vision."

A not-so-worldly-comment by Al Kooper was, "*Sgt. Pepper*, for one thing, was the album that changed drumming more than anything else."

Suzanne Vega later said, "The movement of the '60s had a huge impact on my consciousness. I was very aware of the civil rights movement and the part music played in it." (She was born in 1959, which made her four or five when this was happening.)

A comment with a little more realism by John Lennon was, "Everyone dressed up, but nothing changed."

Drug Glorification

Phil Lesh said, "Most people who are hippies came to it through drugs. I think the more people who turn on, the better world it would be."

Jerry Garcia said, "We had an opportunity to visit highly experimental places, before a highly experimental people, under highly experimental drugs. It was ideal."

Judy Collins declared, "I think LSD has great potential for saving the world."

- And finally, some "musicspeak" comments about Bob Dylan:

Springsteen said, "He predicted some of the fragmentation of thought of images of society itself."

Tom Petty said, "Subject matter opened up for the first time."

Bono said, "He is not just mixing it up album by album or song by song, but line by line. You move into a different world the next line."

Paul Stanley said, "I thought it [Bob Dylan using electrical instruments at the Newport Folk Festival] was a pioneer move to move socially conscious music into another arena." Wrong. When Dylan starting playing electric music, he quit writing socially conscious music.

Answers

5. Beatles; Moody Blues; Byrds; CSNY
10. Byrds, Olivia Newton-John, Jimi Hendrix, Turtles, and of course, Bob Dylan
11. Four Boxes; Jay and the Five Americans
12. "All I Really Want to Do" by both Cher and the Byrds
13. Marty Balin (Jefferson Airplane); Mark Volman (Turtles); Nico (Velvet Underground); Gene Clark (Byrds). It is hard to tell who the primary lead singer was for Peter, Paul, and Mary, so Mary Travers is a possible answer; same for the The Mamas and the Papas, with Michelle Phillips, Denny Doherty, and Cass Elliott.
14. "A Hard Rain's A-Gonna Fall"; "You Ain't Goin' Nowhere"
15. Cliff Richard
16. The Byrds' "Fifth Dimension"
18. "Subterranean Homesick Blues" and "Maggie's Farm"
19. "The House of The Rising Sun" and "Turn! Turn! Turn!"
20. "Come Together," "All Together Now," "Work Together," "Happy Together," "Let's Get Together," "Someday, We Can Be Together"
21. "Barbara Ann" (Beach Boys), "Rainy Day Women" (Bob Dylan), "Secret Agent Man" (Johnny Rivers)
22. Richard Manuel (Band) and Leslie Maguire (Gerry and the Pacemakers)
23. The Byrds (Gene Clark)
27. Easiest to hardest: Bob Dylan ("Subterranean Homesick Blues"); Byrds ("Mr. Tambourine Man"); Turtles ("It Ain't Me Babe"); Olivia Newton-John ("If Not for You"); Jimi Hendrix ("All Along the Watchtower"). "Blowing in the Wind" was Peter, Paul and Mary's third top-forty song, while "Mighty Quinn" was Manfred Mann's fourth.
29. Dave Davies (Kinks)

Songs

13. "Hair," The Cowsills
14. "Fortunate Son," Creedence Clearwater Revival
15. "Sunshine," Jonathan Edwards
16. "Hyacinth House," Doors
17. "Watching the River Flow," Bob Dylan
18. "Pre Road Downs," Crosby Stills and Nash
19. "The Loner," Neil Young
20. "Substitute", The Who
21. "Summertime Blues," The Who or Blue Cheer
22. "The In Crowd," The Mamas and the Papas
23. "Want to Take You Higher," Sly and the Family Stone
24. American Pie," Don McLean; "I Just Stopped In (to See What Condition My Condition Was In)," First Edition
25. "You Can't Always Get What You Want," Rolling Stones
26. "Sympathy for the Devil," Rolling Stones
27. "Peace Frog," Doors
28. "Maggie McGill," The Doors
29. "Roadhouse Blues," The Doors
30. "The Wasp (Texas Radio and the Big Beat)," The Doors (They say "come live with us")
31. "Soft Parade," The Doors
33. "Fire," Jimi Hendrix Experience (probably spelled "Jimi," but that would have given away the answer; maybe he was referring to someone else)
34. "Five to One," The Doors ("we're taking over")
35. "Baby Driver," Simon and Garfunkel
36. "Surfer Girl," Beach Boys
37. "Baby I'm Yours," Barbara Lewis
38. "Insence and Peppermints," Strawberry Alarm Clock, and "Season Of The Witch," Donovan
39. "And When I Die," Blood Sweat and Tears
40. "California Dreamin'", The Mamas and the Papas
41. "Won't Get Fooled Again," The Who
42. "Sympathy for the Devil," Rolling Stones
43. "Blessed," Simon and Garfunkel

44. "Eve of Destruction," Barry McGuire
45. "Down on the Corner," Creedence Clearwater Revival
46. "Games People Play," Joe South
47. "Wear Your Love like Heaven," Donovan
48. "Spirit in the Sky," Norman Greenbaum
49. "American Pie," Don McLean
50. "When the Music's Over," The Doors ("cancel my subscription")
51. "On the Road Again," Canned Heat
52. "Awaiting on You All," George Harrison
53. "Vehicle," Ides of March
54. "Arizona," Mark Lindsay
55. "The Pusher," Steppenwolf
56. "You Can't Do That," The Beatles
57. "Mrs. Robinson," Simon and Garfunkel
58. "Woodstock," CSNY
59. "Fire," Arthur Brown ("of hell fire")

"Since I was ten" (from p. 83, Cream)
"Wine and women" (from p. 83, Cream)

Pictures

Eyes—Ian Anderson
Glasses—Roger McGuinn
White shoes—Janis Joplin
Black shoes—James Brown
Fur hat—John Phillips
White hat—Brian Jones

Band Index